G000124248

Dr. Conze, widely known as a leading Buddhist scholar through his many publications (among them *Buddhism: Its Essence and Development*, which has become a classic), has published during the thirty years of his working life a great number of important articles which are scattered over many periodicals difficult or almost impossible to obtain.

To meet a growing demand for the most important of these articles to be re-published we are presenting this volume which contains both translations and original essays: the indispensable report on Recent Progress in Buddhist Studies; the survey of Mahayana Buddhism which is still the only account based on the actual sources; the comparisons of Buddhist and European philosophy; the essay on Buddhist Saviours. The remaining articles deal with the Prajnaparamita on which the author is the leading authority in the West. The translations included will be specially welcome because reliable English translations of Buddhist texts are still rare.

Thus this volume will be invaluable and indispensable for all students of religion and philosophy.

Thirty Years of Buddhist Studies

Thirty Years of Buddhist Studies

Selected Essays

by

Edward Conze

Munshiram Manoharlal Publishers Pvt. Ltd.

ISBN 81-215-0960-2
This edition 2000
Originally published in 1967
Published with the permission of the original publisher

Printed and published by
Munshiram Manoharlal Publishers Pvt. Ltd.,
Post Box 5715, 54 Rani Jhansi Road,
New Delhi 110 055.

ACKNOWLEDGMENTS

The publishers are grateful for permission to re-print the essays collected in this volume. Permission was kindly given for:

Recent Progress in Buddhist Studies, *published in:* The Middle Way 34, 1959, pp. 6–14; 1960, pp. 144–50; 35, 1960, pp. 93–8, 110.

Buddhist Saviours, *published in:* The Saviour God, ed. by S. G. F. Brandon, 1963, Manchester University Press, pp. 67–82.

Mahayana Buddhism, *published in:* The Concise Encyclopaedia of Living Faiths, ed. R. C. Zaehner, 1959, pp. 296–320.

The Meditation on Death, *published in:* The Middle Way, 29, 1955, pp. 159–163; 30, 1955, pp. 15–18; pp. 54–7.

The Lotus of The Good Law, Chapter 5: On Plants, *published in:* The Middle Way, 37, 1962, pp. 95–6, 1963, pp. 157–60; 38, 1963, pp. 15–7; pp. 49–51.

The Development of Prajñāpāramitā Thought, *publised in:* Buddhism and Culture. Dedicated to D. T. Suzuki in commemoration of his 90th Birthday, ed, by S. Yamagucchi. Kyoto, 1960, pp. 24–45.

The Prajñāpāramitā-hṛdaya Sūtra *published in:* Journal of the Royal Asiatic Society, 1948, pp. 33–51.

The Composition of the Astasāhasrikā Prajñāpāramitā, *published in:* The Bulletin of the London School of Oriental and African Studies, 14, 1952, pp. 251–62.

Hate Love and Perfect Wisdom, *published in:* The Mahabodhi, v. 62, 1954, pp. 3–8.

The Perfection of Wisdom in Seven Hundred Lines, *published in:* Kalpa I 2, 1963, pp. 4–10; Kalpa I 3, 1963, pp. 11–20.

Prajñā and Sophia, *published in:* Oriental Art I 4, 1948, pp. 196–7.

Buddhist Philosophy and its European Parallels, *published in:* Philosophy East and West, 13, 1963, pp. 9–23.

Spurious Parallels to Buddhist Philosophy, *published in:* Philosophy East and West, 13, 1963, pp. 105–115.

The Iconography of the Prajñāpāramitā, *published in:* Oriental Art II 2, 1949, pp. 47–52; III 3, 1951, pp. 104–9.

TABLE OF CONTENTS

Foreword

When teaching recently for a year in North America, it was suggested to me that a re-publication of some of my articles, which have appeared over a period of thirty years in various periodicals, and are now almost unobtainable, might be of assistance to Buddhist scholarship. I therefore submit herewith a first selection of these articles to my readers. If there is sufficient demand, in other words if my patient publisher loses no money on this venture, we plan to bring out a second volume, to be called *Further Buddhist Studies*, later on.

The collection contains two Surveys: The first (p. 1) shows the revolutionary changes which have taken place in the study of Buddhism between 1940 and 1960 with regard to the early period, the Mahayana, the Tantras and Zen; the second (p. 48) still remains the only general survey of Mahayana Buddhism with any claims to scholarly exactitude. Two articles deal with Buddhism as a Philosophy (pp. 210, 229), and one with Buddhism as a religion (p. 33). I have included three translations: Buddhaghosa on the Recollection of Death, the Lotus of the Good Law and a Perfection of Wisdom. The first concerns a standard meditation, followed by a number of my own comments which cannot, I think, be described as an unqualified success, but which may have some merit as a first attempt to do something which will have to be done better and more extensively by others in due course. The second is taken from the *Saddharmapuṇḍarīka*, one of the great classics of Mahayana Buddhism, and greatly revered in the Far East. By consulting the Tibetan translation of the verses I have been able to improve substantially the translation I gave in "Buddhist Texts" in 1954 (nos. 123 and 134). I undertook this translation because at that time the Oxford University Press considered issuing a modernized version of their *Sacred Books of the East* and because I wanted to show what radical changes, as compared with Kern's translation of 1884, would have to be made eighty years later. However, the Oxford University Press found that the scheme was impracticable, and I therefore reprint here only the fifth chapter of my translation which, in the absence of further encouragement, is all that I am ever likely to do. Professor Th. de Bary of Columbia University is, I am glad to hear, arranging for a translation of the Lotus of the Good Law from the Chinese. Thirdly I give the first part of *The Perfection of Wisdom in 700 Lines*. The page-numbers refer to J. Masuda's edition of the Sanskrit text (see my *The Prajñāpāramitā Literature*, 1960, pp. 62–4) which is, alas, confined to the first part of the Sutra. In its second part the text is so corrupt that the meaning cannot always be ascertained with any degree of certainty, and an English translation must await a better edition of the Sanskrit original.

That brings us to the Prajñaparamita which by some obscure karmic dispensation has during this life been my dominant interest. At the present stage of our knowledge of the Mahayana chronological studies of selected literary documents are an especially urgent requirement, and I have attempted to give them for the Prajñaparamita literature in general (pp. 123), and for the version in eight thousand Lines in particular (pp. 168). With regard to the celebrated *Heart Sūtra*, I have not only attempted to submit a better text, but also to reveal its meaning by placing it into its historical context. Two other contributions are rather slight. One (p. 185) attempts to establish some connection between modern psychology and the thought of the Prajñaparamita; the other (p. 207) to indicate some of the similarities between the Indian concept of Prajñaparamita and the nearly contemporary Mediterranean concepts of Sophia and Chochma. The ideas of the latter paper were further developed and presented in a more elaborate lecture on "Gnostic Trends in Buddhist Thought", which I gave in 1960 at the 25th International Orientalist Congress in Moscow, but the opposition to my thesis, particularly from the Indian delegates, was so vehement that it not only propelled me to the front page of *Pravda* but also made me have second thoughts. In the face of so much hostility I have accumulated further data and the July issue of *Numen* 1967 contains my final views on the striking similarities between Buddhism and Gnosis. Finally, the two articles on "The iconography of the Prajñaparamita" are a systemic attempt to survey all the manifold manifestations of this figure. There are few other studies of this kind, and the only other examples which come readily to mind are Mlle. de Mallmann's studies of Avalokitesvara (1948) and Manjusri (1964).

Most of the material has been reprinted *verbatim* as it stood, though there have been some minor adjustments. In the two philosophical articles (pp. 210–242) the loving editorial care of Prof. Charles Moore of Hawaii, editor of *Philosophy East and West*, had so much changed the tone of what I had written that one might have thought it to have emanated from Princeton, Wisconsin or Nebraska. The reprint has nearly everywhere restored the idiosyncrasies of my original text. The article on the Prajñaparamita-hrdayasūtra differs from the original publication in the *JRAS* in two ways: 1. The "Bibliography" at the end (*JRAS*, pp. 48–51) has been lopped off, because it has meanwhile appeared in a much fuller form in *The Prajñāpāramitā Literature*, 1960, pp. 71–75. 2. The Sanskrit text of the Sūtra has been re-edited on the basis of now twenty-nine documentary sources. And in the "Iconography" I have re-cast the list of "Images" so as to take account of post-1950 research on the subject.

It now remains for me to thank those persons and Institutions who have so generously given me their permission to reprint the articles which have appeared in their journals.

Far Eastern and Russian Institute,
University of Washington,
Seattle, Washington, 98105

The usage of diacritical marks, italics, capitals, etc. is that of the articles as they appeared at the time, and therefore varies from place to place.

Recent Progress in Buddhist Studies

The Early Period

Up to about 1935, Buddhist research was divided into three distinct schools.[1] The first was the "Older Anglo-German school". T. W. Rhys Davids and H. Oldenberg were its great masters, and it based itself squarely on the Pali Canon, which it held to have preserved the Buddha's doctrines more faithfully than any other. Until about 1914 it dominated the scene, and from it the general public still derive their ideas of what is the "original", "pure" and "true" Buddhism. To it belongs E. J. Thomas' *History of Buddhist Thought*, which in 1933 summed up the knowledge which had percolated to England by then. But in the meantime active research has moved away from it; in scholarly circles it has few, if any, representatives, and its position has, in fact, become untenable.

Secondly, coming to the fore after 1916, there was the "Leningrad school", headed by Stcherbatsky. Stcherbatsky, Rosenberg and Obermiller devoted themselves to the study of the scholastic literature of Buddhism, which they believed to be nearer the original doctrine than the arbitrary reconstructions of European scholars. It has been the great and indubitable achievement of this school to work out the exact meaning of many Buddhist technical terms, which had so far been translated just anyhow, either on the basis of etymology or of "common sense". But etymology is rarely sufficient to define philosophical terms, which have often quite different connotations in the various Indian systems. And as to "common sense", nothing could differ more radically from nation to nation, from culture to culture, than this alleged "common sense", which is in fact nothing but what Flaubert called the *idées reçues* of a certain set of people. This school interpreted Buddhism in close dependence not only on the Indian

[1] My description and terminology here follow the able exposition of C. Regamey, in: *Der Buddhismus Indiens*, 1951, pp. 244–48; and: *Buddhistische Philosophie* (a bibliography), 1950, pp. 14–17.

commentaries, but on the continuous living tradition of Tibet, Mongolia, China and Japan, in the perhaps not entirely unfounded belief that the mentality of Asiatic Buddhists is probably nearer to that of the Buddha than that of the Protestant Christians of a Europe bursting with imperialistic conceit. Obermiller's translation of Bu-ston's *History of Buddhism* (1931) showed us how Buddhists view their own history, and Bu-ston's masterpiece has been the model for the two general histories of Buddhism which have recently appeared in English, i.e. my own *Buddhism* (1951), and Sangharakshita's *A Survey of Buddhism* (1957). While thus the educated non-specialist has had some taste of the spirit of the Leningrad school, Stcherbatsky's elucidation of the word "dharma"—in the singular, and especially in the plural—has still much to teach him.[1] Far too many people seem still incapable of appreciating the fundamental difference between "dharmas" and "things". So intent had the "Older Anglo-German" school been in making the Buddha appear as a moralist, that the significance of the philosophical analysis of reality into its factors, or dharmas, was overlooked. In fact the dharma-theory is the basis of all forms of Buddhism, and the starting point of all later developments. I cannot here go into the details and must refer to the excellent summary of the situation by von Glasenapp in 1938.[2] With Stcherbatsky's and Obermiller's deaths in the forties the Leningrad school has unfortunately come to an untimely end in the Soviet Union, and no traces of it can be detected at the present time.

Finally, there was the school which Regamey calls "Franco-Belgian", because it was decisively shaped by men like de la Vallée-Poussin, Jean Przyluski, Sylvain Lévi, Paul Demiéville and Etienne Lamotte. Regamey (pp. 247–8) describes their approach as follows: "These scholars continue on the lines of the Russian school. They do not, however, slavishly follow Buddhist scholasticism, but use all the sources which are today available, supplementing their philological and philosophical analysis with the data of ethnology, sociology, etc.

[1] Th. Stcherbatsky, *The Central Conception of Buddhism and the Meaning of the word "Dharma"*, 1923. Reprinted in 1956.

[2] *Zur Geschichte der buddhistischen Dharma-Theorie*, ZDMG 1938, pp. 383–420.

They have abandoned as fruitless the attempt to reconstruct a pure Buddhism, are convinced that Buddhism is as much the work of the Buddhists as of the Buddha himself, and find the entire wealth and the true face of this religion in the manifoldness of its aspects, and the multiplicity of its sects or schools." While the "Older Anglo-German school" has died out from inanition, and the Leningrad school has perished through unfavourable social conditions, the principles of the Franco-Belgian school have now been universally adopted by all scholars working in this field, whatever the country they may live in. This is the basic change which has taken place in the last twenty years.

At present we are concerned only with the first period of Buddhist history, its first five hundred years, from the time of the Buddha to about the beginning of the Christian era. The status of the Pali Canon is here the basic problem, and there has been quite a landslide in its evaluation. It is now well known that Pali was not the language of the Buddha, but a dialect of the West of India. The Buddha himself spoke some kind of Magadhi, and all his sayings, like those of Jesus, are lost in their original form.

The Pali Canon, as we have it, is no older than that of other schools, say that of the Sarvastivadins. Its prestige among Europeans owed something to the fact that it fitted in with their own mood, in being more rationalistic and moralistic than some other traditions, and much less given to religious devotion, mythology and magic. The Pali Canon stresses the ethical side of Buddhism, to which Protestants would readily respond. The treatment of the Buddha's last words provides a curious example. In *Dīghanikāya* XVI they appear as *vayadhammā saṃkhārā appamādena sampādetha*, i.e. "doomed to extinction are composite things; exert yourselves in wakefulness!" But in the Sarvastivadin *Mahāparinirvāṇasūtra* (p. 394) we have only *vyayadharmāh sarvasaṃskārāh*, i.e. "doomed to extinction are all composite things". A mere statement about the facts of life, and no word about the need for "striving", so dear to the European moralist!

The fact of the matter is that there were eighteen schools in the first period of Buddhist history, that most, if not all, had their own set of Scriptures, and that each of them can equally well claim to represent the teaching of the Buddha. If the Canon of one school only, that of the Theravadins, has reached us intact and in its entirety, this is not due to its greater antiquity or intrinsic merit, but to the accidents of historical transmission. The fanatical fury of the Mohammedans which destroyed all Buddhist documents in Northern India never reached Ceylon. The Scriptures of the Northern schools were largely lost, and fragments only are preserved in Sanskrit manuscripts from Nepal and Tibet, and chiefly in Chinese and Tibetan translations. In England the Pali Scriptures in addition owe much of their position to the further accident that they caught the eye of British administrators, and have almost completely been translated by the devoted zeal of the Pali Text Society. In the perspective of those who only read English, the Theravadins have therefore come to occupy a quite disproportionate importance.

One of the main advances in the period under review is that the writings of at least two of the other schools, of the Sarvastivadins and Mahasanghikas, have been made more accessible to European readers. The Sarvastivadins were for long the dominant school in India. Prof. Waldschmit and other German scholars have edited, and are editing, many of their most important canonical writings, which the sands of Turkestan have preserved in their Sanskrit form. Of quite outstanding value is Prof. Waldschmidt's work on the *Mahāparinirvāṇa-sūtra*, which describes the events connected with the Buddha's last days. Not only has he published a sumptuous edition of the Sanskrit text, with the Pali and versions from a Tibetan and Chinese Vinaya in parallel columns,[1] but we also owe him a most careful analysis of the material.[2] Three-quarters of the text, so he shows (p. 336), have a common basis, which has, however, in many places been worked over at a later time. We may conclude that these common parts go back to 250 B.C., if not further.[3] It is quite obvious that in future this rich

[1] *Das Mahāparinirvāṇasūtra*, 1950–1, three vols., Abh. d. dtschen Ak. d. Wiss. zu Berlin.

[2] *Die Ueberlieferung vom Lebensende des Buddha*, two vols., 1944, 1948, Abh. d. Ak. d. Wiss. Goettingen.

[3] This assumes, of course, that the Theravadins can be identified with the Vibhajyavadins—a particularly thorny and unrewarding problem of Buddhist history.

Sarvastivadin material must be consulted by all students with as much care as the Pali sources.[1]

Likewise there has been an increase in our information about the Mahasanghikas, from whom the Mahayana developed later on. There is first the translation of the *Mahāvastu* ("The Great Event") by J. J. Jones, in three volumes (1949 to 1956). Sénart's edition of this important book, in 1882–1897, had not contributed overmuch to the appreciation of Buddhism, because the language of this text is extremely difficult and wearisome. Now, thanks to Dr. Jones, the English reader can study at his leisure this wonderful collection of stories, legends and discourses, which distinctly and eloquently exhibits the religious, as distinct from the philosophical, and moral, side of Buddhism. Another important document is the Vinaya of the Mahasanghikas. Most of it is still hidden away in Chinese. In 1946 Hofinger examined eight canonical accounts of the Council of Vaisali (380 B.C.), and came to the conclusion that the one in the Mahasanghika Vinaya is indubitably the oldest of them all.

There can be no doubt, therefore, that all students of the first period of Buddhism must henceforth pay equal attention to all the sources, whether Theravadin, Sarvastivadin or Mahasanghika. As Prof. Waldschmidt (1948, II 353) says, "it is not infrequently the (Sanskrit) *Mahāparinirvāṇasūtra* which has probably preserved the original tradition more faithfully, and it has at least the same value as the Pali text", and he adds (p. 354) that "both 'Northern' and 'Southern' sources are equally important for ascertaining the oldest tradition". Similarly J. J. Jones (II p. x) agrees that we "must proceed from the assumption that both Pali and Sanskrit texts preserve as a fixed core a very primitive tradition". "In all texts, irrespective of language, earlier and later strata may be distinguished". Sometimes the Pali is "more original", and sometimes the *Mahāvastu*. Hofinger (p. 257) expresses the same opinion, i.e. "once again the Pali Canon has come down from the pedestal on which it has stood for so long; it has no more value than the Chinese and Tibetan canonical documents, and occasionally it is even somewhat inferior to them".

[1] And that applies not only to the canonical writings, but also to the rich meditation literature of this school, the study of which P. Demiéville began in 1954 with his book on Sangharaksha's *Yogācārabhūmi*.

But if all the Scriptures, as we have them, date back no further than the beginning of the Christian era, how can we know anything about the earlier phases? Some of the contents of the Canon must surely be quite early, while others are certainly rather late, and it is often hard to determine the age of the various layers. Many examples show that the Buddhists were quite in the habit of keeping their holy books up-to-date by repeated additions over the centuries. We cannot study their attitude in Ceylon, where all documents representing earlier stages have perished. In the North, however, we sometimes have, thanks to the Chinese translations, successive dateable versions of the same text. A good example is the *Suvarṇaprabhāsa*, which Prof. Nobel[1] has, over the last twenty years, studied with great care. This large Sūtra began as a relatively short *Confession of Sins*, which is now chapter three of the extant Sanskrit version in nineteen chapters. A few centuries later, that had in I-tsing's (A.D. 700) Sanskrit text grown to thirty-one chapters, and been enriched with numerous *dhāraṇīs*, and many additional treatises—about the three bodies of the Buddha, the removal of the obstacles which one's own past deeds cause to the spiritual life, the goddess Sarasvati, etc. Likewise, we can compare Dharmaraksha's translation of the *Question of Rāṣṭrapāla*[2] (270 A.D.) with our Sanskrit text which is at least three centuries later, and find that such passages as the prophecy of the decline of the Samgha, the list of Jatakas, and many of the verses are later additions. I myself have proved a similar process of accretion for the *Prajñāpāramitā in 8,000 Lines*,[3] and made it probable for the *Diamond Sūtra*.[4]

We must further bear in mind that the arrangement of the Scriptures, and their division into a Tripitaka is very late, if only because by common consent the third part, i.e. the Abhidharma, took shape only after Asoka's time. Before that there were only the Dharma and Vinaya, with the Dharma divided

[1] Sanskrit edition 1937; Tibetan translations 1944 and 1958; German translation from Chinese of I-tsing, 1958.

[2] Trsl. by J. Ensink, 1952.

[3] Bulletin of the London School of Oriental and African Studies, XIV 2, 1952, pp. 251–62. See below pp. 169 sq.

[4] *Vajracchedikā Prajñāpāramitā*, 1957, pp. 6–7.

into twelve, or nine, different classes.[1] The twelve are: Sūtra, Geya, Vyakaraṇa, Gatha, Udana, Nidana, Avadana, Itivrttaka, Jataka, Vaipulya, Abdhutadharma, Upadesa. This may be roughly translated as, "Sermons, Mingled Prose and Verse, Prediction, Verses, Verses of Uplift, Origins, Tales, Thus-was-said, Birth-stories, Expanded Texts, Marvels and Expositions".[2] The Scriptures arranged in this manner are now lost, although the arrangement itself has left its imprint on the *Kṣudrakanikāya* of the various sects.

It is difficult to know when and at what stage this Nine- or Twelvefold Scripture came into being, but we may reasonably assign it to pre-Aśokan times, because it fails to mention one class of literature which decisively changed the character of Buddhism, and made it into what it is today. I refer to the *Mātṛkas*, the "Summaries" or "Numerical Lists". In 1944 E. M. Hare in his fine English translation of the *Suttanipāta*, which is generally held to be one of the earliest Pali writings, brought to light the fact that "the well-known formulae of the four Nikayas are nearly all omitted in the *Suttanipāta*" (p. 216). He lists the eightfold Path or Way, the four Truths, the three refuges, the three gems, the three signs (i.e. impermanence, etc.), the five skandhas, the five (or six) superknowledges, and the four, eight (or nine) *jhānic* abidings. This is indeed a really startling fact, particularly when taken together with the well-known observation that Asoka's inscriptions likewise never mention any of these items. Their omission in the inscriptions could be accounted for by saying that Asoka, as a layman, spoke only of those aspects of the dharma which are relevant to laymen. But such an argument would clearly not apply to the *Suttanipāta*. It seems probable that at a certain stage in the history of the order, fairly late, meditation was increasingly based on numerical lists, which it was the purpose of the *Matṛkas* to enumerate. The *Matṛkas* in their turn developed among the rationalists into the Abhidharma, among the mystics into the Prajñaparamita.

In view of these considerations it would be quite uncritical

[1] The ninefold division belongs to the Theravadins and Mahasanghikas, the twelvefold to all the other schools.

[2] The Theravadins drop Nidana, Avadana, Vaipulya and Upadesa, and have instead a somewhat mysterious item called "Vedalla".

to jump from the existing Scriptures straight back to the Buddha's time. It is certainly not good enough any longer to go through the Pali Scriptures, take out the bits which take one's fancy, and call them "the original gospel". That method, easy to apply, and therefore unduly popular, yields no objectively valid results. In fact, all one can attempt to do is to go back from stage to stage and here is a diagram of the stages one has to bear in mind:

		The doctrine of the Buddha	
480		Nirvana of the Buddha	
		The doctrine of the most ancient community	
		"Pre-canonical" ideas	
340		Mahasanghikas / / / Sthaviras	
			Skandhaka
280	Ninefold or Twelvefold Scripture	Pudgalavadins / / / Sthaviras	Aśoka 274–236
244		Vibhajyavādins / / / Sarvastivadins	
100–			Mātṛkas
	Tripitaka	Scriptures written down	Abhidharma Prajña-paramita
100			

In other words, before we can come to the Buddha we must first get beyond Asoka. In a remarkable piece of inspired detective work Prof. Frauwallner in *The Earliest Vinaya and the Beginnings of Buddhist Literature* (1956) has proved almost conclusively that before Asoka a great work, the *Skandhaka*, was produced, which divided and arranged the enormous material concerning monastic rules according to a well-conceived plan. It regulates the fundamental institutions of Buddhist monastic life, the admission to the Order, the confession ceremonies, the retirement during the rainy season, and discusses clothing, food and drugs for the sick, as well as the rules to be observed in the punishment of offenders. This *Skandhaka* is in fact the earliest Buddhist literary work of which we have any definite knowledge.

For the rest, we must patiently compare the recensions of the different schools. The information which has been handed down to us about the "eighteen sects" is in rather a chaotic condition, but in 1955 A. Bareau brought order into the chaos in his *Les sectes bouddhiques du petit véhicule* (308 pp.), a work quite indispensable to all scholars from now on. What has to be done is to compare the documents of various sects, say a Theravadin text from Ceylon with a Sarvastivadin text from Turkestan. Where we find passages in which these two texts, the one in Pali and other in Sanskrit, agree almost word by word, we can assume that they belong to a time antedating the separation of the two schools, which took place during Asoka's rule. Where they do not agree we may, in the absence of evidence to the contrary, infer their post-Asokan date. Much work has been done on these lines during our period, but no systematic survey of the results has yet been possible. This approach cannot, however, get us beyond 340 B.C. with the Sūtra texts, because their Mahasanghika version is lost. Comparing ten recensions of the Pratimoksha rules, W. Pachow has, on the other hand, shown in 1955 that all sects agree about most of them, and that therefore they must have been formulated within the first century after the Buddha's Nirvana.

Some attempts have been made to get back to the original Canon through linguistic studies. Where we have similar texts in both Pali and Sanskrit, we may well believe that the Sanskrit has been translated from the Pali, or vice versa. It is the merit of Prof. Lueders[1] to have demonstrated that in many cases this is impossible and that in fact large portions of both recensions have been translated from a Magadhi original. Quite often this enables us to spot a corruption of the tradition, which is either due to a misunderstanding on the part of the original translator, or, where the text is in verse, to the difficulty of finding a Sanskrit or Pali equivalent which would not spoil the metre. In Dhp. 259, for instance, occurs the senseless *dhammam kāyena passati*, "he sees dharma with his body". The Prakrit version has *phaṣai* ("touches"), the Sanskrit *vai spṛṣet*; the Magadhi original was *phāsai*, the Pali equivalent of which, *phusati*, would not fit the metre (pp. 162–3). This small example may indicate how the method works. Its conclusiveness lies in the philological detail, which we cannot present here. Most of Lueders' material seems to substantiate his thesis, but, of

[1] H. Lueders, *Beobachtungen ueber die Sprache des buddhistischen Urkanons*, Abh. dtsche Ak. d. Wiss. zu Berlin, 1954, 196 pp.

course, this proves no more than that parts of the existing Canon were translated from Magadhi. Other parts must go back to a Middle-Indian original, as Edgerton[1] has clearly shown. In fact, from the very start Buddhism was preached in a variety of dialects, and in the *Cullavagga* (5.33) the Buddha gives his consent to this practice. These linguistic investigations are still at their beginning. It should be clear, however, that before they are completed it will be extremely hazardous to make any statements about the contents of the original Canon, and much more so about the Buddha's actual words.

No sane man can, in fact, say anything conclusive about the doctrine of the Buddha himself. Even that of the most ancient community is difficult to ascertain. Some Polish scholars, like St. Schayer (1935–8), Constantin Regamey[2] and Maryla Falk[3] have tried to penetrate at least to what they call "Pre-canonical Buddhism". Their views are on a completely different level from the arbitrary speculations of Jennings (1947), Guenther (1949) and Bahm (1958), in that they keep in touch with the actual facts of Buddhist tradition. They assume that wherever the Canon contains ideas which conflict with the orthodox theories of the Theravadins and Sarvastivadins, and wherever these ideas are taken up and developed by the Mahayana, we have to deal with a very old, "pre-Canonical" tradition, which was too venerable to be discarded by the compilers of the Canon. How otherwise could one account for the numerous references to a "person" (*pudgala*)[4] or the assumption of an eternal "consciousness" in the *ṣaḍdhātusūtra*, or the identification of the Absolute, of Nirvana, with an "invisible infinite consciousness, which shines everywhere" (*viññānam anidassanam anantam sabbato pabham*) in *Dīghanikāya* XI 85? Side by side with the oft-repeated negation of an *ātman* there are traces of a belief in consciousness as the non-impermanent centre of the personality which constitutes an absolute element in this contingent world. Though generally

[1] *Buddhist Hybrid Sanskrit Grammar and Dictionary*, 1953.

[2] *Der Buddhismus Indiens*, 1951, pp. 248–64. *Le problème du Bouddhisme primitif et les derniers travaux de Stanislaw Schayer*, Rocznik Orientalisticzny, xxi, 1957, pp. 37–58.

[3] *Il mito psicologico nell' India Antica*, 1939. *Nāma-rūpa and dharma-rūpa*, 1943.

[4] See my *Buddhist Scriptures*, Penguin Classics, 1959, pp. 195–7.

Nirvana is kept transcendentally remote and defined only by negations, there are distinct remnants of a more positive concept, and of an unorthodox ontology, which regards Nirvana as a place (*pada*) or an entity (and not merely a state), identical with the eternal and absolute reality (*dharma*), and with the translucent (*prabhāsvara*) Thought (*citta*) or consciousness. Deliverance is then conceived as the gradual purification of this consciousness which finally attains to the summit of the "Realm of Dharma" (*dharmadhātu*), from which it will no longer fall back (*acyuta*). The treatment of the Buddha shows a similar inconsistency. Normally presented as a man who has found the truth, at times he is shown as a supernatural being, the mythical pre-Buddhistic Tathagata, the earthly manifestation of the absolute principle (*dharma*). The faithful are recommended to have trust in His spiritual authority, which is guaranteed by the radiant blaze of his supernatural body, whereas in general the Theravadin Scriptures play down the rôle of faith, teach that no one can save another, and that each one should judge for himself.

The suggestion that these "aberrant" doctrines represent a "pre-Canonical" stratum of Buddhism, is proffered by our Polish friends as merely a tentative hypothesis, and it is no more than that. It is equally possible that they were later concessions to popular demand, just as the lower goal of birth in heaven (*svarga*) was admitted side by side with Nirvana. The real issue is this: Did Buddhism originate among an élite of intellectuals, of philosophical ascetics, and then become a popular religion only at the time of Asoka?[1] Or was it, even from the earliest times onwards, a popular religion based on the cult of the Bhagavan, of the Lord Buddha? And if so, was this religious side a part of its very essence,[2] or just as propagandistic concession to laymen?[3] As Regamey (1957, p. 43) puts it, "is it more probable that a system which was originally a simple religion, developed in time an increasingly subtle and elaborate theology and scholastic philosophy, or that the philosophical doctrines of an élite were, as they gradually spread, vulgarized and diluted into something more accessible to the masses?" Although I personally am inclined to see in Buddhism from the very beginning a popular mass movement, I must admit

[1] So von Glasenapp. [2] So the Polish school. [3] So Mayrhofer, 1952.

that no decisive argument can be found for either alternative. Nor is this really surprising. A hundred and forty years after the Nirvana this very same question was already debated, no agreement could be reached on it, and it led to the first split in the community. Now, 2,500 years later, how can we hope to reach any certainty on this issue?

This brings us to the Life of the Buddha. Can we, with our present knowledge, separate legend from fact? In 1947 Prof. Lamotte showed[1] that the historical facts are beyond our reach, and that we must be content to study the successive stages of the Buddha legend. In 1949 appeared A. Foucher's *Life of the Buddha*,[2] the last work of the great archaeologist. This is a real masterpiece, and the truest and most convincing account we have had so far. It is based not only on the texts of all the schools, but also on the numerous works of art, dating from the second century B.C. onwards, of which Prof. Foucher had over fifty years acquired an unrivalled knowledge. As a vigorous traveller, M. Foucher had spent many years in India, had become thoroughly familiar with Indian conditions and habits of thought, and had himself made the Eight great Buddhist pilgrimages. The inspection of the locality of the legends throws a surprising light on many of their features, for not a few of our traditional accounts are stories told to pilgrims by their guides. As no one before him, Prof. Foucher has thus succeeded in re-establishing the actual Indian tradition about the Buddha, and in describing the state of the legend as it existed at the beginning of the Christian era.

We may conclude our account with a few words about the relation of early Buddhism to the Upanishads. This is important for the question of the *anattā* doctrine, which is, of course, central to any understanding of Buddhist doctrine. There has been a persistent tendency to attribute to primitive Buddhism the Upanishadic teaching of the Self, or *ātman*. Little can be adduced from the existing Scriptures in support of this thesis, but it has been the curse of Buddhist studies that people will persist in believing that the Buddhists must have radically

[1] *La légende du Bouddha*, Revue de l'histoire des religions, cxxxiv, pp. 37–71.

[2] *La vie du Bouddha d'après les textes et les monuments de l'Inde*, 1949, 383 pp.

misunderstood the Buddha, and so they hanker, in the words of Prof. Murti, after a "soul-affirming primitive Buddhism followed by a soul-denying scholastic Buddhism". To again quote from Prof. Murti (p. 177), "if the *ātman* had been a cardinal doctrine with Buddhism, why was it so securely hidden under a bushel that even the immediate followers of the Master had no inkling of it? The Upanishads, on the other hand, blaze forth the reality of the *ātman* in every page, in every line almost". The word *ātman* was to such an extent a "bad word" for the Buddhists, that they carefully avoid using it for Nirvana, and that even the "Personalists" always speak of a *pudgala*, and never of an *ātman*. The question has meanwhile once and for all been settled by Prof. von Glasenapp's article on "Vedanta and Buddhism".[1] He shows that the Upanishadic doctrine is mentioned in the Buddhist Scriptures only very rarely, and then always polemically, that most of the confusion is due to "arbitrary translations which contradict the whole of Buddhist tradition", and he points out that the researches of the Leningrad school have made "the attempts to find room for the *ātman* in the teachings of the Buddha" "quite antiquated". "There can", as he says, "be no doubt that the works of Rosenberg and Stcherbatsky have for the first time put the understanding of Buddhism as a well-balanced philosophical system on a new and firm basis, which is all the more solid because it can enlist the agreement of all Buddhist schools of Asia." And "it is the basic idea of the whole system that all dharmas are devoid of ātman, and without cogent reasons one ought not to claim that the Buddha himself has taught anything contrary to that which his disciples have for more than two thousand years been regarding as the quintessence of their doctrine". It is well known, of course, that theories often manage to linger on, long after their validity has been exploded. So it will be here also. As long as people insist on writing about the orthodox *nairātmya* theory without practising the meditations which were designed to disclose it, misconceptions are bound to crop up.

[1] "Vedanta und Buddhismus, 1950", Ak. d. Wiss. and d. Lit. in Mainz, 18 pp.—Parts of the article have appeared in English in *The Buddhist*, xxi, 1951, in *The Middle Way*, xxxi, 1957, and as a pamphlet of the Buddhist Publication Society in Kandy, 1958.

The Mahayana

One hundred years after the Nirvana the Buddhist community divided itself into a "rationalist" and a "mystical" section. The "mystical" wing formed the Mahasanghika school, which three centuries later developed into the Mahayana. In using the words "rationalists" and "mystics" we must, of course, beware of taking them in their European sense. No Buddhist "rationalist" was ever bitterly hostile to religion in the sense in which Gibbon, Hume, Lady Wootton and The Rationalist Press Association hate it as a degrading superstition. No Buddhist "mystic" ever turned against rational thinking as such with the fervour of a Petrus Damiani, a William Blake, or the "obscurantist" wing of the French, Spanish or Irish Catholic Church.

The difference was really one between the *rational mysticism* of the Mahayana, and the *mystically tinged rationalism* of the Theravadins or Sarvastivadins. They had much common ground on the middle ranges of the path where the ascetic strove for emancipation in a quite rational and businesslike manner. Neither side denied that below these there was the comparative irrationality of popular religion, and above it the super-rationality of the higher stages of the path and of the top levels of *samādhi* and *prajñā*. They differed only in the emphasis which they gave to these phenomena. The proto-Mahayanists and the Mahayanists themselves looked more kindly upon the religious needs of ordinary people, and in addition they had much more to say about the higher stages of the path, and in particular about the transcendental knowledge, or intuition, of the Absolute, the Unconditioned.

The author of an interesting and valuable book[1] on the essentially rationalistic Buddhism of Burma sees the specifically religious element in the assumption of a "thought-defying ultimate", i.e. of "The Immortal" or Nirvana, which "is marked by the paradox of affirmation and negation, of sustaining faith and halting language". When they talk so much more freely about the Absolute and its immediate approaches we need not necessarily assume that the Mahayanists were

[1] R. L. Slater, *Paradox and Nirvana*, 1951.

more familiar with them. Quite possibly the non-Mahayanists were perfectly contented with formulating only that which could be formulated with some ease, and deliberately left the remainder to look after itself. The Mahayanists, on the other hand, regarded it as a worth-while task to combat mistaken verbal formulations of the highest and most unworldly spheres of spiritual experience. I cannot help feeling that this was connected with some loss of expertise within the Samgha after the first five hundred years had passed.

The slow gestation of the Mahayana within the Mahasanghika schools is still wrapped in obscurity. What we believe to know is that between 100 B.C. and A.D. 100 it emerged as a separate trend of thought, which increasingly turned against the "Disciples and Pratyekabuddhas", who stood for what is now awkwardly called "the Hinayana". Where this process took place is still a matter of dispute. The traditional view that the Mahayana originated in the South of India has been challenged by E. Lamotte[1] and A. Bareau[2] who want to assign it respectively to the North-west of India or to the Northern Dekkhan. A definite decision on this issue is, however, still premature.

In fact, when assessing the progress made in Mahayana studies, the main observation we have to make is that in comparison with the vastness of the field there has been almost no progress at all. Recent research into the first five hundred years of Buddhist history has at least led to a quite new perspective and re-orientation. The new picture which has begun to shape itself has been most admirably outlined by E. Lamotte in his huge book on *The History of Indian Buddhism.*[3] As regards the Mahayana we are still in the first stage of painfully gathering any material that may be at hand. Our picture of it is still that of the old nineteenth-century maps of Africa, with some coloured patches here and there at the edges, but with the vast interior left empty and white, filled only with conjecture and surmise.

The vast literature of the Mahayana falls into two groups:

[1] *Sur la formation du Mahayana*, in *Asiatica*, 1954.

[2] *Les sectes bouddhiques du petit véhicule*, 1955, pp. 296–305.

[3] *Histoire du Bouddhisme Indien. Des Origines à l'ère Saka.* 1958. 862 pp.

1. Sūtras. 2. The scholastic works of the Madhyamikas and Yogacarins. As to the Sūtras, their interpretation has for long been difficult and uncertain because their language often differs from classical Sanskrit, and no grammar or dictionary was available. In 1953 this deficiency was mended by F. Edgerton.[1] His self-denying labours have greatly eased the task of future students, and translations are likely to become more accurate than they were in the past. As a philologist Edgerton is, however, much more reliable on ordinary everyday words than on technical terms, which he did not bother to understand. In our modern universities a linguist would lose caste if he were caught out actually thinking about the contents of the texts he studies. Much of the technical vocabulary of the Mahayana is therefore still unexplored, and even scholars are forced to guess where they do not know.

1. The Sūtras of the Mahayana consist of *a*) the early seminal Sūtras, and *b*) later expanded (*vaipulya*) Sūtras. The "seminal Sūtras" all very brief, rarely exist separately, but are usually embedded in the later expanded texts. Many comparative studies and much critical acumen will be needed before we learn to isolate them. At present we possess no more than a few hints scattered through various periodicals. Until we are better acquainted with these seminal Sūtras we cannot really know what the Mahayana was like at its inception, and still less how it originated and developed, or how it is related to earlier forms of Buddhism. Some people surprise me by the amount of thought they expend on the problem of how the Mahayana derives from the Theravada. Theirs is a fruitless labour, since in fact the Mahayana did *not* derive from the Theravada which, in the words of Prof. Murti (p. 69), "had little or no direct influence on the development of Buddhist schools in India". In the later stages of scholastic elaboration some of the formulations of Mahayana beliefs arose from controversies with Sarvastivadins and Sautrantikas, but never with Theravadins. In so far as the Mahayana "derives" from anything it is from the Mahasanghikas, and there we are faced with the difficulty that only the Vinaya of that school is preserved, and nothing of the Sūtra Pitaka. My study of the first two chapters of the *Ratnaguṇa*, which I regard as the original

[1] *Buddhist Hybrid Sanskrit Grammar and Dictionary*. Two vols.

Prajñaparamita, has led me to the tentative conclusion that at first the Mahayana introduced no innovations at all, but relied on placing a new emphasis on certain parts of the commonly accepted traditional material.[1]

The real glory of the Mahayana lies, however, in the Expanded Sūtras and here the situation is, if possible, still more unsatisfactory. The *Lotus of the Good Law*, for instance, is a religious classic of breath-taking grandeur, and still we have no reliable translation. In 1884 H. Kern published a translation from the Sanskrit which is as good as it could possibly be 80 years ago when nearly all the necessary data were unknown. I am not lacking in respect for this great pioneer scholar when I say that by now his rendering has become quite inadequate, and is positively misleading on many vital points of doctrine. In 1930 W. E. Soothill attempted an abbreviated version from the Chinese which has not stood the test of time, and merely demonstrates that China missionaries were ill-equipped for grasping the sublimities of Buddhist thought.

During this century only two of the large Sūtras have been translated—the *Perfection of Wisdom in 8,000 Lines* into English[2] and the *Sutra which is Splendid like the Finest Gold* into German.[3] Neither of these translations can be pronounced an unqualified success. Apart from actual errors, which others are more likely to spot than myself, my translation of the *Aṣṭasāhasrikā* is disfigured by innumerable misprints, and the occasional omission of lines must add to the reader's mystification.[4] As with incredulous dismay I watched the bungling slowness of the Calcutta Asiatic Society which took eight years to print 225 pages of straightforward text, I reluctantly decided against entrusting them with the notes, Introduction and Indices, however necessary they might be. Their inclusion would have further postponed publication for an indefinite

[1] For the details see pages 125-9 of this volume.

[2] 1958, by E. Conze, The Asiatic Society, Calcutta.

[3] 1958, by J. Nobel, *Suvarṇaprabhāsottamasūtra*, E. J. Brill, Leiden.

[4] For instance, at the bottom of p. 96 the following lines got lost in the second proofs which I never saw: "synthesis, and that it is in this sense that they are concentrated thought, the same as space. The Tathagata knows *unconcentrated* thoughts for".

number of years, and much of what I had said would have become nearly unrecognizable. By contrast Prof. Nobel has benefited from the superb craftsmanship of the house of Brill, and the printing and layout of his book are as good as they can possibly be. Nor can he be accused of undue haste. From 1927 onwards he has devoted to the intensive study of the *Suvarṇaprabhāsa* more than thirty years, which is about the time a European needs to become really familiar with any of these Sūtras. And yet the result of all this labour is a sad disappointment. Prof. Nobel's translation conveys none of the music, the magnificence, the ethereal glory of this Sūtra, crude misunderstandings of Mahayana thought very often distort it and some of the footnotes betray an almost staggering misapprehension of quite ordinary technical terms.[1] This translation compares most unfavourably with Prof. Nobel's own editions of the Sanskrit and Tibetan text of the *Suvarṇaprabhāsa*, which are models of almost faultless accuracy. The reason is that our professor is a self-confessed "philologist" who puts words before sense and takes no living interest in what he translates. Buddhist thought has never aroused his curiosity, and the veil of haziness which he throws over it shows that he fails to appreciate how precise and unambiguous it is. These Sūtras are spiritual documents, and the spirit alone can fathom them. An uncomprehending attention to the letter will easily turn the sublimest record of wisdom teaching into a string of lifeless absurdities. It is indeed difficult to see how a satisfactory translation of a Mahayana Sūtra can be expected from anyone but a devout and believing Mahayana Buddhist.

For the rest there is little to report. In 1952 J. Ensinck gave us a conscientious translation of a minor Sūtra, the *Question of Rashtrapala*.[2] A few years later I managed, against great odds, to publish a new edition and an annotated translation of the *Diamond Sūtra* (1957–8). But that is about all. Of the Large Prajñaparamita, the key to the entire Mahayana, not even an edition of the Sanskrit text has been accomplished, though I

[1] See e.g. p. 67 n. 7, 70 n. 2, 102 n. 5, 155 n. 6, 161 n. 1, 263 n. 5, 179 n. 4, 260 n. 5, 362 n. 1 (where he admits not knowing what the "four brahmaviharas" are).

[2] Zwolle, Holland.

could bring out a tentative English translation in 1961 and 1964. W. Baruch's text of the *Saddharmapuṇḍarīka* was ready for printing in 1937, but owing to the general indifference it seems to have just vanished with his death a few years ago. In 1953 R. Robinson sent me a full translation of Kumarajiva's Chinese version of *The Exposition* of *Vimalakirti*, but it has remained in typescript and nothing has been done about it since. There are no funds available for this kind of thing. As a result of its apathy the public is not only denied access to scholarly works but is positively misled by substandard books which continue to circulate in default of anything better. Each time I look into the translation of the *Śikshāsamuccaya* (1922), a unique collection of extracts from Mahayana Sūtras, I am shocked by its almost incredible carelessness, especially in the later parts not supervised by C. Bendall. Numerically speaking, perhaps five per cent of the Mahayana Sūtras have been reliably edited, and perhaps two per cent intelligibly translated. It is clear that inferences drawn from the scanty material at our disposal must remain extremely dubious.

This neglect of the Mahayana is rather strange at a time when the most obscure writings of other traditions elicit floods of ink from scholars all over the world. The complete lack of encouragement for these studies seems to point to their having no relation to the needs of any significant section of contemporary society. In consequence the study of Mahayana Sūtras is either left to outsiders lodged precariously on the margin of society, or is carried on for reasons which have little to do with their actual message,—such as an interest in linguistic problems, or a desire to foster Indian national self-esteem. This deep-seated antipathy of the presentage for the revelations of the Mahayana, which was dramatically confirmed recently by the wanton destruction of their Tibetan stronghold, would deserve a more ample explanation. But this is not the place for it.

2. We now turn to the *scholastic literature*. First, as concerns the Madhyamikas, E. Lamotte's translation of one-fourth of Nagarjuna's commentary to the Large Prajñaparamita[1] was a huge step forward. The first volume deals with the Mahayana

[1] *Le Traité de la Grande Vertu de Sagesse*. I, 1944, chaps. 1–15; II, 1949, chaps. 16–30. 1118 pp.

conception of the Buddha and Bodhisattva, and the second gives a very detailed description of the six perfections. The third volume will in the main contain Abhidharma material and to my great joy I heard recently from Prof. Lamotte that he has nearly completed it and that it will appear in the near future. It is still uncertain whether the author of this commentary is the Nagarjuna of the *Verses on the Madhyamika Doctrine*, but no one doubts that it expounds authoritatively the point of view of the Madhyamika school. An almost unbelievable wealth of information is spread before us in this truly encyclopaedic work which was composed at the period when the vigour of Buddhist thought was at its very height. It is rather sad to reflect that the immensely wealthy Anglo-Saxon nations have taken no steps whatsoever to make this masterpiece accessible to the English-speaking public.

The standard commentary on Nagarjuna's *Verses on the Madhyamika Doctrine* is Candrakirti's well-known *Prasannapadā*. Although it calls itself the "Clear-Worded", it has defied European scholarship for more than half a century after de la Vallée Poussin's edition of the Sanskrit text, and scholars have been content to just nibble at the text chapter by chapter.[1] During our period J. W. de Jong has done chapters 18–22 into lucid French,[2] and Jacques May's excellent French translation of the remaining twelve chapters came out in 1959. But what a higgledy-piggledy way of dealing with a great classic all this is! What we really need is a uniform translation of the whole book into English and there is almost no one who would be willing or able to do it.

Essentially an exposition of Candrakirti's point of view is also Prof. T. R. V Murti's *The Central Philosophy of Buddhism* (1955), which combines sustained intellectual effort and lucidity with scrupulous scholarship and metaphysical passion. The book has to be read to be properly appreciated, and I will say no more about it. But its title is a challenge to Western Buddhists which so far they show little sign of heeding, with the result that their faulty perspective vitiates both their

[1] This is the record up to 1940: English: chap. 1, 25, Stcherbatsky, 1927; French: chap. 17 Lamotte, 1938; German: chap. 5, 10, 12–16, S. Schayer, 1930–1.

[2] *Cinq Chapitres de la Prasannapadā*, 1949.

theory and their practice. The central tradition is that of Emptiness, represented by Sarvastivadins, Madhyamikas, and Tibetan Lamas. By contrast, the Theravādins and Zen, which alone have caught on so far, are peripheral. As I said in 1957: "Both in Christianity and in Buddhism we can distinguish between a *central* and a *sectarian* tradition. Christianity originated in the Eastern Mediterranean, and it is there that the central tradition developed. In the outlying districts of Europe, e.g. in Wales, Scotland and Sweden, at the confines of the sea, or in Wittenberg and Bohemia, at the very borders of Mediterranean culture, the Christian faith then appeared in quite new and unexpected guises. As the living tradition had not sufficient strength to penetrate quite to this distance, it was replaced by fanciful ideas which claimed to go back directly to the 'original gospel', and which represented the battered remains of a mighty tradition as the 'only pure' doctrine."

A similar state of affairs can be discerned in Buddhism, which originated in the North of India. It is thereabouts that its central tradition took shape, and it is near there, in Tibet, that it has been best preserved. But when in the course of its expansion Buddhism spread from the *madhyadeśa*, the "middle region" (see *Aṣṭa* xvii 336) to the *pratyantajanapada*, to the border regions, there, at the confines of the sea, in Ceylon and Japan, its mentality became not unakin to that of the Protestants in the outlying districts of Europe. In fact, Ceylonese Theravada, and Japanese Zen both reject the living tradition of Buddhism, the latter in the name of a "direct transmission outside the Scriptures", the former in the name of a Pali Canon which alone is alleged to preserve the original "Buddha-word".[1]

Or, as Christmas Humphreys has put it much more succinctly: "Western Buddhism is now in a curious condition. There are those to whom Theravada Buddhism is all-sufficient, and there is a rapidly increasing group of those interested only in Zen. These are the wings of the bird, but where is the body?"[2] Though I would add that "wing-tips" rather than "wings" might be nearer the mark.

[1] *The Aryan Path*, July 1957, pp. 319–20.

[2] In B. L. Suzuki, *Mahayana Buddhism*, 3rd ed., 1959, p. xi.

So prolific has been the literary output of the Madhyamikas that even after Lamotte and Murti a large part of it has barely been touched. Much of their religious teachings is still buried in the untranslated Chinese pages of Nagarjuna's gigantic commentary. Aryadeva, Nagarjuna's great contemporary, has so far had almost no attention. We still have no clear idea of Bhavaviveka's Svatantrika system,[1] which can be studied only in Tibetan translations, and which seems to have upheld the well-night incredible thesis that in Madhyamika logic valid positive statements can be made. Likewise we continue to be baffled by the teachings and affiliations of the Yogacara-Madhyamikas who worked out the final synthesis of the Mahayana in India. My translation of Maitreya's *Abhisamayālankāra*,[2] a verse summary of the Large Prajñaparamita, was meant as a contribution to the understanding of the Prajñaparamita, and did little to clarify the doctrinal position of this somewhat elusive school. Finally, the all-important art of Meditating on Emptiness seems to have got lost almost completely. It is the one serious shortcoming of Prof. Murti's book that he treats the views of the Madhyamikas as if they were the result of philosophical reasoning, when in fact they derive from meditational experience. The spiritual potency of the Madhyamika teachings can re-assert itself only if and when it can be reintegrated with meditational practice. Emptiness is essentially an object of rapt contemplation, and no amount of inconclusive chatter about it being, or not being, "nothingness", and so on, will be of any avail.

The almost complete neglect of the *Yogācārins* during the last twenty years may perhaps be explained by the numerous pre-1940 studies which have temporarily satiated our curiosity. The views of the Yogacarins have, in any case, never stirred the East to the extent that the Emptiness doctrine has moved it. The contemplation of the Void manifestly sets the mind free, whereas speculations about the "store-consciousness" only

[1] See my *Buddhism*, 1951, p. 125.

[2] Rome 1954. This was followed by an article in *East and West*, Vol. 3, 1954, pp. 192–7, which took the place of an Introduction to the book, and another article in the *Liebenthal Festschrift*, Sino-Indian Studies, Vol. 3, 1951, pp. 21–35, which amplifies some of my comments and in particular gives a survey of the stages of the Path as they appeared to the Mahayana.

provide it with additional puzzles. Prof. E. Frauwallner of Vienna is somewhat partial to this school and has produced several technical articles about it which do not concern the general reader. Every student of Buddhism who knows German will, however, derive great profit from turning to his anthology of philosophically relevant passages from the Sūtras and Shastras.[1] There the Yogacarins are described as "the most important school of the Mahayana" (p. 264), but Prof. Frauwallner is too good a scholar to allow this bias to distort his perspective. His almost invariably accurate translations allow the reader to get a fair idea of first the "doctrine of the Buddha" (pp. 9–60), then the Hinayana schools (pp. 61–142), and finally the Madhyamikas (pp. 143–254) and Yogacarins (pp. 264—407). Experts will grumble at some of his renderings and comments, but no one at present could do better than he has done.

Tantra and Zen

The Tantra has always been the step-child of Buddhist studies. By 1940 W. Y. Evans-Wentz's classical editions of Kazi Dawa-Samdup's translations[2] were almost the only sources of intelligible information to which the English-speaking reader could turn. In addition there were a somewhat inadequate translation, from the Tibetan, of just one chapter of one Tantra,[3] B. Bhattacharya's instructive survey of *The Indian Buddhist Iconography*,[4] based chiefly on the *Sādhanamālā*, and L. A. Waddell's (1895) factual, but hostile and contemptuous description of Tibetan beliefs and rituals.

In the last twenty years the situation has somewhat improved. The outstanding event has been the publication and translation, in 1959, of the *Hevajra Tantra* by D. L. Snellgrove, the first full-length Tantra to have been treated scientifically by a really competent scholar. Celebrated though this Tantra may be, it turns out to be a work of slight literary merit,

[1] *Die Philosophie des Buddhismus*, Berlin 1956.

[2] *The Book of the Dead*, 1927. *Milarepa*, 1928. *Tibetan Yoga*, 1935.

[3] Kazi Dawa-Samdup, *Śrīcakrasambhāra Tantra*, 1919, pp. 1–68.

[4] The "second and enlarged edition" of 1958 is not exactly an improvement, as I have shown in *Oriental Art*, Vol. 1, 1959, p. 31.

composed by members of the lower classes who knew Sanskrit only imperfectly. Its construction is positively chaotic, and each topic is dropped almost as soon as it has been raised. The primitive swing and vigour of the original, naturally lost in the English version, will often stir the modern reader, but the contents will rarely edify him. This Tantra attempts in fact to combine the lofty Madhyamika philosophy with the magical and orgiastic rites current in Indian villages living on the level of the Old Stone Age. That was certainly worth doing at the time, but the result can scarcely have an immediate message to people living in our own extremely artificial and urbanized social environment. Readers should therefore be warned that this text, though a document of great historical importance, contains little that could at present be assimilated by Western Buddhists.

Three of the more important strands of the Tibetan tradition have also become better known in recent years: The Nyingmapa through Evans-Wentz's *The Tibetan Book of the Great Liberation* (1954), the Kahgyutpa by H. V. Guenther's admirable translation of Sgam-po-pa's *The Jewel Ornament of Liberation* (1959), and the Gelugpa by the information which Alex Wayman has provided on Tsongkhapa's *Stages of the Path of Enlightenment.*[1] Nor should we omit to mention G. N. Roerich's translation of Gshon-nu-dpal's *The Blue Annals* (1949, 1953) which throws much light on the development of Tibetan thought up to 1478.

In addition there have been four reliable and authoritative accounts of Tantric Buddhism, by H. von Glasenapp in 1940,[2] G. Tucci in 1949,[3] S. B. Dasgupta in 1950[4] and D. L. Snellgrove in 1957.[5] They all agree in presenting the Tantra as a perfectly intelligible system of great religious value, which emerges quite logically from the preceding phases of Buddhist doctrinal formulation.

[1] A rather inaccessible synopsis has appeared in *Phi Theta Annual Papers of the Oriental Languages Honor Society*, University of California, III (1952), pp. 51–82.

[2] *Buddhistische Mysterien*. Also in French.

[3] *Tibetan Painted Scrolls*. Three vols.

[4] *An Introduction to Tāntric Buddhism*. Also: *Obscure religious cults as background of Bengali literature* (1946).

[5] *Buddhist Himalaya*.

By themselves these scholarly productions must, however, remain relatively barren, since a knowledge of the Sanskrit and Tibetan alone cannot provide the clue to the Tantric systems which are essentially psychological in their purpose and intention. For it is the specific contribution of the Tantra to deal with the repercussions of the traditional Buddhist practices on the unconscious mind which they irritate and on the occult forces which they activate. In the long run our mental health will, of course, greatly benefit from Buddhist methods of living and contemplation. In the short run the reverse often happens. The stresses of an unnatural mode of living may well bring latent neurotic tendencies to the fore. Spiritual progress requires long periods of solitude. Social isolation begets anxiety, which is a fear of nothing in particular, all the more intense, heart-rending and bowel-shaking for its inability to find anything tangible to be afraid of. The constant curb imposed on our egoistic inclinations and desires must cause a sense of frustration with all its attendant mental disturbances, particularly because the resulting anger should not be "sublimated" into religious fanaticism and the zealous persecution of others, nor the resulting depression dulled by drugs or alcohol. What is more, self-restraint must bring with it a severe conflict between the conscious and the unconscious minds, because the conscious effort to suppress an instinctual urge intensifies it in the Unconscious. Finally, a number of unsuspected forces, both occult and spiritual, are awakened, slowly or suddenly. Without the help of a really competent spiritual guide we may frequently be at a loss how to handle them.

These psychic disturbances were well known to medieval contemplatives under the name of *accidia*, and Hakuin spoke of them as the "Zen sickness", which he described in his *Yasen Kanna*.[1] The complacency of people who never exert any pressure upon themselves is startled, and secretly gratified, by the spiritual, mental and physical disorders of those who really attempt to do something. These disturbances, like the "Dark Night of the Spirit", are not signs of failure, as the untutored worldling is apt to suppose, but signs of growth—the creaking

[1] H. Dumoulin, *Zen*, 1959, pp. 259–62. This work was translated into English by R. D. M. Shaw and Wilhelm Schiffer. pp. 127. *Monumenta Nipponica* XIII, 1957, pp. 101.

of the rheumatic joints foretelling their eventual mobility. Nevertheless, a great deal of suffering and waste of time could be avoided if we knew how to dispel these disorders. In the heyday of the dharma, people took these troubles in their stride, and dealt with them just anyhow. One thousand years after the Buddha's Nirvana, when social conditions became increasingly adverse to the spiritual life, they began to constitute a real problem, and the Tantra was evolved to cope with them by special methods which allowed the practitioner to regain his innate radiance and calm.

This is not the place for showing the abundance of psychological knowledge hidden away in the cryptic language of the Tantric writings. Two extremely elementary examples must suffice to show its presence. The Oedipus Complex, a potent source of a constant sense of guilt, far too often dismissed as Freud's invention, is clearly described as a normal pre-conceptual experience by the *Tibetan Book of the Dead* (p. 179), which here only reproduces the older tradition of the *Abhidharmakośa*. Secondly, a beginner who wishes to direct his energies into really fruitful channels must first of all determine the type he belongs to.[1] Only then can he decide which one of the numerous methods of salvation to pursue. In this connection he should take notice of such things as the equivalence of Prajñaparamita with Akshobhya and the hate-family, and that of Amitabha, whose paradise is described in the *Sukhāvatīvyūha*, with the greed-family.

What I am trying to say is that, in order to disclose to us people of the twentieth century the living meaning of the Tantra, a scholar must not only know Sanskrit and Tibetan, but also be familiar with modern psychology and one or other of the occult arts. G. Tucci has made some useful remarks about the relation of the Tantra to the psychology of the Unconscious,[2] and it is H. V. Guenther's merit to have perceived the task,[3] although wilfulness has so far prevented him from saying much of lasting value. Likewise, though many readers will not believe it, it is obvious that no one can do justice to the occult side of the Tantra without knowing at least one of the

[1] See my *Buddhist Scriptures*, 1959, pp. 116–21.
[2] In his book on *The Theory and practice of the Mandala*, 1961.
[3] *Yuganaddha, the Tantric view of life*. 1952.

magical arts, such as astrology,[1] and without some actual experience of the working of the magical forces within and all around us. If such a marriage of linguistic scholarship with first-hand psychological and occult knowledge should ever take place, then and only then will the Tantra become a vital ingredient of Western Buddhism. At present it is likely to be merely the object of an idle and invariably baffled curiosity, or an outlet for interests more easily gratified by a perusal of Boccaccio's *Decamerone*, or of *Lady Chatterley's Lover*.

Ch'an arose simultaneously with the Tantra. The more we learn about both, the more we see how much they have in common. For Ch'an and the Tantra are the two characteristic creations of the third phase of Buddhism, which began about A.D. 500, and they both respond to similar problems in similar ways.[2] In the thirties D. T. Suzuki put Ch'an, or rather Zen, on the map, and for long he was the only source of what we in the West believe we know about Zen. In recent years the inevitable reaction has set in.

The spread of literacy has filled the world with minor intellectuals who regard any kind of eminence as a personal reproach, and undisputed eminence as altogether unendurable. Few of their mutterings against Suzuki have found their way into print. For years, however, they assured one another in confidential whispers that Suzuki utterly failed to present Zen as the Chinese and Japanese actually understand it. An article of Hu-shih's, extant only in Chinese, was for a long time said to have exploded Suzuki's pretensions once and for all. At last Hu-shih's criticisms appeared in English,[3] and it turned out that Suzuki had a perfect answer.[4] So the tune has now changed, though the melody remains the same.

[1] How different the spirit of academic scholarship! When I suggested to a scholar who works on the *Kālacakra* that a knowledge of astrology might be useful to him, he thought I was mad or joking.

[2] For details see my *A short history of Buddhism*, 1960, chap. III, 1 and 6.

[3] Ch'an (Zen) Buddhism in China: Its history and method. *Philosophy East and West*, III, 1953, pp. 3–24.

[4] Ibid. pp. 25–46. Reprinted in *Studies in Zen*, 1955, pp. 129–64. This tremendously interesting controversy was continued in *Philosophy East and West* up to 1956, with P. Ames and Arthur Waley joining in. It is very important for the whole problem of the relation between the historical and spiritual approach to the dharma.

Hu-shih is an historian who wants to know exactly what happened, how, and in what sequence. For Suzuki, on the other hand, "Zen is above space-time relations and naturally above historical facts". Arthur Waley tried to mediate between the two with a parody of Han Shan:

> "Water and ice do one another no harm;
> History and religion—both alike are good".

There is no time here to give the reasons why excessive attention to the facts of Buddhist history must do harm to the spiritual vision of the dharma. I must be content to distinguish between three kinds of historian—the scientific, the humanistic and the transcendental. The first studies a butterfly after killing it and fixing it with a pin into a glass case, where it lies quite still and can leisurely be inspected from all angles. The second lets it fly in the sun, and looks wonderingly at its pretty ways. The third assures us that a man will know a butterfly only if he becomes one. As a creative thinker Suzuki tells the descriptive historian, whether scientific or humanistic, that Zen must be grasped within, and not as an outside historical fact, and that only by actually becoming Zen can one know it. Although his demands may be rather hard on the average historian, I see no reason to disagree with him.

Apart from Suzuki's overtowering eminence, his effect on some Western intellectuals has provoked unfavourable reactions. Unsuspectingly Suzuki fed an Eastern form of spirituality into a predominantly ex-Protestant environment which, having lost all touch with spiritual tradition, gravitated inevitably towards a self-assertive nihilism. Stirred by his message, a vast literature on "Zen" arose in England, France, Italy, Germany, and the U.S.A., ranging from positively stuffy and ultra-respectable "square" Zennists to the wild whoopees of Mr. Kerouac and his Beatniks.[1] All that there is in these books about Zen comes from Suzuki, and he is held responsible for the misunderstandings they contain.[2] If Suzuki is to be

[1] In this connection Allan Watt's pamphlet on *Beat Zen, Square Zen and Zen* (1959) is of some interest.

[2] So Chen-chi Chang, "*The nature of Ch'an (Zen) Buddhism*", *Philosophy East and West* VI 4, 1958. Though it makes some telling points against some of the vulgarizers, this article makes the essential soundness of Suzuki's own work quite apparent.

blamed for anything, it is an insufficient awareness of the aridity of the desert into which he transplanted his lovely azalea tree.

Zen was designed to operate within emptiness. When coming West it is transferred into a vacuum. Let us just recollect what Zen took for granted, as its antecedents, basis and continuing background: a long and unbroken tradition of spiritual "know-how"; firm and unquestioned metaphysical beliefs, and not just a disbelief in everything; a superabundance of Scriptures and images; a definite discipline supervised by authoritative persons; insistence on right livelihood and an austere life for all exponents of the Dharma; and a strong Sangha, composed of thousands of mature and experienced persons housed in thousands of temples, who could keep deviations from Buddhist principles within narrow bounds. As I have said elsewhere, the Ch'an sect "found a situation in which the fervour of the faithful had so multiplied the means of salvation, in the form of Sūtras, commentaries, philosophical subtleties, images and rites, that the goal itself was apt to be lost sight of, and the spiritual life was in danger of being choked by the very things which were designed to foster it. In their reaction against the overgrown apparatus of piety they advocated a radical simplication of the approach to enlightenment. They never tired of denouncing the misuse of this apparatus, which could so easily become an end in itself".[1] It is the fundamental error of many Europeans to mistake these denunciations for a desire to do away altogether with traditional spiritual practices. Suzuki could not possibly have foreseen that. Likewise, when he condemned the intellect as inhibiting our original spontaneity, Suzuki took it for granted that, once the intellect is eliminated, the Tao will take over. He was unfamiliar with Western irrationalist philosophy, where the elimination of the intellect makes room for nothing more than the uninhibited assertion of self-willed instincts. When speaking of spontaneity he meant the spontaneity of Sages, and not that of overgrown schoolboys.

Finally, Suzuki represents only one form of Zen, the Rinzai sect of Japan. Post-Suzukian Zen studies have tried to fill in

1 *A short history of Buddhism*, 1960, pp. 74–5. *Buddhismo*, 1958, pp. 811–2.

our knowledge of other sects, thereby hoping to gain a fuller view and a more correct perspective:

1. H. Dumoulin, a Jesuit of the Catholic Sophia University at Tokyo, has placed Ch'an into the context of Chinese history and thought. So intent had Suzuki been on explaining the spiritual message of the Ch'an masters, that it is very hard from his books alone to form an idea of their localization in time and space, or of their doctrinal affiliations. In an admirable article, later on admirably edited by Ruth Fuller Sasaki,[1] Dumoulin describes the development of Ch'an during the T'ang and Sung periods, i.e. during the time when Ch'an was at the acme of its creativity, produced a great number of strong personalities, and achieved a startling originality of expression. In 1959 Dumoulin published in German a general survey of Zen history[2] which was in 1963 translated into English. This handbook is a most conscientious and relatively unbiassed piece of work which gives all the relevant facts as known at present. One may complain that it is confined to the external historical facts, but they are surely worth knowing, as long as they are not taken too seriously. Nothing prevents his readers from suffusing the facts with their own religious experience, if they have any.

2. Rinzai Zen has become so closely bound up with the "Japanese national character", or rather the mentality of the Samurai, that it is unlikely to be the same as Ch'an, a creation of the essentially pacific Chinese genius. Zen, in fact, is *not* Ch'an, but a response of the Japanese mind to Ch'an, just as Ch'an itself had been the response of the Chinese mind to Indian Buddhism. The study of Ch'an thought has in recent years been advanced by Fung Yu-lan[3] to whom we owe a masterly exposition of the philosophical views of the Ch'an masters, and partly by a number of translations, which range from the T'ang masters[4] to the later Ch'an literature of the seventeenth to

[1] *The development of Chinese Zen*, 1953 (First in German in 1941).

[2] *Zen Geschichte und Gestalt*. 1959.

[3] *A history of Chinese philosophy*, vol. II, 1953.

[4] Shen-hui (668–760) into English in *Asia Major*, III, 1952, 132–55, and into French by J. Gernet in various places. Hui Hai (ca. 800) by J. Blofeld, 1948, 1959. The *Mumonkan* into German by G. H. Dumoulin, Monumenta Serica, VIII, 1943, pp. 41–102.

twentieth centuries,[1] which turns out to be surprisingly interesting, vigorous and elevating. It must, however, be pointed out that generally speaking these translations, especially of the earlier literature, leave much to be desired and will have to be revised in due course. They are inaccurate for two reasons: *a*) Far from rejecting the Sūtras, the Ch'an masters were absolutely saturated in them, and many of their sayings are either direct quotations from the Sūtras, or contain allusions to them. A translator who does not know the Sūtras, or believes that they are irrelevant, will make many mistakes. What, for instance, can he make of Tsung-chih's reply to Bodhidharma's query about her achievement if he does not know that it refers to chap. 28 of the *Perfection of Wisdom in 8,000 Lines*?[2] *b*) Like the Tantra, Ch'an was largely a movement of the lower strata of society. In consequence the koans and other sayings of the masters are couched in colloquial Chinese, which differs from the language of the Mandarins. It is impossible to ascertain the meaning of the terms used by looking them up in a dictionary of classical Chinese, and Prof. Demiéville is at present engaged in determining their exact connotation by studying the language of the Chinese documents from Tun-huang.

3. Prof. P. Demiéville[3] and G. Tucci[4] have revealed the presence of numerous adherents of Ch'an in Tibet in the eighth century, and the Tibetan material will one day have to be co-ordinated with the Chinese.

4. Even in Japan itself, Rinzai with 6,000 temples is in a minority compared with Sōtō which has 15,000.[5] Sōtō prefers ordinary people to Samurais, has always remained aloof from political affairs, cultivates "gentleness of spirit" (*nyunanshin*), expects little from the koan technique, and does not altogether reject logic and intellect, but is ready to reason and to make sense. As it becomes better known in the West, it will prove more congenial and attractive than Rinzai to some tempera-

[1] Charles Luk, *Ch'an and Zen Teaching*, I, 1960.

[2] pp. 192–193 of my translation (1958).

[3] *Le Concile de Lhasa*, I, 1952.

[4] *Minor Buddhist Texts*, II, 1958.

[5] There is also Obaku, the smallest sect, with 550 temples. About its special approach see Tetsugen (1630–1683), *Sermon sur le Bouddhisme Zen*, by M. Shibata. *Présence du Bouddhisme*, France-Asie, 1959, pp. 633–53.

ments. So far, however, the literature available on Sōtō[1] seems rather uninteresting and elusive. This may be because the sect has so far not been able to mobilize any great literary talent, and its books are usually badly written by persons none too familiar with the English language. Or perhaps the Sōtō monks are really serious about their not theorizing and having no thought, and confine themselves to sitting in Zazen, an activity which has little entertainment value for onlookers. The future will show.

This concludes the three articles in which I have described to the best of my knowledge the progress made in Buddhist studies during the last twenty years. Concentrating on essentials and on publications of unimpeachable scholarship, I have tried to indicate the extent to which our knowledge of Buddhist history has been revolutionized since the end of the last war. Through the devoted labours of scholars all over the world we now have gained access to a very wide range of documents representing the different lineages in which the holy doctrine has been handed on. It is up to us to see to it that the rain which has descended so abundantly from the Rain-cloud of the dharma actually nourishes our spiritual faculties, and does not just go down the drain of a mere intellectual curiosity.

[1] R. Masunaga, *The Sōtō approach to Zen*, 1958, contains on pp. 81–192 extracts from Dōgen's writings. The only well written accounts are those translated by R. T. Leggett in my *Buddhist Scriptures*, 1959. pp. 134–44.

Buddhist Saviours

I

In the interest of terminological precision the Sanskrit terms corresponding to "save" and "saviour" must first be ascertained. When the Baptists of Serampore translated the New Testament in 1808, they used *trāṇa* for "salvation" and *trātur* for "saviour", the root being *trai*, to protect. Just so the Bactrian coins had translated *sōtēr* as *trātur*. Monier Williams's *A Dictionary of English and Sanskrit* (1851) gives further equivalents derived from the roots *raksh, pāl, gup*, to guard, defend, protect, *tṛī* cs. to carry across ((*nis*) *tāraka*, etc.), *uddhṛi*, to extricate and *muc*, to liberate ((*pari*)*mokshaka*). In addition we may mention *nātha*, helper, protector and *śaraṇa*, refuge. In fact, however, Buddhist terminology has no exact equivalent to the Christian conception of a "saviour". H. A. Jaeschke in his *Tibetan-English Dictionary* tells us that in Tibet Protestant missionaries used *skyabs-mgon* (*śaraṇa* + *nātha*) for "Saviour, Redeemer, Christ", whereas Catholics seem to prefer *blu-pa-po*, from *blu-ba*, to redeem (a pawn, pledge, or security). Neither of these words was ever used by Buddhists, as the dictionaries of Das and Lokesh Chandra make quite clear.

It will be best to first describe the Buddhist beliefs about "saviours" in the actual words of the texts themselves. In many ways they are so similar to Christian views that missionaries have often seen them as a counterfeit gospel deliberately created by the Devil to deceive the faithful. At the same time, when the exact words of the originals are faithfully rendered into English it becomes obvious that there are no precise equivalents to the key terms, that the finer shades of meaning and the emotional flavours and overtones differ throughout, that much of this teaching must seem strange to Christians and that in fact the logic behind it is at variance with all the basic presuppositions of Christianity. From the very start we must be careful to eschew such loaded words as worship, prayer, sin, love, eternal or supernatural, and instead use more neutral terms such as revere (= to regard with extreme respect), vow, evil, devotion, deathless and supernormal, and we must also distrust any description of the Buddhist doctrine which, without many qualifications, attributes to the saviours "grace", "mercy" or "forgiveness".

1. The famous twenty-fourth chapter of the *Lotus of the Good Law*[1] contains all the main ingredients of our theme. There we read that all those beings "who experience sufferings will, on hearing the name of Avalokiteśvara, the Bodhisattva, the great being, be set free (*parimucyeran*) from their ills". What they have to do is "to learn" (*grahaṇa*) his name and to "bear it in mind" (*dhārayati*), to "invoke" or "implore" him (*ākrandaṃ kuryuḥ*), to "pay homage" to him, to "recollect" (*smarato*) and to "revere" him (*pūjayati*). "Think of him (*smarathā*), think of him, without hesitation, / Of Avalokitesvara, the being so pure! / In death, disaster and calamity, / He is the saviour, refuge and resort (*trāṇu bhoti śaraṇaṃ parāyaṇam*)."

The "merit" derived from bearing in mind his name, or of even once paying homage to him, is "immeasurable" and lasts through many aeons. Avalokitesvara is "endowed with inconceivable virtues". For aeons he has "purified his Vow (*praṇidhāna*)". Great "might" (*prabhāva*) is attributed to him, and much is made of his miraculous, psychic and magical powers (*maha-rddhika, vikurvaṇa-prātihārya, māyopama-samādhi*). "He has reached perfection in wonderworking power (*ṛddhībala*), / He is trained in abundant (*vipula*) cognition and skill in means." He "gives fearlessness to frightened beings", he is their "saviour" (*trātaru*) and "destroys all sorrow, fear and ill".

There is, however, nothing unique about Avalokitesvara, and he does no more than all Bodhisattvas are bidden to do. In the *Prajñāpāramitā*, for instance, we read:

Desirous of the welfare of the world with its gods, men and asuras, desirous to benefit it, to make it happy, to make it secure, the Bodhisattva, when he has seen those ills which afflict beings on the plane of Samsara, produces an attitude of mind (*cittotpāda*) in which he reflects: "Having crossed over (*tīrṇa*), we shall help across

[1] *Saddharmapuṇḍarīka-sūtram*, ed. U. Wogihara and C. Tsuchida (1958), 362–74.

(*tārayema*) those beings who have not yet crossed! Freed we shall free those beings who are not yet free! Comforted we shall comfort those beings who are as yet without comfort! Gone to Nirvana we shall lead to Nirvana those beings who have not yet got there!"[1]

More specifically the Bodhisattvas promise that, on having won full enlightenment, "we will become a shelter (*trāṇam*) for the world, a refuge, the place of rest (*layanam*), the final resort (*parāyaṇam*), islands, lights and leaders of the world!"[2]

2. From the earliest times onwards the Buddhists have described salvation as a process of crossing over.[3] In later times *Tārā*, the deity who ferries across (*tārayati*), became the "Saviouress" *par excellence*. At one stage of her development she is closely connected with Avalokitesvara,[4] and conceived analogously to him, as a kind of female counterpart who in China then evolved into the female Kwan Yin. She is said to have emerged from a tear he shed when beholding the misery of the world, or from a blue ray emanating from his eyes, or, alternatively, she 'arose from the countless filaments of the lotus-face of the Saviour of the triple world',[5] i.e. of Avalokiteśvara. Or, again, the Taras are 'the mothers of the world, born of the power of Amitabha's vow and understanding, endowed with great compassion, created for the world's

[1] E. Conze, *The Gilgit Manuscript of the Ashṭādaśasāhasrikāprajñāpāramitā* (1962), 248.

[2] *Ashṭasāhasrikā Prajñāpāramitā*, ed. R. Mitra (1888), 293. These terms are then explained in pp. 294–9.

[3] For the details see I. B. Horner, *The Early Buddhist Theory of Man Perfected* (1936).

[4] But after A.D. 750, under the influence of the theory of the *Five Jinas*, the green Tara was assigned to Amoghasiddhi (as in the *Sādhanamālā*, trans. E. Conze, *Buddhist Meditation* (1956), 137) and the Vajratara to Vajrapaṇi, of the Akshobhya family. At about the same time "Tārā" became a general term for "saviouress", or "helpful goddess", or "beneficent deity", and this resulted in great indefiniteness and gave her a truly Protean character. Long lists of Taras were elaborated, some due to separating the services which she may render, while others refer to the localities in which she had a shrine. One of these lists is *The book of praises of the 21 forms of Tārā*, ed. and trans. into German by S. Hummel, *Lamaistische Studien* (1950), 97–109.

[5] Hummel 97, of the *rab-tu dpa'-ba'i sgrol-ma*.

saving.'[1] And so, intent on freeing all beings from birth-and death, the Tara can say:

It is for the protection of the world that I have been produced by the Jinas. In places of terror, which bristle with swords, and where dangers abound, / When only my (108) names are recollected, I always protect all beings, I will ferry them across (*tārayishyāmi*) the great flood of their manifold fears. / Therefore the great Seers sing of me in the world under the name of Tara.

What is needed is to "correctly repeat her names" and Tara will "fulfil all hopes". "These 108 names have been proclaimed for your welfare; / They are mysterious, wonderful, secret, hard to get even by Gods; / They bring luck and good fortune, destroy all evil, / Heal all sickness and bring ease to all beings." Then follows a catalogue of the benefits derived from their recital, and they include everything that worldly or unworldly men may desire, from wealth, health, cleverness and success in litigation to spiritual virtues and the promotion of enlightenment. "Whoever meditates on our Blessed Lady in a lonely mountain cave, he will behold her face to face with his own eyes. And the Blessed Lady herself bestows upon him his very respiration, and all else. Not to say any more, she puts the very Buddhahood, so hard to win, in the very palm of his hand.[2] She "alone by herself, effectively removes all evil by the fact of her name being heard or recollected (*smṛtyā*)",[3] for "her mercy flows out to all creatures without distinction."[4]

3. In Buddhist mythology Avalokitesvara and Tara, two Bodhisattvas, are held to be dependent on a perfectly enlightened Buddha—the Buddha *Amitābha*. The texts contain some information about Amitabha's antecedent "Vow".[5] Aeons ago, when he was the monk Darmakara he pronounced forty-eight Vows in front of the Buddha Lokesvararaja. The

[1] *The* 108 *Names of the Holy Tārā*, trans. E. Conze, ed. *Buddhist Texts* (1954), no. 176, p. 197. Also the following quotations are from this source.

[2] *Sādhanamālā* in E. Conze, *Buddhist Meditation* (1956), 138–9.

[3] Sarvajñamitra, *Sragdharāstotram*, ed. S. Ch. Vidyabhushana (1908), v. 8.

[4] *Ibid*. v. 3.

[5] See *Hobogirin*, ed. P. Demiéville (1929), 26; H. de Lubac, *Amida* (1955), 65–7; *Buddhist Texts*, 206. I have glossed over the considerable divergences between the different sources, which would be of interest only in a specialized study.

eighteenth Vow is generally held to be the most important, and its essence is the promise that "when the time comes for me to become a Buddha, I will not enter into full enlightenment unless all beings who believe in me and love me with all their hearts are able to win rebirth in my kingdom if they should wish to do so". Once reborn in this Buddha-realm, they can be trained for enlightenment, "because no being can be turned back from the supreme enlightenment if he has heard the name of the Lord Amitabha, and, on hearing it, with one single thought raises his heart to Him with a resolve connected with serene faith". As a result of this Vow those who rely on Amitabha's "promise" and "solemn oath" will be reborn in the "Happy Land" where they will receive further training from Him. The faithful express their belief by invoking the Buddha's name ("Homage to the Buddha Amitabha!", "Nembutsu" in Japanese). Shinran has formulated the doctrine in a somewhat extreme form:[1]

At the very moment the desire to call the Nembutsu is awakened in us in the firm faith that we can attain rebirth in the Pure Land through the saving grace of the Inconceivable Grand Vow, the all-embracing, none-forsaking virtue of Amida is conferred on us. Once belief in Amida's Vow is established, no other virtue is necessary, for there is no goodness that surpasses Nembutsu. . . . One who strives to accumulate merits through his own efforts is not in accord with Amida's Grand Will, since he lacks absolute, pure faith in its power. But if he re-orients his ego-centred mind and acquiesces in Amida's Grand Will, he will attain rebirth in the True Land of Fulfilment. . . . To be egoless means leaving good and evil to the natural working of karmic law and surrendering wholeheartedly to the Grand Vow. . . . For rebirth in the Pure Land cleverness is not necessary,—just complete and unceasing absorption in gratitude to Amida.

4. Avalokitesvara, Tara and Amitabha are three Saviours who belong to one "family" (*kula*). They are connected with the world-system of Sukhavati, the Paradise or "Buddha-field", which is situated far in the West. This Western Paradise has made an exceptionally strong impact on the imagination of the Buddhists, in accordance with a so far unexplained propensity of the archaic mythological imagination which in

[1] *Tannisho*, trans. Higashi Honganji (1961), 2, 6, 33, 45.

many cultures has placed the "Islands of the Blessed" into the West.[1] But there are many, many more. The Scriptures mention thousands of Buddhas and Bodhisattvas, and dozens have become objects of cults in various parts of Asia. Though they may differ in minor details from the Amitabha family, they are all variations on the same theme of which the main outlines have been given, and there is no point in describing them any further.

II

What is common to all these "saviours", however, is that they were unknown to original Buddhism and that the "Hinayana" continued to ignore them, with the solitary exception of Maitreya, the coming Buddha. In fact, Amidism and similar cults may well be considered as almost a new religion, which arose five hundred years after the founder's death and owed much to contact with the non-Indian world. According to some it has completely departed from the original doctrine, turning it into the exact opposite of itself. The protagonists of the older Buddhism often claim that the "historical Buddha" was not a "saviour", that, as distinct from Christianity, Buddhism knows no external saviours, and that everyone must save himself and no one can save another. With the somewhat extreme views of Shinran we may contrast the equally extreme views of the present Theravada orthodoxy in Ceylon. It will suffice to quote just one representative, the Ven. Walpola Rahula,[2] who, in the words of Prof. Demiéville, presents an "aspect of Buddhism"—"humanist, rational, Socratic in some respects, Evangelic in others, or again almost scientific"—which "has for its support a great deal of authentic scriptural evidence" (see below, p. 44). Now let us listen to the Ven. *bhikkhu*:

A man has the power to liberate himself from all bondage through his own personal effort and intelligence. . . . If the Buddha is to be called a "saviour" at all, it is only in the sense that he discovered and showed the Path to Liberation, Nirvana. But we must tread the Path ourselves. . . According to the Buddha, man's emancipation

[1] E. Conze, *Buddhism* (1951), 205; H. de Lubac, *Amida* (1955), 63.

[2] *What the Buddha Taught* (1959), 1–15.

depends on his own realization of the Truth, and not on the benevolent grace of a god or any external power as a reward for his obedient good behaviour. . . . Almost all religions are built on faith,—rather "blind" faith it must seem. But in Buddhism emphasis is laid on "seeing", knowing, understanding, and not on faith or belief.[1]

Though we must, of course, bear in mind that the extreme positions of Shinran and Rahula are rare and untypical. Far from sharing Shinran's exclusive reliance on Amida's Vow, the bulk of the Mahayanists advocated innumerable additional practices as aids to salvation. Far from sharing Rahula's excessive rationalism, even the non-Mahayanists have at all times and to a varying extent made provision for attitudes which can be properly called "religious". Rahula assures us that "among the founders of religions the Buddha was the only teacher who did not claim to be other than a human being, pure and simple". It is true that to win enlightenment the Buddha used only resources which are open to all humans and not beyond the capacity of human nature as such, and that his powers are supernormal merely because they are based on highly developed moral purification and mental concentration.[2] But though the Buddha was a human being, he was certainly a most extraordinary one. Like Jesus and Mohammed he had supernormal powers and could work miracles; his body had thirty-two special marks and much of it refused to burn up on his funeral pyre; and, though essentially a teacher who exhorts and instructs, he was more than an ordinary human teacher because omniscient, infallible and completely dependable. At least that is the tradition of all the schools. In addition he is often called *Bhagavad* and *Tathāgata*, and both these words

[1] As Winston L. King well expresses the Theravada theory in a book soon to be published: "The Buddha is not a saviour in the religious sense. For one cannot address a prayer to him, saying 'save me!' Nor make an offering to him to 'please' him. Nor expect acts of grace to emanate from him nor experience his love. One reveres the memory of the Buddha as a supreme teacher and example." For a more extensive explanation of the Theravada position see *Devotion in Buddhism*, Buddhist Publication Society (1960), Kandy, Ceylon.

[2] Though if we go more deeply into these things, they become also more complicated. The Son of God was also called the Son of Man, and Buddha, the man, was also known as "the god above the gods."

have distinctly numinous connotations.[1] His followers appreciated not only his teaching, but also his mere presence, they craved for the very sight of HIM and expected protection from being "brought to mind" by the Buddhas and Lords. They habitually venerated relics, Stupas, Caityas and the Bodhi-tree, which were the visible signs of his presence on earth. Though, of course, a Buddhist's devotions are not so much petitions to a God, but a means by which he renews his own courage and confidence. The rationalist orthodoxy of Ceylon has a vision of Buddhism which is as truncated and impoverished as the fideism of Shinran, and it is no accident that they are both geographically located at the outer periphery of the Buddhist world.

III

Even the basic act of "taking refuge" with the Buddha, Dharma and Samgha, which is common to all followers of the Dharma, involves a certain amount of faith, and may call forth devotion on the part of those who are thus inclined.[2] Essentially, however, it implies trust in the Buddha as a "saviour" in the strictly limited sense that he had discovered the doctrine (*dharma*) which, if properly applied, must without any doubt lead to salvation. More than this is implied when we speak of Avalokitesvara, etc., as "saviours". They effect the salvation of beings by more than the enunciation of a transcendental doctrine.[3] But all that is said about them respects in every way the framework of the original teaching from which the later developments have not radically departed and from which they can be derived without a break. Though the activities of these Bodhisattvas must seem quite miraculous and extraordinary, they operate strictly within the law of *karma*, and their power to do good is based on the enormous amount of "merit" (*puṇya*) which they have accumulated, on the vast

[1] See my *Buddhist Thought in India* (1962), 27.

[2] E.g. sGampopa, *The Jewel Ornament of Liberation*, trans. H. V. Guenther (1959), 103 sq.

[3] In fact they rather exert the three functions of the Blessed Lord which are enumerated in *Bhagavadgīta*, IV, 8.

extent of the "roots of good" (*kuśalamūla*) which they have "matured". "Merit" is that quality of an action which leads to future happiness, either worldly or supramundane. As long as we stay within the strictly *moral* sphere, there is some correspondence and proportion between virtue and reward, between crime and punishment. So we are told in *Majjhima Nikāya* no. 135[1] of the karmic effects of seven wholesome and seven unwholesome modes of action. The first normally lead to rebirth in the hells, the second to rebirth in the heavens. But in case the offender is reborn as a human being, then the punishment fits the crime. Killers will be short-lived, the jealous will be people of little account, the stingy will be poor, and so on. And likewise, those who have abstained from killing will be long-lived, etc. From other sources we learn that a gluttonous person becomes a hog, a rapacious one a tiger, etc.

But this correspondence no longer holds good when we move into the *spiritual* sphere. An action is "spiritual" when it is 1. Directed to a transcendental object; or 2. completely disinterested. Whereas the reward of moral actions is limited, that of spiritual acts has no limit, and "bears no comparison" to the merit of moral actions. This has two consequences:

1. A simple act of faith, when turned on the Buddha or on a proclamation of his Dharma, produces an inconceivable amount of merit which may outweigh countless moral defaults. A well-known stanza which must be fairly old, because common to many traditions,[2] tells us that the Buddha is inconceivable, and so is his Dharma, and in consequence faith in the inconceivable also produces an inconceivable reward. The commentary explains "inconceivable" (*acintiya*) as "that which seems incredible to unbelievers",[3] and alludes to what is said in a Sūtra about the enormous consequences of "one single thought of faith".[4] In consequence a faithful and devout longing for the Transcendental purifies the believer to quite an extraordinary extent, and through faith he jumps ahead by

[1] A more elaborate account on the same lines is the *Mahā-Karmavibhanga*, ed. and trad. S. Lévi (1932).

[2] S. Lévi, 153–5, 169–70, 176.

[3] *Ibid.*, 154–5.

[4] See also *Apadāna*, 336, for the miraculous results (*acchariyam*) of one single act of devotion.

leaps and bounds, whereas morality, meditation and wisdom can advance him only at a comparative snail's pace.

2. A Bodhisattva reaches on the seventh stage a condition where, now a "celestial Bodhisattva",[1] he is quite disinterested in what he does, and acts exclusively out of consideration for others. He has solved all his own personal problems, he could enter Nirvana, but during the seventh, eighth and ninth stages of his career he chooses to stay in the world. The fact that he could enter Nirvana shows that he has enough merit for himself, and that all the further merit generated by his good deeds has no karmic effects on him and cannot benefit him personally. So he bestows it on others through what is called the "dedication of merit",[2] drawing on what is known to Catholics as the *thesaurus ecclesiae*, or the *thesaurus meritorum Christi et Sanctorum*.[3]

In this way the believer's progress is immensely accelerated, partly because he generates extra merit by his acts of faith, and partly because he benefits from the merits generated by the celestial Bodhisattvas. For the Mahayana salvation does not depend on the teaching alone, but on manipulating "merit" in such a way that conditions are produced in which it can be appreciated and understood. What is the use of preaching the holy doctrine to the mill hands of Manchester?

So far about the karmic side. A few words must still be said about three other aspects of the Bodhisattva's activity. 1. His *motive* is compassion, pure and simple. 2. One important step in *carrying out* his compassionate intentions is the Vow (*praṇidhāna*), which occurs twice in his career. First at the beginning, when he resolves to win enlightenment and to save all beings,[4] and then again on the ninth stage of his career, when the Vow has become a completely disinterested intention (*anābhoga-praṇidhāna*)[5] which, as a purely spiritual act, can have the

[1] *Buddhist Thought in India* (1962), 236–7.

[2] Har Dayal, *The Bodhisattva doctrine in Buddhist Sanskrit Literature* (1932), 188–93; *Buddhist Texts* no. 128.

[3] For the fascinating details see H. Denzinger, *Enchiridion Symbolorum*. Also H. Bechert, *Bruchstücke buddhistischer Versammlungen* I (1961), 38–9.

[4] A very beautiful poetical description of the Vow is *Samantabhadracaryāpraṇidhānarāja*, now critically edited by S. Devi (1958).

[5] *Daśabhūmikasūtra*, ed. J. Rahder (1926), 73–81.

most marvellous effects. And then 3. Most difficult to understand for modern Europeans, there are his *wonderworking powers*. They are the normal concomitants of the fourth stage of trance[1] and the celestial Bodhisattva has completely mastered them. In consequence, subjectively his body is no longer the gross material body of earthlings, but the "dharmic" body of the sages, an "adamantine" body far surpassing all terrestrial circumstances; objectively, the world he deals with is not the world of brutish, given facts which hem in the average worldling, but a world of artefacts, conjured up by his magical power, a magic show generated by his unwavering concentration (*māyopama-samādhi*). The good which he does to others lies not only in his teaching, but in his magical transformations which open the minds of people to its message. This is hard to believe, but essential to Mahayana doctrine.

IV

We can now return to the problem of the apparent antithesis between the Buddhism of Faith and that of Self-exertion. In Japan it is known as the contrast between *Tariki* (Other-Power) and *Jiriki* (Self-Power),[2] the first being represented by the Pure Land schools which thereby seem to side with the theistic religions, and the second by Zen which has Taoism for one of its principal antecedents. It is, however, arbitrary and misleading to postulate a real opposition between those who just passively sit about waiting for somebody else to release them from their troubles, and those who nobly and strenuously exert themselves. The fact is that those who exert themselves must have plenty of faith to induce them to turn their energies in that particular direction,[3] and that those who wait for Amitabha to take them to his Paradise will have plenty of opportunity to exert themselves when they get there. "Self-power"

[1] *Buddhist Scriptures*, trans. E. Conze (1959), 121–33.

[2] The advantages and disadvantages of the two have been well discussed by Chr. Humphreys in *Young East* (1961), 2–4. Of outstanding importance in this context are the studies of D. T. Suzuki, especially *A Miscellany on the Shin Teaching of Buddhism* (1949); *Mysticism, Christian and Buddhist* (1957), 161–214; *The Eastern Buddhist*, III (1925), 285–326, and VII, 1–58 (offprint).

[3] *Buddhist Thought in India*, 47–51.

and "Other-power" constitute a duality, and all duality is *per se* falsely imagined and cannot possibly be ultimately valid.

Moreover, in a system of thought in which there is no "self", the distinction between "self" and "other" is at best provisional only. Likewise, from a system which declares all dharmas to be "inactive" (*nirīhaka*), no dogmatic statement about the agent of salvation can be expected. The situation differs greatly from that prevailing within Christianity. As conceived by both Christians and Buddhists, salvation, or emancipation, must obviously involve the co-operation of the individual with some spiritual force. To Christians it has seemed a meaningful undertaking to find some overall dogmatic formulation which would define the relative strength of the two factors for all cases. In consequence innumerable discussions of incredible subtlety have tried to determine the relative weight of divine grace and the power of man's own good works, as well as the relation of the Divine Will to the freedom of the human will. Dogmatic formulations of this kind have not been attempted by Buddhists, who believe that circumstances alter cases.

For instance, we may read that it is the Tathagata who "gives" (*dāsyāmi*) to suffering beings "both pleasures and the Final Rest".[1] On the other hand we have, "you yourself must make the effort (*kiccam ātappam*), the Tathagatas do but point the way (*akhātāro*)".[2] "Everyone is his own protector (*nātha*); what other protector could there be?[3] "Dwell in such a way that you are an island and a refuge to yourselves, and do not seek any other refuge!"[4] Buddhists offer two distinct explanations for the discrepancy between such *ad hoc* pronouncements. The Theravadins believe that those which stress "self-striving" belong to an earlier and more authentic tradition, whereas the stress on faith and the power of the Buddhas represents

[1] *Saddharma-puṇḍarīka*, V, v. 18.

[2] See *Dhammapada*, 276. Also M. N., iii, 6, "A shower of the Way is the Tathāgata"; so also *Saddharmapuṇḍarīka*. V, 115, 20–1.

[3] *Dhammapada*, 160. My translation takes *attā*, etc., as reflexive pronouns; other take them as substantive nouns.

[4] *Dīghanikāya*, in E. Waldschmidt, *Das Mahāpariṇirvāṇasūtra* (1951) 200. Though this is much less convincing when the context and sequel are considered. Miss I. B. Horner tells me that also the following passages are relevant: A, i, 189, 11, 191; S, iii, 108–9, iv, 179–81, A, ii, 5–6, Iti., 113–15, Sn. 1053, 1064, Dhp. 168–9.

later concessions to human weakness. Their assertions are incapable of proof, and I personally prefer the Mahayana explanation according to which all statements for or against "self-activity" are pedagogic devices, not propositions aiming at universal theoretical validity. They are advice given to people of different temperament and situated on varying levels of spiritual maturity and endowment, suitable to some and unsuitable to others, and there is no antagonism between the higher and the lower.

In its true reality salvation (*moksha*) is the fading away of the bonds which imprison men in the conditioned and defiled world of Samsara, and the restoration of the absolute freedom of the unconditioned and undefiled reality of Nirvana. What or who then is saved? Nothing and nobody. None of what is here can be carried over there, for Nirvana is *das ganz Andere*. Nor is anyone ever saved, for "anyone who distinguishes between self and other is still under the influence of karma",[1] and therefore unsaved.

Ineffable in its true reality, the process of salvation can nevertheless be viewed from three points of view: 1. As the result of an external personified agent accepted in faith. 2. As the result of self-striving guided by an infallible teacher. 3. As the doing of the Absolute, or the *dharmadhātu*, with which Amitabha is readily identified. Of the three viewpoints the third would be the most valid because, as against the first it is based on wisdom, so much superior to faith, and as against the second it realizes that no one can really rely on a "self" which is a mere fiction, and that, in any case, a puny individual is unlikely to have the strength to direct his own spiritual destiny. And as to the division between viewpoints 1) and 2), mystics generally tend to blur the dividing lines between the external and the internal. "Look within, thou *art* Buddha." "I and my father are one." "I am not the doer, mine is not the doer." "It is not I that speak but my Father who is speaking in me." And so on. " 'Not my will but thine be done', he says to the universe, and begins to feel that the Power which he seeks within, by which he heals and teaches and makes one, is not *his* power within or without, but a force which works in its own sweet way."[2]

[1] Candrakīrti, *Prasannapadā*, XVI v. 9.
[2] Chr. Humphreys, *Young East* (1961), 4.

V

These doctrines obviously cry out to be compared with Christianity. From a Christian point of view this comparison has been ably carried out by the Père de Lubac S.J.[1] for the Roman Catholics, and by H. Butchkus[2] for the Lutherans. My own comparison, made from a Buddhist point of view, is here constrained by the need for brevity which must excuse a certain bluntness which, in any case, should not offend those who were told to turn the other cheek.

1. While Buddhists would be willing to accept Jesus as one Bodhisattva among many, the idea that he is unique, as the one son of God, and so on, is anathema to them, as likely to lead to intolerance, persecution and bloodshed. Buddhists desire to multiply saviours, not to restrict them. 2. The great stress laid on "the blood of Jesus Christ" and on the Crucifixion[3] is distinctly distasteful to Buddhists. 3. Salvation consists in the removal of ignorance. It cannot be effected by the extirpation of a sin which is seen as a rebellion against God. A man may be morally without blemish, and yet for aeons to come he may have to remove the vestiges of his ignorance before he can become fully enlightened. 4. There is no "forgiveness of sin". Karma takes its course, and the consequences of acts can never be annulled, though in time they may wear off and though spiritual practices may to some extent whittle them away. 5. Buddhists have no historical sense, and no one wants to know exactly when Amitabha made his Vow, or when the Bodhisattva sacrificed himself for the tigress.[4] Nor is this regarded as a weakness. The "historical basis" of Christianity is not always an aid to faith, and the dissection of the Resurrection accounts has often appeared to leave them without much solid foundation in fact. 6. Centuries of theological controversy have habituated Christians so much to the opposition between "good

[1] *Amida* (1955).

[2] *Luther's Religion und ihre Entsprechung im japanischen Amida-Buddhismus*, n.d. (*c.* 1950?).

[3] The mild Suzuki says in *Mysticism, Christian and Buddhist* (1957), 136: "The crucified Christ is a terrible sight and I cannot help associating it with the sadistic impulse of a psychically affected brain."

[4] E. Conze, *Buddhist Scriptures* (1959), 24–6.

works" and "grace" that they find it not easy to see how "grace" can be based on good works, or "merit", as explained in III. 7. It comes natural to Buddhists to subordinate the personal to the suprapersonal, i.e. the Buddha to the Dharma, Amitabha to the *dharmadhātu*. This goes very much against the grain of Christian thought. 8. The higher stages of a "celestial" Bodhisattva's life show close analogies to the doctrine of the *communicatio idiomatum*. 9. The Mahayana assertion that all saviours, Buddhas and Bodhisattvas alike, are mere fictions and images in a dream, that they have issued from the Void and are projections of man's inner consciousness, is well nigh incomprehensible to Christians, who find it hard to believe that anyone can maintain such a thesis in good faith.

This is a rather fumbling way of dealing with a great problem. When we compare the doctrinal formulations of two such religions as Buddhism and Christianity we often feel that they converge so closely that they seem bound to meet at some point. But in fact they never actually do meet, and when we remember the roots and aspirations behind those formulations, a gulf yawns at once. Leaving behind the doctrinal formulation, we may turn to the ideal type of person whom these religions tend to produce. The gulf then widens still more. I once read through a collection of the lives of Roman Catholic saints, and there was not one of whom a Buddhist could fully approve. This does not mean that they were unworthy people, but that they were bad Buddhists, though good Christians. Ultimately, when viewed as pure germinal intuitions, all religions are probably inspired by the same vision of man's true and original nature. In their doctrinal formulations no such unity can be discerned, they seem to be mutually incommensurable, and constant misapprehensions are unavoidable.

MAHAYANA BUDDHISM

Introduction

The word *Mahāyāna*, or "Great Vehicle", is the name generally given to those ideas which dominated the second phase of Buddhist thought. One speaks of a "vehicle" because the Buddhist doctrine, or Dharma (Pali, Dhamma, from *dhṛ*), is conceived as a raft, or a ship, which carries us across the ocean of this world of suffering to a "Beyond", to salvation, to Nirvana. Its adherents called it "great" by way of praising the universality of its tenets and intentions, in opposition to the narrowness of the other Buddhist schools, which they describe as the "Hinayana", as the "inferior" vehicle, a term naturally not much cherished by those to whom they apply it. At present the Mahayana is confined to the Northern half of the Buddhist world, and the Buddhists of Nepal, Tibet, China, Korea and Japan are nearly all Mahayanists. The South, on the other hand, is entirely dominated by the Theravadins, one of the eighteen traditional sects of the Hinayana, and their form of Buddhism is the national religion of Ceylon, Burma and Siam. The other seventeen Hinayana sects disappeared seven hundred years ago when the Muhammadans swept into Northern India and destroyed its flourishing Buddhist monasteries.

In point of *time* the rise of the Mahayana coincides with the beginning of the Christian era. It must have gathered momentum in the first pre-Christian centuries, but many of its basic ideas go back, as we shall see, to the fourth or fifth century B.C., if not to the Buddha himself. But the literature which sets out the specific Mahayana doctrines is attested only for the beginning of the Christian era, and this raises an interesting, and so far unresolved, historical problem. How can we account for the observation that Buddhism, just at the time when Christianity itself arose, underwent a radical reform of its basic tenets which made it much more similar to Christianity than it had been before? To show the nature of the problem, I will mention just three parallels between the Mahayana and Christianity. First of all, loving-kindness and compassion, subordinate virtues in the older Buddhism, are stressed more and more, and move right into the centre of the picture. This may remind us of the Christian emphasis on "love". Secondly, we hear of compassionate beings, called "Bodhisattvas", whose main claim to our gratitude lies in that they sacrifice their lives for the welfare of all. This may remind us of the Christ who died for us all so that our sins may be forgiven. And thirdly, the Buddhists of this period show eschatological interests, and fervently hope for a "second coming" of the Buddha, as Maitreya (Pali, Metteya), the "Loving One". Thus we have at least three innovations of the Mahayana, of which each is as near to the spirit of early Christianity as it is to the older Buddhism.

Nor is this all. Occasionally we find close verbal coincidences between the Christian and the Mahayana Scriptures. Just one instance must suffice. At the time when the *Revelation of St. John* was written down in Greek in the Eastern Mediterranean, the Mahayanists produced in the South of India one of their most revered books, *The Perfection of Wisdom in* 8,000 *Lines. Revelation* (v. 1) refers to a book "closely sealed" with seven seals, and likewise the *Perfection of Wisdom* is called a book "sealed with seven seals". It is shown to a Bodhisattva by the name of "Ever-weeping" (*Sadāprarudita*), and St. John "weeps bitterly" (v. 4) because he sees no one worthy to open the book and to break its seals. This can be done by the Lamb alone, slaughtered in sacrifice (v. 9). In the same way, chaps. 30 and 31 of the Mahayana book describe in detail how Everweeping slaughtered himself in sacrifice, and how he thereby became worthy of the Perfection of Wisdom (*see* pp. 62–4). This parallel is remarkable not only for the similarities of the religious logic, but also for the fact that both the number seven and the whole notion of a "book with seals" point to the Judaeo-Mediterranean rather than to the Indian tradition. Here is a fruitful field for further study. At present we cannot account for the parallels between the Mediterranean and Indian developments which occur at the beginning of the Christian era. For the interpretation of the Mahayana they are significant and should not be ignored.

It was in fact, *geographically* speaking, in the two regions of India which were in contact with the Mediterranean that the

Mahayana seems to have originated. On the one hand we have the South of India, which was in close trading relations with the Roman Empire, as is shown by the huge hoards of Roman coins found there in recent years. And it was in the region round Nagarjunikonda, in the South, near the temple of Amaravatī, which has rightly been called a "Dravido-Alexandrian synthesis", that tradition places the development of the first Mahayana Scriptures, i.e. the Sūtras on Perfect Wisdom, and where also Nagarjuna (*c.* A.D. 100), the greatest philosopher of the Mahayana, appears to have lived. The second centre of the incipient Mahayana was in the North-West of India, where the successor states of Alexander the Great kept open a constant channel for Hellenistic and Roman influences, as the art found in that region amply demonstrates. Its openness to foreign, non-Indian influences was indeed one of the features which distinguished the Mahayana from the older forms of Buddhism.

We know little about the actual *causes* which brought about this revolution in Buddhist thought. Two, however, seem certain, the exhaustion of the *Arhant* ideal, and the pressure of the laity.

As for the first, the older Buddhism was designed to produce a type of saint known as *Arhant*—a person who has been liberated once and for all from the cycle of birth and death. Three or four centuries after the Buddha's Nirvana the methods which had at first produced *Arhants* in profusion lost their potency, fewer and fewer monks reached the goal, and the conviction gained ground that the time for Arhants was over. When the expected fruits were no longer forthcoming, it was natural for a section of the community to explore new avenues, and they replaced the Arhant ideal by the Bodhisattva ideal (pp. 54–67).

Relations of the monks with the laity had always been precarious. Here at its base was the Achilles' heel of the whole soaring edifice. The Mahayana gave much greater weight to laymen. It could count on much popular support for its emphasis on active service, for its opinion that people are as important as "*dharmas*" (Pali, *dhammā*, 'events'), for its attacks on the selfishness of monks who think only of their own welfare, for its censure of "haughty" and "conceited" monks for its stories of wealthy householders, such as Vimalakirti, who surpassed the oldest and most venerable monks in the splendour of their spiritual attainments, and for its belief that the saints should accept a common fate with their fellow men. Popular pressure would also induce the monks to become more manifestly useful to their lay followers. They increasingly interested themselves in their daily problems, and by acting as astrologers, exorcizers, weather makers, physicians, etc., inserted themselves into the magical side of their lives. The wishes of the dumb common people, so despised by the monkish party, in the end proved paramount.

Our knowledge of the Mahayana is derived from its very extensive *literature*, which was composed over about 2,000 years, most of it in Sanskrit, but some also in Chinese, in Tibetan and in Central Asian languages. Although many Mahayana works have been lost, the bulk of what is left is so huge that no one has ever read through it. Our views on the subject must therefore remain tentative, and future discoveries may compel their revision. This literature falls into three main classes—*Sūtras*, *Śāstras* and *Tantras*. The *Sūtras* are the most authoritative, and no follower of the Mahayana would wish openly to repudiate anything they contain; the authority of the *Śāstras* is more limited, and they are binding only on the members of the philosophical school which they represent; that of the *Tantras* is even more restricted, its range being confined to the few adepts of a small esoteric sect.

Sūtras claim to be sayings of the Buddha himself, and they always give at the beginning the exact place, either on earth or in heaven, where the Buddha is believed to have preached this particular sermon. In the case of Mahayana Sūtras, written more than five centuries after the historical Buddha's death, this is obviously a pious fiction. If an historian were asked to define a Sūtra, he would have to say that it is an anonymous document elaborated usually collectively over many centuries, which has to be significant without being controversial or sectarian. The most beautiful of all Mahayana Sūtras is the *Lotus of the Good Law*, a work of great power and magnificence. There are a few European translations, but none of them is even remotely accurate. The most instructive Sūtras are those on *The Perfection of Wisdom*. Of that we have about thirty different recensions, composed in the course of six or seven centuries. Many other Sūtras are preserved, several hundred of them, but there is little point in further enumeration. The continuous, slow, and measured growth of these Sūtras makes them appear as more than the works of mere men, and some of their majesty is still felt in Japan, Tibet, and even in Europe.

A *Śāstra* is a treatise written by a known person, either in the form of a commentary to a Sūtra, or in the form of a systematic text book. When I say "a known person", I do not, of course, mean that we know the actual author, but only that it is ascribed to some actual doctor of the "Church". For there has been a tendency to simplify matters by attributing the works of many writers to a few big names. The four biggest names are, about A.D. 150, Nagarjuna and Aryadeva, and, about A.D. 400, Vasubandhu and Asanga. The first two are the founders of the philosophical school of the Madhyamikas, while the second two initiated the rival school of the Yogacarins (see p. 78). These two schools were engaged in constant disputes, and the works of the one have no authority for the other. The limited authority of a "doctor of the Church" is based on three factors: a saintly life, great learning, and inspiration by one of the mythical Buddhas or Bodhisattvas (pp. 67 sq.). Wonder-working powers, though desirable, are not indispensable.

Sūtras and *Śāstras* are public documents available to anyone sufficiently interested to procure them. The *Tantras*, by contrast, are secret documents destined only for a chosen few who are properly initiated, or consecrated, by a properly initiated teacher or *guru*. To let the uninitiated into their secret is an unpardonable crime. In order more effectively to hide their contents from outsiders they employ a deliberately mysterious and secretive language. Without the oral explanations of an initiated master they are practically meaningless, and reveal nothing of any importance. Tantras give to the initiated instructions for the practical realization of certain Yogic practices. They were composed in profusion from about A.D. 500 onwards, and we have literally thousands of them. Their historical study has barely begun, and as outsiders we seldom have a clue to their meaning. Thousands and thousands of pages are filled with statements about "cosmic tortoises" and "sky dogs", or about gods dressed in "fur coats" or "tiger skins", living in "iron palaces" or "copper fortresses", and "holding a black trident with four heads stuck on it and a blood-dripping heart, at which two black vipers are sucking" (see R. de Nebesky-Wojkowitz, *Oracles and Demons of Tibet*, 1956). What are we to make of all that? In their desire to shock the profane, the authors of the Tantras are prone to the use of obscene and sexually suggestive language. Again we are at a loss to know what their jokes really meant. We can well imagine, to give a parallel case, an earnest Japanese anthropologist of the year A.D.3242 pondering over a choice piece of ornithological information he has found in an English soldier's letter of 1942, "Two wrens went into the sea, and four blue tits came out again". Some initiation into the lore of the British Army would soon tell him the meaning of that statement. In its absence he would have to resort to wild guesses, without having much to go on. Most of the words used in the Tantras can be found in our dictionaries—but then it does not help very much to know that a "red herring" is a "pink fish". We can at present form some idea of the general principles of the Tantras (see pp. 84–5), though the concrete detail quite passes us by. The authority of a Tantra is usually derived from a mythical Buddha who is said to have preached it in the remote past to some other mythical person, who transmitted it to a human teacher who stands at the beginning of a long line of initiated *gurus* who hand the secret wisdom down from generation to generation.

This ends the survey of the literary sources. In addition we can derive much information from innumerable *works of art* which express the spirit of the doctrine accurately and impressively. Buddhist works of art allow little scope to the arbitrary inventions of individual artists. The images are too holy for that, for they are supports, though inadequate, for meditation, as well as reservoirs of supernatural power. They are made according to formulae elaborated by the scholars and mystics, which the artist just invests with a visible form. About the mythological and ritual aspects of the Mahayana these works of art can teach us a great deal.

The Mahayana is first of all a way of life, with a clear-cut idea of spiritual prefection and of the stages which lead to it. In addition, it puts forth a number of mythological concepts and ontological doctrines. Finally, in an effort to maintain itself against hostile influences, it enlists the help of female deities and magical forces. These are the three sides of the Mahayana which we shall now survey one by one.

The Bodhisattva Ideal

The creation of the Bodhisattva ideal and the elaboration of the doctrine of "Emptiness" are the two great contributions which the Mahayana has made to human thought. While the philosophy of Emptiness has proved an unfailing source of attraction to generations of scholars and intellectuals, it was to its teachings about the "Bodhisattva" that the Mahayana owed its success as a religion, and that it proved capable of converting the whole of Central and East Asia, and of winning, for a time, more adherents than any other religion. Here was the image of an ideal man, who could stir the hearts of all, whether rich or poor, learned or ignorant, strong or weak, monks or laymen. It could easily win their admiration, for it reflected what was best in them. It could also become a basis for immediate action, because it could be adjusted to the infinite variety of human circumstances. Put forth with self-sacrificing zeal, with all the resources of eloquence and all the refinements of art, the Bodhisattva-ideal has been one of the most potent ideas of Asian thought. So irresistible was its power that even the Hinayana schools were prepared to incorporate it to some extent into their own systems.

What then is a "Bodhisattva"? It will be best first to explain the Sanskrit term: *Bodhi* means "enlightenment", and *sattva* "being" or "essence". A Bodhisattva is thus a person who in his essential being is motivated by the desire to win full enlightenment—to become a Buddha. Destined to become a Buddha, he nevertheless, in order to help suffering creatures, selflessly postpones his entrance into the bliss of *Nirvana* and his escape from this world of birth and death.

From another angle a Bodhisattva is said to be dominated by two forces—compassion and wisdom. Compassion governs his conduct towards his fellow beings, wisdom his attitude to Reality. The Mahayana teachings on compassion are easy, those on wisdom hard to understand. Everyone listens gladly when the talk is about himself, but gets rather bored when feeling himself ignored. So we begin with compassion, leaving wisdom for later on.

Buddhists, as is well known, regard the difference between human beings and animals as unimportant, and equal compassion should, in any case, be extended to all. Scrupulous respect for the life and dignity, for the rights and wishes of all living beings is a Bodhisattva's first and most elementary duty. During a debate with the Saskya Pandita which the Venerable Tsong-kha-pa had about A.D. 1400 his opponent, probably absent-mindedly, crushed a louse between his nails. Tsong-kha-pa interrupted him, exclaiming, "While we are here debating these abstruse metaphysical subtleties, I hear the laments of a fellow-creature rising to the sky!" The Saskya Pandita was so much taken aback by the reproof that his hat fell off, he left the tent in confusion, and victory remained with Tsong-kha-pa and his "Yellow Church" (R. Bleichsteiner, *Die gelbe Kirche*, 1937, p. 84). Likewise, it is quite usual for Bodhisattvas to sacrifice their own lives for animals. When he was a prince of Benares, the Bodhisattva who subsequently became the Budda Gautama (= Pali, Gotama), threw himself down in front of a tigress who had given birth to five cubs and was exhausted from hunger and thirst. "But she did nothing to him. The Bodhisattva noticed that she was too weak to move. As a merciful man he had taken no sword with him. He therefore cut his throat with a sharp piece of bamboo and fell down near the tigress. She noticed his body all covered with blood, and in no time ate up all the flesh and blood, leaving only the bones" (*Suvarṇa-prabhāsottama-sūtra*, ed. J. Nobel, 1937, p. 214). On another celebrated occasion, as king Śibi, the Bodhisattva ransomed a pigeon by giving a pound of his own flesh to the hawk who had caught it (E. Lamotte, *Le Traité de la grande Vertu de Sagesse*, 1944, vol. 1, pp. 255–6). This fellow-feeling for all living beings, whoever they may be, is much akin to Dr. Schweitzer's "reverence for life", which, as I read some time ago, he extends to "gazelles, pelicans, ants, mosquitoes, worms and even bacilli". Even the bacteria had already been thought of by the Buddhist monks, who took special precautions against harming the invisible creatures who were said to abound in water and in the air.

And not only are all beings alike in that they dislike suffering, but they are also all capable of enlightenment. Each one of them is a potential Buddha. Hidden away within each being there exist in embryonic form the factors needed for the attainment of Enlightenment. So "the road to Buddhahood is open to all" (*Buddhist Texts*, p. 181). "Even in animals the personality of a Buddha should be discerned, concealed though it be by the taints of manifold defilements" (*Buddhist Texts*, p. 183). One day these adventitious defilements will disappear, the moment they are seen to be unreal they will vanish away, and the Buddha-nature then manifests itself in its full glory. A small minority of Mahayanists, it is true, claimed that there are some beings called Icchantikas, who are for ever excluded from enlightenment. But the overwhelming majority rejected this heresy which had crept in from Gnosticism, probably through the Manichaens, and took their stand on the belief that every living organism has it in him to win enlightenment sooner or later. Who, then, would have the temerity to "hinder it on its upward path"?

It is the essential feature of a Bodhisattva's compassion that it is "great", i.e. boundless, and that it makes no distinctions. "He radiates great friendliness and compassion over all beings, and he resolves, 'I shall become their saviour, I shall release them from all their sufferings' "(*Buddhist Texts*, no. 124). Or this is how Santideva, a poet of the seventh century, expresses it:

The merit I achieved by all these pious actions, may that make me
Quite able to appease the sufferings of all beings.
A medicine for the sick I'll be, their healer, and their servant,
Until the day that sickness is a thing no more remembered.
With showers of food and drink I'll quench the pains of hunger and of thirst;
In the dearth at the end of the aeon I'll turn into food and drink.
And for the needy I'll be a source of wealth quite unfailing,
Serving them well with all that their needs may require.
Heedless of body, of goods, of the merit I gained and will gain still,
I surrender my all to promote the welfare of others.

(*Buddhist Meditation*, p. 59.)

So far so good. The modern age, while it may deplore the Mahayana tendency to hyperbole, is sure to applaud its concern for the welfare of others. But what it has the greatest difficulty in grasping is that compassion cannot stand on its own feet, that it cannot do its work without the help of wisdom, and that the Bodhisattva, instead of doing something useful all the time, continues to push forward to the remote, otherworldly goal of Enlightenment. I must therefore give some of the reasons which make the Mahayanists combine compassion with wisdom and Enlightenment.

What then is a Bodhisattva's compassion? It is the selfless desire to make others happy. Now it is 1. Not self-evident what is good for others, nor is 2. Self-interest easily shunned.

1. In order to make others happy, one must have some idea of what *can* make them happy. Being inherently foolish, the other people are not always the best judges of that. Even if the louse had not been crushed, it would still lead the life of a louse. Even though the tigress was fed, she was still only a tigress. And so on. As soon as we get down to actual details, we find it hard to decide what is good for others, and what of real benefit to them. Is it, for instance, an act of kindness to kill an animal in pain, or to give whisky to a tramp? But these are only comparatively trifling problems pertaining to the casuistry of love. Far more fundamental difficulties arise from the fact that one good thing can be the foe of another. The highest good is said to be the gift of the Dharma. In that case the gift of anything else, in so far as it increases people's worldly welfare, may militate against the development of their spiritual potentialities, for it may bind them still further to this world and increase their worries and anxieties. Should we then wish to increase the material welfare of the people, or should we not? In the Mahayana texts we find a great deal of rhetoric about this, but the actual achievements of Buddhist countries fell far short of it. This is not surprising because social services are not only a matter of good will, but of the productivity of labour. Before the advent of modern technical developments there simply did not exist the means to raise what is nowadays called the "standard of living" of the common people to any appreciable extent. Our attitude to these developments is not easy to determine. On the one side our compassion would probably make us glad

to see that people are becoming less poor, that they live longer, that their sicknesses are treated with some care and skill, that justice is dispensed with greater humanity, and so on. On the other hand all these benefits depend on the technical organization of modern society, which makes a spiritual life next to impossible. Whatever the answer, it is clear that only a great deal of wisdom can decide a dilemma of this kind.

2. Not only the effects, but also the motives of doing good to others present serious problems. "Charity" has so much fallen into disrepute because too often it was motivated by a sense of guilt, by the desire to humiliate the poor, or to buy them off with a few crumbs. If others are so often ungrateful for what we have done for them, if they hate us for the help we gave, they are in most cases quite justified because somehow they divine that we considered ourselves first in what we did, and them only in the second place, degrading them into a mere means or material of our desire to do good. The benefits of generosity to ourselves are not in doubt. It is the benefit to others which is in question. A very high degree of sanctity is necessary to do good to others without harming or irritating them. Only the pure in heart can have the vision necessary to decide what is really beneficial to others, and only they have the purity of motive. In the Scriptures the ability really to benefit others is regarded as a very high and rare virtue, the last and most sublime flowering of a mature development of perfect wisdom. Eight hundred years ago Milarepa, the great Tibetan saint, was asked by his disciples "if they could engage in worldly duties, in a small way, for the benefit of others". Milarepa replied:

"If there be not the least self-interest attached to such duties, it is permissible. But such detachment is indeed rare; and works performed for the good of others seldom succeed, if not wholly freed from self-interest. Even without seeking to benefit others, it is with difficulty that works done even in one's own interest are successful. It is as if a man helplessly drowning were to try to save another man in the same predicament. One should not be over-anxious and hasty in setting out to serve others before one has oneself realized the Truth in its fulness; to do so, would be like the blind leading the blind. As long as the sky endures, so long will there be no end of sentient beings for one to serve; and to every one comes the opportunity for such service. Till the opportunity come, I exhort each of you to have but the one resolve, namely to attain Buddhahood for the good of all living beings" (W. Y. Evans-Wentz, *Tibet's Great Yogi Milarepa*, 1928, p. 271).

It is a general Buddhist conviction that ordinary life is hopelessly unsatisfactory, exposed to constant pain and grief, and in any case quite futile, since death swallows all so soon. Without the Dharma no lasting happiness is possible. But if the gift of the Dharma is the highest gift of all, one must oneself possess the Dharma in order to give it to others. And the only way to get hold of it is through Enlightenment. It is for this reason that the Bodhisattva wishes to win full Enlightenment, so that he may be really useful to others. And, of course, his usefulness to them increases as he comes nearer and nearer to Enlightenment.

What then is this Enlightenment, of *bodhi*, which is the ultimate goal of a Bodhisattva's endeavours? It is a thorough and complete understanding of the nature and meaning of life, the forces which shape it, the method to end it, and the reality which lies beyond it. Indian tradition is quite wont to see the highest achievement of man in a cognitive insight into a Reality which transcends this fleeting world, and all the beings in it. But then—and there is a definite problem—the man who has cognized this reality, which is so much more satisfactory than anything he sees around him, will want to withdraw into it and away from his fellow creatures. No more re-born, he will be lost to the world. Measuring the concerns of the world by the yardstick of true reality, he will be unable to take them very seriously. Humanity will appear to him as a mass of non-entities constantly worrying over nothing in particular. This is a specially important point in Buddhism, which has always taught that persons are not really "persons", but only imagine that they are, whereas in strict fact they *are* non-entities.

The Mahayanists agreed that enlightenment does not automatically entail the desire to assist others. Among the enlightened they distinguished four types, of whom two do not appreciably help others, whereas the other two do. And although the Mahayanists insist that different people must reach the goal by different ways, they regard the unselfish types as superior to the others.

The "selfish" enlightened persons are first the *Arhants* or "Disciples", who are said to represent the ideal of the Hinayana, and who are aloof from the concerns of the world, intent on their own private salvation alone. And then there are the *Pratyekabuddhas*. They differ from the Arhants in that, independent of the instructions of a Buddha, they can gain Enlightenment by their own private efforts. But once they have gained Enlightenment, they keep their knowledge to themselves, and do not communicate it to others.

The unselfish types are the Buddhas and the Bodhisattvas. Omniscience is the chief attribute of a *Buddha*, the distinctive feature of his enlightenment. The Buddha is essential to the Buddhist religion in all its forms as the founder who guarantees the truth and reliability of the teaching by the fact that he is "fully enlightened". It was always agreed that he knew everything necessary to salvation, his own and that of others, and that therefore in spiritual matters he is a sure and infallible guide. The Mahayana now claims that he knows also all other things, that he is omniscient in the full sense of the term. But since it is one of the peculiarities of a Buddha's gnosis that therein the subject is identical with the object, the fact that he knows everything there is, implies that he also *is* everything there is. In consequence the Buddha becomes identical either with the Absolute, or with the sum total of existence, with the totality of all things at all times. It is only because he has merged with everything that the Buddha has cast off all traces of a separate self, and has attained complete and total self-extinction.

We can well believe in the selflessness of a Buddha conceived in this way. But when the Mahayana goes on to say that this Buddha—all knowing, all-wise, all there is—is also all-compassionate, we remain slightly unconvinced. In an effort to humanize the Buddha the Mahayanists called him a "Father" of all those who are helpless and afflicted, but this attribute never quite comes to life. Matrceta, a fine Mahayana poet of the second century, has this to say on the Buddha's compassion:

> Which shall I praise first, you or the great compassion, which held
> You for so long in *samsāra*, though well its faults you knew?

Your compassion, given free rein, made you pass your time
Among the crowds, when the bliss of seclusion was so much
more to your taste.

(*Buddhist Texts*, p. 192.)

The first of these verses refers to the Buddha when he was a Bodhisattva, the second to the forty-five years of his ministry on earth after his Enlightenment. It was, however, the compassionateness of a Buddha after his death, after his final Nirvana, which has always seemed barely credible. Originally, before the Mahayana, the Buddha after his final Nirvana was conceived of as totally extinct as far as this world and its inhabitants are concerned, and no longer interested in them. No amount of ingenuity could quite move Buddhism away from that original position, and really graft compassion on the Buddha who had "passed away". While it is possible to see that he helps beings by the gift of the perfect Dharma, the emotion of compassion must appear to be alien to him. The doubts which have always remained on that point are in part due to the transcendental and truly inconceivable nature of all that concerns the Buddha. Everything about him lies outside the range of our own direct experience. For selfish and limited people like us, even-mindedness and compassion seem mutually incompatible, and we are apt to think that in one vast Emptiness compassion must get lost and become inapplicable. But then what light does this kind of reasoning shed on the selfless Buddhas, who are said to have all these states to perfection—imperturbable even-mindedness, boundless compassion, and full emptiness? From our lowly perspective the transcendental world of self-extinction teems with apparent inconsistencies—but whom should we blame for that?

The *Bodhisattvas*, on the other hand, are much nearer to us in their mentality, and they take good care to remain in touch with the imperfect by having the same passions as they have, although, as distinct from them, these passions neither affect nor pollute their minds. Not yet having become everything, the Bodhisattvas are not quite beyond our ken, and we can appreciate that, while all the time intent on their transcendental goal, they remain during their struggles always aware of their solidarity with all that lives, in accordance with the famous saying:

Can there be bliss when all that lives must suffer?
Shalt thou be saved and hear the whole world cry?
(H. P. Blavatsky, *The Voice of Silence*, p. 78.)

But if a Bodhisattva wishes to become a Buddha, and if a Buddha is defined as the sum total of everything there is, then the distance between a given person and the state of Buddhahood will obviously be a very large one, and nearly infinite. In one life it could not possibly be traversed. Countless lives would be needed, aeons and aeons would have to pass, before a Bodhisattva can reach his goal. And yet—and this is somewhat of a paradox—only one single little obstacle separates him and us from Buddhahood, and that is the belief in a self, the belief that he is a separate individual, the inveterate tendency to indulge in what the texts call "I-making and Mine-making". To get rid of himself is a Bodhisattva's supreme task, and he finds that this is not an easy thing to do. He takes two kinds of measures to remove this one obstacle to Buddhahood—actively by self-sacrifice and selfless service, cognitively by insight into the non-existence of a self. The latter is due to wisdom, defined as the ability to penetrate to true reality, to the "own-being" of things, to what they are in and by themselves, and held necessary to disclose the ultimate inanity of a separate self. And in this scheme action and cognition always go hand in hand, and are closely interrelated.

The self-sacrifices of Bodhisattvas are the subject of many edifying stories. By way of example, I will re-tell that of the Bodhisattva "Ever-weeping" mentioned before (p. 49). I will relate it in some detail and largely in translation, because it has all the typical features of a Mahayana story, and exemplifies Mahayana mentality to perfection. It tells us how Everweeping searched for the Perfection of Wisdom, and how he found it in the end, "because he did not care for his body and had no regard for his life". He goes to see the Bodhisattva Dharmodgata, who can answer all his questions, but he feels that "it would be unseemly to come empty-handed to him". So he decides to sell his body, goes to the market place, and cries, "Who wants a man? Who wants to buy a man?" But Māra the Evil One fears that Everweeping, if he succeeds in "selling himself out of concern for Dharma, from love for Dharma, so as to do worship to Dharma", will then in due course win Enlightenment, and remove himself and others from Māra's sphere of influence. So he brings it about that no one can see or hear the Bodhisattva. Then Śakra, chief of the gods, decides to test Everweeping, and conjures up a young man who says to him that his father wants to offer a sacrifice. "For that I require a man's heart, his blood and the marrow of his bones." Everweeping, "his mind bristling with joy", agrees, and says, "I will give you my body, since you have need of it!" "He then takes a sharp sword, pierces his right arm, and makes the blood flow. He pierces his right thigh, cuts the flesh from it, and strides up to the foot of a wall in order to break the bone." Śakra "thereupon throws off his disguise as a young man, and in his proper body he stands before the Bodhisattva", applauds his resolution and asks him to choose a boon. Everweeping asks him for the "supreme dharmas of a Buddha", but Śakra has to admit that this is beyond his powers, and begs him to choose another boon. Everweeping replies: "Do not trouble your mind about the mutilated condition of my body! I shall now make it whole again by the magical power of my enunciation of the Truth. If it is true that I am bound to win full Enlightenment, if it is true that the Buddhas know of my unconquerable resolution—may through this Truth, through this utterance of the Truth, this my body be again as it was before!" "That very moment, instant and second, through the Buddha's might and through the perfect purity of the Bodhisattva's resolution, his body became again as it has been before, healthy and whole." The story then goes on to tell how Everweeping, accompanied by a merchant's daughter and her 500 maidservants, goes to see Dharmodgata, who lives in great wealth and splendour; how they hear a sermon on Perfect Wisdom; how then they spend seven years in deep trance; and how thereafter, on meeting Dharmodgata once more, they find that "Māra the Evil One had hidden away all the water"; so, to prevent "the rising dust from falling on Dharmodgata's body", they sprinkle the earth with their own blood; and as a reward Everweeping acquires millions of trances, "sees the Buddhas and Lords in all the ten directions, in countless world systems, surrounded by their congregations of monks and accompanied by numerous Bodhisattvas". And wherever he was henceforth re-born, it was always in the presence and within the sight of a Buddha (*Aṣṭasāhasrikā Prajñāpāramitā*, ed. R. Mitra, 1888, chaps. 30 and 31).

This story is not after the taste of our hard-headed age, which will condemn it as rather airy-fairy, positively puerile and out of touch with social realities. It is indeed a pure fairy-tale, showing complete disregard for commonsense and this mundane world. Everything about it is otherworldly, the excessive regard for the Dharma and its representatives, the intervention of mythological beings like Mara and Śakra, and also the almost naïve belief in the power of Truth. To the spiritually minded it nevertheless illustrates the inescapable fact that the readiness to sacrifice all is an indispensable condition for the acquisition of wisdom.

The unity of compassion and wisdom is acted out by the *six perfections*, or *pāram-itā*, "methods by which we go to the Beyond". A person turns into a Bodhisattva when he first resolves to win full enlightenment for the benefit of all beings. Thereafter, until Buddhahood, he passes many aeons in the practice of the *Pāramitās*. So important is this concept that the Mahayana often refers to itself as the "Vehicle of the *Pāramitās*". The six are: the perfections of giving, morality, patience, vigour, concentration, and wisdom. The terms are not really self-explicative, and require some comment.

First of all a Bodhisattva must learn to be *generous*, with everything he has, his possessions, his family, and even his own body. By *morality* is then meant the observation of the moral precepts, and the Bodhisattva will rather give up his life than offend against them by lying, stealing or killing. The Mahayana, in contradistinction to the Hinayana, has much to say about *patience*, but the word is used in a much wider sense than is usual with us. "Patience" is both a moral and an intellectual virtue. As a moral virtue it means the patient endurance of all sufferings, as well as of the hostile acts of others, without ever feeling any anger, ill-will or discontent. As an intellectual virtue it means the emotional acceptance, before one has properly understood them, of the more unpalatable, incredible and anxiety-producing ontological doctrines of the Mahayana, such as the non-existence of all things, which leaves us with nothing much to live for. Perfect in his *vigour*, the Bodhisattva, in spite of all discouragements and obstacles, indefatigably perseveres in his work, without ever yielding to despondency or dismay. In addition his energy is so great that he shirks no task, however difficult, however impossible:

> However innumerable sentient beings are, I vow to save them!
> However inexhaustible the defilements are, I vow to extinguish them!
> However immeasurable the *dharmas* are, I vow to master them!
> However incomparable Enlightenment is, I vow to attain it!
> (After D. T. Suzuki, *Manual of Zen Buddhism*, 1935, p. 4.)

The practice of the perfection of *concentration* then enables the Bodhisattva to gain proficiency in trances and meditations "numerous as the sands of the Ganges". These disclose to him new facets of reality unsuspected by the average worldling, and at the same time convince him of the insufficiency and unreality of all merely sensory experience. The perfection of *wisdom* finally is the ability to understand the essential properties of all processes and phenomena, their mutual relations, the conditions which bring about their rise and fall, and the ultimate unreality of their separate existence. At its highest point it leads right into the Emptiness which is the one and only Reality.

All the six perfections are dominated by the perfection of wisdom which alone makes the others into *Pāramitās*, or practices which actually lead to the Beyond. Just as blind people cannot find their way unguided into a city, so only the perfection of wisdom imparts to the other perfections an "organ of vision which allows them to ascend the path to all-knowledge and to reach all-knowledge" (*Aṣṭasāhasrikā* VII 173). What matters is not only what the Bodhisattva does, but the spirit in which he does it. When giving, he is constantly admonished to have no thought of what he gives, to pay no attention to the person to whom he gives, and, chief of all, to remain unaware that it is he who gives. Convinced by perfect wisdom of their ultimate unreality, he should "have no perception of self, no perception of others, no perception of a gift" (*Buddhist Texts*, no. 131). Likewise, without strong wisdom some of these virtues, such as patience, cannot possibly be practised to perfection, In the *Diamond Sūtra* the Buddha tells of the occasion when he remained unperturbed although the King of Kalinga hacked him to pieces. "At that time I had no notion of a self, a being, a soul or a person. If I had had such notions, then I would also have felt ill-will at that time" (*Vajracchedikā Prajñāpāramitā*, ch. 14e.) Compassion itself is capable of three degrees of perfection: at first the Bodhisattva is compassionate to living beings; then he realizes that these do not exist, and directs his compassion on the impersonal events which fill the world; finally, the compassion operates within one vast field of Emptiness. The last two stages are unattested by our everyday experience. Nevertheless, it is not necessarily absurd to speak of a compassion which "has no object at all", for we know of other emotions which arise inwardly, without the stimulus of outside objects. Under the influence of excessive adrenalin a person may feel very angry, and will then look round for an object to vent his wrath on. An elderly spinster is full of more love and tenderness than she knows what to do with, and accordingly she will not rest until she has found someone to bestow it upon, even if only a cat or a parrot. Similarly a Bodhisattva's compassion springs from the depths of his heart, and from there it spreads over to that which he knows to be illusory.

The Mahayana distinguishes *ten stages* through which a Bodhisattva must pass on his way to Buddhahood. This is another of its distinctive contributions which, slowly maturing over the centuries, found its final formulation before 300 in the *Sūtra on the Ten Stages*. These "stages" refer to fairly exalted conditions, for Nagarjuna, the greatest thinker of the Mahayana, was a Bodhisattva of the first stage only. The first six stages correspond to the perfections, and with the sixth the Bodhisattva has by his understanding of Emptiness come "face to face" with Reality itself.

At that stage he is entitled to Nirvana, but renounces it voluntarily. From now onwards he is always re-born miraculously, and acquires many unearthly qualities which qualify him to become a saviour of others, and raise him to the condition of a celestial being. In the course of the seventh stage he acquires "sovereignty" over the world, nothing can prevent him any longer from becoming a Buddha, he is now a "Crown Prince" of the Dharma, and his representations in art show him as a royal personage. It is clear that the Bodhisattvas on the last four stages differ in kind from those on the first six, and in future I will speak of them as "celestial Bodhisattvas".

Mythological Doctrines

The celestial Bodhisattvas were well suited to becoming objects of a religious cult, and soon the faithful increasingly turned to them. Many were given names and endowed with both spiritual and visible attributes. There we have Avalokitesvara, a bodhisattva of the ninth stage, who is governed by compassion, holds a lotus, and in his mercy helps all beings in distress, assisted by a positively Protean capacity for transforming himself into any shape desired. There is Manjusri, who excels in wisdom, holds a sword, and imparts wisdom to those who implore him. There is Maitreya, the coming Buddha, now in the Tushita heaven, who represents friendliness, holds a flask filled with the elixir of immortality, and will lead many to Enlightenment at a future time. There is Kshitigarbha, a Lord of the nether world, who holds a staff and looks after the welfare of the dead, particularly in the hells. And, riding on a white elephant Samantabhadra dispenses talismanic formulas which avert all dangers.

The conception of these Budhisattvas often shows foreign, non-Indian, and particularly Iranian, influence. The twenty-fourth chapter of the *Lotus*, which deals with Avalokitesvara, shows remarkable parallels to certain passages in the *Avesta*. Avalokitesvara wears in his crown an image of Amitabha, his spiritual sire. A similar arrangement can be observed in the headdress of the priests of Palmyra and of those of the Great Goddess of Phrygia. Maitreya owes much to Mithra. His epithet is *a-jita*, "the unconquered", just as Mithras in his Roman mysteries was called *in-victus*.

The Bodhisattvas are as worthy of worship as the Buddhas, and some Mahayanists thought that they are more so (*see* p. 61). In the *Lotus Sūtra* it is said that to adore Avalokitesvara is as rewarding as the worship of countless Buddhas (*Saddharma Pundarīkā*, p. 364). And elsewhere, "Indeed, O Kashyapa, just as one worships the new and not the full moon, just so those who believe in me should honour the Bodhisattvas, and not the Tathagatas." Or: "From the Buddha arise only the Disciples and *Pratyekabuddhas* (p. 60), but from the Bodhisattva the perfect Buddha himself is born."

The development of mythical Bodhisattvas was accompanied, and even preceded, by that of mythical Buddhas. This side of the Mahayana went back to within a century of the Buddha's death. It took shape in the school of the Mahasanghikas, the majority faction in a dispute with the so-called "Sthaviras" or "Elders", proud of their greater seniority and orthodoxy. The Mahasanghikas were the popular and democratic party, through which popular aspirations entered into Buddhism. The conception which they formed of a Buddha is of central importance, and one cannot understand the Mahayana without appreciating the logic behind it.

The concept of a "Buddha" had from the very beginning contained a duality which became the starting point of far-reaching developments. The word "Buddha" itself is not a proper name, but a title, or epithet, which means the "Enlightened One". It refers to the condition of a man who is a completely unobstructed channel for the spiritual force of the dharma. The proper name of the historical Buddha was Gautama (Pali, Gotama), or Siddhartha (Pali, Siddhattha), or, after his tribe, he is often called Sakyamuni. The Buddha is thus on the one hand an historical individual, on the other a channel for the spiritual teachings about dharma. This duality is normal in authoritative Asian religious leaders, In recent years we met it again in Karamchand Gāndhī, who was also the Mahatma, the "Great-souled One". The actually observable historical effects of his actions remain a mystery to all those who cannot look through the personal mask of Gandhi to the spiritual force which worked through him, and fail to understand that his significance lay in his Mahatma side, for which the personality of Gandhi was just a vessel.

In this way the individual, called Gautama or Sakyamuni, somehow co-exists with the spiritual principle of Buddhahood which is variously called "the Tathagata", or "the Dharma-body", or the "Buddha-nature", although the Buddhists regarded the exact relation between the individual and the spiritual sides of his being as incapable of definition. And at all times all Buddhists have also consistently opposed the tendencies of the unregenerate to put their faith in a living person, and have done everything to belittle the importance of the Buddha's actual physical existence. It is the Buddha himself who, in a Hinayana Sūtra, is reported to have said to Vakkali: "What is there, Vakkali, in seeing this vile body of mine? Whoso sees the spiritual Dharma, he sees me; whoso sees me sees the spiritual Dharma. Seeing Dharma, Vakkali, he sees me; seeing me, he sees Dharma" (*Buddhist Texts*, no. 103).

Within the Hinayana the Mahasanghika school now initiated a process, centuries before the rise of the Mahayana, by which the historical Buddha becomes less and less important. They regarded everything personal, earthly, temporal and historical as outside the real Buddha, who himself was transcendental, altogether supramundane, had no imperfections and impurities whatsoever, was omniscient, all-powerful, infinite and eternal, for ever withdrawn into trance, never distracted or asleep. In this way the Buddha became an ideal object of religious faith. As for the historical Buddha, who walked the earth about 500 B.C., he was a magical creation of the transcendental Buddha, a fictitious creature sent by him to appear in the world and to teach its inhabitants. While on the one side intent on glorifying the otherworldliness of the Buddha, the Mahasanghikas at the same time tried to increase the range of his usefulness to ordinary people. The Buddha has not disappeared into Nirvana, but with a compassion as unlimited as his length of life, he will until the end of time conjure up all kinds of forms which will help all kinds of beings in diverse ways. His influence is not confined to those few who can understand his abstruse doctrines, but as a Bodhisattva he is even re-born in the "states of woe", becomes of his own free will an animal, or a ghost, or a dweller in hell, and works the weal of beings who have the misfortune to live in places where wisdom teaching must fall on deaf ears. Nor are Buddhas found on this earth alone. They fill the entire universe, and are to be met everywhere, in all the world systems.

The Mahayana took over this Buddhology in its entirety.

The historical Buddha faded away, leaving the Buddha as the embodiment of Dharma as the only reality. In the *Diamond Sūtra* occur the famous verses:

Those who by my form did see me,
And those who followed me by voice,
Wrong the efforts they engaged in,
Me those people will not see.
From the Dharma should one see the Buddhas,
For the Dharma-bodies are the guides.
Yet Dharma's true nature should not be discerned,
Nor can it, either, be discerned.

(*Vajracchedikā Prajñāpāramitā*, chap. 26.)

The Buddha himself tells us in the *Lotus of the Good Law* that many Buddhists believe that "the Lord Sakyamuni, after going forth from his home among the Sakyas, has quite recently awoken to full Enlightenment on the terrace of Enlightenment, by the town of Gayā. But not thus should one see it. In fact it is many hundreds of thousands of myriads of kotis of aeons ago that I have awoken to full Enlightenment. Fully enlightened for ever so long, the Tathagata has an endless span of life, he lasts for ever" (*Buddhist Texts*, pp. 140, 142).

As the manifestation of a type, the historical Buddha is not an isolated phenomenon, but only one of a series of Buddhas who appear on earth throughout the ages. Knowledge of the non-historical Buddhas seems to have grown as time went on. At first there were seven, then we hear of twenty-four, and so the number grew steadily. The Mahayana went further and populated the heavens with Buddhas. In the East lives Askhobhya, the "Imperturbable". In the West the Buddha of "Infinite Light", Amitabha, whose cult owed much to Iranian sun worship, probably originated in the Kushana Empire in the borderland between India and Iran, and was first brought to China, between 148 and 170, by an Iranian prince, the Arsacid Ngan che-kao. Other popular Buddhas are the "Buddha of Healing" (Bhaishajyaguru), as well as Amitayus, the Buddha who "has an endless life-span", a counterpart to the Iranian Zurvan i Akanarak ("Unlimited Time"). Most of these innumerable Buddhas were endowed with a "kingdom", or "field", or "mystical universe" of their own, a world which is not of this world, a land which is "pure" because free from sin and the states of woe. Later on the Tantra added still further Buddhas, for instance Vairocana, Vajrasattva, Vajradhara, and so on. Even as an object of devotion the Buddha Sakyamuni receded into the background, and sometimes he is reduced to the status of a mere phantom body of a celestial Buddha, like Vairocana.

About A.D. 300 the Buddhology of the Mahayana was finally formulated in the doctrine of the *Three Bodies*. A Buddha exists on three levels: he has (1) a fictitious, conjured-up body (*nirmāṇa-kāya*); (2) a communal body (*sambhoga-kāya*); and (3) a Dharma-body. The first and third are easy to understand. The Dharma-body is the Buddha seen as the Absolute. The fictitious, conjured-up body is the one which people can see at a given time, in other words, it is an historical Buddha. In the fifteenth century this doctrine of "fictitious bodies" took in Tibet a form which has somehow stirred the imagination of the West, where everyone has heard of Dalai Lamas and "Living Buddhas" (*Tulkus* = *sprul-sku* = *nirmāṇa-kāya*). People usually misunderstand the theory behind them because they pay no attention to the essential difference between ordinary persons and accomplished saints in their manner of coming into the world. An ordinary person was someone else before being re-born here, but his re-birth was determined by his unexhausted *karma*, and he was pushed where he is more or less against his will. No such ties bind the celestial Bodhisattvas or Buddhas to this world, which they could quite easily leave behind, if their compassion would permit them to do so. Now it is a quite old tradition that perfected saints can conjure up phantom bodies which are to all intents and purposes indistinguishable from ordinary bodies, and which they use as a kind of puppet to help and convert others. These are in no way "incarnations" of the saint in question, but free creations of his magical power, which he sends out to do his work, while he himself remains uncommitted. One might more appropriately speak of "possession", and the idea is not unlike that of St. Paul who claimed that it was not he who spoke but the Christ who was in him (*Galatians* ii, 20). So it is not the Tulku who acts, but the spiritual force which directs him.

All this is common property to all Buddhists. The innovation of Lamaism in the fifteenth century consisted in teaching (*a*) that certain Bodhisattvas and Buddhas would send into certain places a certain number of phantom bodies to act as the priestly rulers of that area. In this way Avalokitesvara would appear thirteen times as the ruler of Lhasa, Maitreya seven times in Urga, and so on. (*b*) They claimed that it is possible to discover the spiritual principle of the old ruler in the body of a child who had been conceived forty-nine days after his decease. Government by Tulkus, carefully chosen by skilled monks on the basis of rules as elaborate as those which enable the Congregation of Rites to differentiate genuine from spurious miracles, was the distinguishing feature of the Lamaist world during the last four hundred and fifty years, though in the case of the highest ruler, the Dalai Lama, it was tempered by a few judicious assassinations.

All this is quite simple and straightforward. The same cannot be said of the second or "communal" body. Even the exact meaning of the term is in doubt, and "enjoyment-body" may be a better translation. It is a supernatural refulgent body in which the Buddha appears to superhuman beings and to the celestial Bodhisattvas in unearthly realms which his merit has created, and where he preaches the Dharma to them, while generating joy, delight and love for it. We must leave it at that, but may add that this glorified body provided a much-needed justification for the new Scriptures of the Mahayana (*see* p. 51), which could be traced back to its activities.

Skill in Means

And yet, if the truth be told, everything we have spoken about so far is not real at all, but is part of the vast phantasmagoria of this world of illusion. In actual reality there are no Buddhas, no Bodhisattvas, no perfections, no stages, and no paradises—none of all this. All these conceptions have no reference to anything that is actually there, and concern a world of mere phantasy. They are just expedients, concessions to the multitude of the ignorant, provisional constructions of thought, which become superfluous after having served their purpose. For the Mahayana is a "vehicle", designed to ferry people across to salvation. When the goal of the Beyond has been reached, it can safely be discarded. Who would think of carrying a raft along with him once he had got to the other shore?

In the *Perfection of Wisdom* the anxious gods ask the Venerable Subhuti: "Even Nirvana, Holy Subhuti, you say is like an illusion, is like a dream?" and they receive this reply: "Even if perchance there could be anything more distinguished, of that also I would say that it is like an illusion, like a dream. For not two different things are illusions and Nirvana, are dreams and Nirvana." (*Buddhist Texts*, no. 165). Nirvana, as the true Reality, is one single, and it has no second. All multiplicity, all separation, all duality is a sign of falseness. Everything apart from the One, also called "Emptiness" or "Suchness", is devoid of real existence, and whatever may be said about it is ultimately untrue, false and nugatory, though perhaps permissible if the salvation of beings requires it. The ability to frame salutary statements and to act in conformity with people's needs, springs from a faculty called "skill in means", which comes to a Bodhisattva only late, on the seventh stage, after the "perfection of wisdom" has thoroughly shown him the emptiness of everything.

"Skill in means" made the Mahayanists much more effective as missionaries outside India than the Hinayanists. Not that the latter were deficient in missionary zeal. They were, however, handicapped by being rather inflexible literalists, whereas the Mahayana claimed much greater freedom in interpreting the letter of the Scriptures. This applied to both monastic rules and doctrinal propositions. The books on *Vinaya* state that the monks must wear cotton robes. The Hinayanists took this as a final ordinance, and in consequence they had great difficulties in establishing themselves in a cold climate, and could not efficiently operate in Tibet, Northern China, Mongolia and Japan. Mahayana monks, on the other hand, wear wool and felt without any qualms. Similarly, if the rules about eating meat are strictly interpreted, nomadic populations must remain without the consolations of the Dharma. Mahayana monks quickly found a way round unworkable rules and re-interpreted them to fit the circumstances. Of particular importance for the success of their missionary enterprises was their attitude to the Vinaya rule which forbids monks to practise medicine. The history of Christian missions in recent centuries shows that, violence apart, the medical missionaries effected more conversions than anyone else. The Buddhists disdained to use the sword, but the scalpel, the herb and the potion opened to the Mahayanists the houses of poor and rich alike. Convinced that compassion and their responsibilities to their fellow-men counted for more than a well-meant monastic rule, they zealously gave themselves over to the study and practice of medicine, which formed part of the curriculum for instance of Nalanda University, and also in the monastic institutions of Tibet.

The same easy-going attitude was practised with regard to doctrinal questions. Great care was taken to minimize the differences between Buddhist and non-Buddhist opinions, to absorb a great deal of the pre-existing views of the converts, and to effect, regardless of the purity of the doctrine, some kind of syncretism with Taoist, Bon, Shinto, Manichaean, shamanist or other views. This latitudinarianism is, of course, in danger of lapsing into laxity in the moral, and into arbitrary conjectures in the doctrinal field. The latter danger was on the whole more effectively avoided than the former, and the best Mahayana literature contains little, if anything, which to any fair-minded Buddhist would seem positively unorthodox.

If "skill in means" is detached from its background of a continuous and living spiritual tradition, it may well appear to amount to sheer opportunism. What then, we must ask, was it that limited and restrained the "skill in means" of these men? The first restraining factor was the belief in the inexorable force of *karma*, by which everyone "knew that he will experience the fruit of any *karma* that he may have done." For instance, it was an application of skill in means, though stretched rather far, when a monk in A.D. 842 killed the Tibetan king Langdarma who persecuted the holy religion, his ostensible motive being compassion, because he wanted to prevent the king from doing any more evil which could only result in a most unfortunate re-birth. But in spite of this high-minded motive he well knew that he had done wrong. When the persecution had abated and new monks could be ordained, he refused to officiate in the ordination ceremony, since as a murderer he had forfeited the right to do so, and would first have to be purified by a sojourn in purgatory. This kind of reasoning is quite taken for granted, and treated as self-evident. Once I had lunch with a Mongol Lama, and tried to get him vegetarian food. He declared that this was quite unnecessary, "We Mongol monks always eat meat, because there is nothing else". So I said, "Well, I only thought of the Vinaya", meaning the monastic disciplinary code. But he rejoined at once, "Yes, we know that by habitually eating meat we act against the ordinances of the Lord Buddha. As a result of our sin we may well be re-born in hell. But it is our duty to bring the Dharma to the Mongol people, and so we just have to take the consequences as they come."

The Mahayanists were further restrained by the *meditations* on traditional lines which for many years moulded and disciplined their minds, and which exert a uniform influence on all Buddhists alike. Nor did they ever swerve from the *aim* of all Buddhist endeavour, which is the "extinction of self", the dying out of separate individuality, to which all these devices are subservient. Long familiarity with the history of Buddhism reveals two further stabilizing factors, which are no less real and vital for being rather intangible, and apt to strike the casual observer as fantastic. Buddhism throughout its history has the unity of an *organism*, in that each new development takes place in continuity from the previous one. Nothing could look more different than a tadpole and a frog, or a chrysalis and a butterfly, and yet they are stages of the same animal, and evolve continuously from one another. The Buddhist capacity for metamorphosis must astound those who see only the end-products separated by long intervals of time. In fact they are connected by many gradations, which only close study can detect. There is in Buddhism really no innovation, but what seems so is in fact a subtle adaptation of pre-existing ideas. Great attention has always been paid to continuous doctrinal development, and to the proper transmission of the teachings from teacher to teacher. These are no anarchic philosophizings of individualists who strive for originality at all costs.

Furthermore, all Buddhist writings have a *flavour* of their own, and for thirty years I have not ceased marvelling at its presence in each one of them. The Scriptures themselves compare the Dharma to a taste, saying that the Buddha's words are those which have the taste of peace, the taste of emancipation, the taste of Nirvana. Tastes can unfortunately not be described, and even the greatest poet could not tell the taste of a peach and say how it differs from that of an apple. Those who refuse to taste the Scriptures for themselves are therefore at a serious disadvantage in their appreciation of the unity which underlies all forms of Buddhism.

Ontological Doctrines

Having so far spoken about the way to the Beyond, we next turn to the Beyond itself. From the outer buildings of the palace of the Mahayana we now move into the inner sanctum, the wisdom teachings which concern ontology, or the nature of reality. These doctrines are extremely subtle and abstruse, and I cannot hope to expound them within the space allotted to me. It may console us to know that their true understanding is said to require not only many years but many lives even, and the Mahayana authors do not cease to warn their readers about the difficulties in front of them. The situation has been neatly summed up in the Sūtra on "Perfect Wisdom", where we read: "Thereupon the thought came to some of the gods in that assembly, 'What the fairies talk and murmur, that we understand though mumbled. What Subhuti has just told us, that we do not understand!' Subhuti read their thoughts, and said, 'There is nothing to understand, nothing at all to be understood! For nothing in particular has been indicated, nothing in particular has been explained.' " In fact, "no one can grasp this perfection of wisdom, for no dharma at all has been indicated, lit up or communicated. So there will be no one who can ever grasp it" (*Buddhist Texts*, no. 165). In spite of this warning I will now proceed to enumerate the chief ontological doctrines of the Mahayana. They will here be presented as bald dogmatic propositions, although this does violence to their true character. For they were never meant as definite statements about definite facts.

The foundations for the ontological doctrines of the Mahayana, as those for its Buddhology, were laid in the school of the Mahasanghikas, who developed two philosophical theories of outstanding importance: 1. Thought, in its own nature, "own-being" or substance, is perfectly pure and translucent. The impurities never affect its original purity and remain accidental or "adventitious" to it. 2. As against the philosophical realism of the other Hinayana schools, the Mahasanghikas became increasingly sceptical about the value of empirical knowledge. Some of them taught that all worldly things are unreal, because they are the result of ignorance and perverted views. That which transcends worldly things is the only reality and the absence of all of them is called "Emptiness". Others went even further, and regarded everything, both worldly and supramundane, both absolute and relative, as fictitious. They believed that nothing real ever corresponds to verbal expressions which give us a mere illusion of knowledge.

On this basis the Mahayana evolved the following propositions:

1. All things are "empty". The Hinayana, in rejecting the "heresy of individuality", had taught that persons are "empty of self", and are in fact conglomerations of impersonal processes, called *dharmas*. The Mahayana now adds that also these impersonal processes are "empty of self", in the sense that each one is nothing in and by itself, and is therefore indistinguishable from any other *dharma*, and so ultimately nonexistent.

The speculative contents of this concept of Emptiness are so rich that I must refer for further information to Prof. Murti's *Central Philosophy of Buddhism*. Here it must suffice to say that "emptiness" means an absolute transcendental reality beyond the grasp of intellectual comprehension and verbal expression. Practically it amounts to an attitude of perfected even-mindedness. One should not "seize" on anything, or "grasp" at it, because that would involve an act of preference bound up with self-interest, self-assertion and self-aggrandizement, ill-becoming to the selfless. "As contrary to the ways of the whole world has this dharma been demonstrated. It teaches you not to seize upon *dharmas*, but the world is wont to grasp at anything" (*Aṣṭasāhasrikā* XV 305) The attitude of the perfected sage is one of non-assertion.

2. This Emptiness is also called "Suchness" or the "One". It is "Suchness" if and when one takes it "such as it is", without adding anything to it or subtracting anything from it. It is the

"One" because it alone is real. The multiple world is a product of our imagination.

3. If all is the same, then also the Absolute will be identical with the relative, the Unconditioned with the conditioned, Nirvana with Samsara. It is a practical consequence of this that the Bodhisattvas aim at a Nirvana which does not exclude Samsara. Ordinary people choose the Samsāra, the Disciples and Pratyekabuddhas wish to escape into Nirvana. The Bodhisattvas do not leave or abandon the samsaric world, but it no longer has the power to defile them.

4. True knowledge must rise above the duality of subject and object, of affirmation and negation. To be is just the same as not to be, "yes" and "no" are both equally true and untrue, and everything is identical with its own negation. If statements must be made, self-contradictory propositions are the ones most likely to bring out the truth of what there actually is.

The attempt to define the exact nature of this ultimate reality led to the one serious disagreement which occurred within the Mahayana, otherwise singularly free from doctrinal disputes. Two philosophical schools slowly crystalized themselves, the Madhyamikas and the Yogacarins. The Madhyamikas maintained that no positive statement whatsoever can be made about the Absolute, that our linguistic resources are hopelessly inadequate for the task, and that the Buddha's "roaring silence" is the only medium by which it can be communicated. The Yogacarins, developing the first thesis of the Mahasanghikas (p. 76-7), believed by contrast that the Absolute can usefully be described as "Mind", "Thought", or "Consciousness". The Madhyamika philosophy is primarily a logical doctrine, which by the successive self-annihilation of all propositions arrives at an all-embracing scepticism. Kant is the nearest European equivalent. The Yogacarin philosophy is a metaphysical idealism, which teaches that consciousness can exist by itself without an object, and that it creates its objects out of its own inner potentialities. Berkeley is the nearest European equivalent. The Madhyamikas believe that salvation is attained when everything has been dropped, and absolute Emptiness alone remains. For the Yogacarins salvation means to have "an act of cognition which no longer apprehends an object", an act of thought which is "Thought-only", pure consciousness, and altogether transcends the division between object and subject.

Help From Above

Many are the obstacles which beset the Bodhisattva in the course of his career. On all sides hostile forces rise up against him, not only from his own passions, but also from the powers of darkness and from adverse historical trends.

As for the powers of darkness, it was never doubted that disembodied spirits could help or hinder spiritual progress, and it is a simple matter of experience that, as they advance on the spiritual path, people become more and more sensitive to psychic, and presumably magical, influences. "For we wrestle not against flesh and blood, but against principalities, against powers, against the rulers of the darkness of this world, against spiritual wickedness in high places" (*Ephesians* vi, 12).

As for the pressure of their social environment, far from believing in progress, the Buddhist, like the Hindu, philosophy of history assumes a continuous decline in the age in which we live. Prophecies dating back to the beginning of the Christian era tell us that the Dharma will become progressively weaker, and that a decisive change for the worse will take place every five hundred years. Each generation will be spiritually more obtuse than the previous one, and as time goes on the wisdom of the sages will be understood less and less. In the West Horace said nearly the same thing at the same time:

> Our father's age ignobler than our grandsires
> Bore us yet more depraved; and we in turn
> Shall leave a race more vicious than ourselves.
>
> (*Odes* 3. 6.)

From A.D. 400 onwards the Buddhists of India were filled with expectations of the coming end. For Vasubandhu

> The times are come
> When flooded by the rising ride of ignorance
> Buddha's religion seems to breathe its last.
>
> (*Abhidharmakośa*, ch. 9.)

Two centuries later Yüan-tsang's account of his travels breathes the same spirit, and he met with gloomy forebodings in many parts of the Buddhist world. The pressure of the times exacted many undesirable concessions, such as married monks and wealthy monasteries. The times were bad and would get worse and worse. This conviction has coloured all Buddhist thinking for the last 1,500 years.

The help which the Bodhisattva needs for his gigantic struggles comes from two sources, from personal spiritual force and from more impersonal magical and occult powers.

The help of unseen beings had always been taken for granted. The new mythological figures of the Mahayana added to their number. An important innovation, which profoundly affected the whole tone of Buddhism, and which perhaps divides the Mahayana from the Hinayana more than anything else, consisted in the introduction of *feminine deities*. Religions tend normally to be either matriarchal or patriarchal. The Protestant interpretation of Christianity centres round God the Father and God the Son, and views with considerable distaste the devotion to the "Mother of God" which is accorded so much prominence among Catholics. In some schools of Buddhism the central person is the Buddha himself, a Father figure, whereas in others the Buddha is subordinated to a female force, the Prajñaparamita, who is the "Mother of all the Buddhas". In the older Buddhism, the higher planes of the spiritual life were considered beyond the reach of women. Even the early Mahayana teaches that in Amitabha's Pure Land there are no women, and in the *Lotus of the Good Law* we have the story of the daughter of a Dragon king who, the moment she becomes a Bodhisattva, automatically turns into a man (*Saddharma Pundarīkā*, pp. 226–8, tr. H. Kern, 1909, pp. 251–4).

Nevertheless, the feminine element was with the Mahayana from the very beginning, owing to the importance it attributed to the *Perfection of Wisdom*. E. Neumann, in *The Great Mother* (1955), has recently studied all the manifestations of what he regards as the "archetype" of the "Mother", and he describes Sophia, or Wisdom, as the sublimest and most spiritual form of femininity, the last refinement of a Mother image dreamt up in remote times in the caves of Palaeolithic man. The Prajña-paramita is not only feminine by the grammatical form of her name, but on statues and images the femininity of her form is rarely in doubt. The Mahayana believed that men should in their meditations complete themselves by fostering the feminine factors of their personality, that they should practise passivity and a loose softness, that they should learn to open freely the gates of nature, and to let the mysterious and hidden forces of this world penetrate into them, stream in and through them. When they identify themselves with the Perfection of Wisdom, they merge with the principle of Femininity (Jung's *anima*), without which they would be mutilated men. Like a woman the "*Perfection of Wisdom*" deserves to be courted and wooed, and the Sūtras on Perfect Wisdom constitute one long love-affair with the Absolute. Meditation on her as a Goddess has the purpose of getting inside her, identifying oneself with her, becoming her. In the later Tantra a sexual attitude to Prajñaparamita is quite explicit. Disguised by the use of ambiguous terms it was already present in the older Prajñaparamita Sūtras themselves.

And it is interesting to notice that these writings show many feminine features, in which we learn to participate by their recitation, and by meditation on them: argumentations almost entirely rely on intuition, and attempts at reasoning are scanty and far from conclusive. The Sūtras win over by fascination, and not by compulsion. Timeless, they are not obsessed with time, but ignore it. They urge on to a contemplation of the world, and not to its conquest by manipulation. They show some of the amoralism which later on hardened into the antinomianism of the Tantra, and which did not fail to provoke protests from the more tight-laced monks. They are indifferent to sensory facts, and in vain do we search through thousands of pages for one single "hard fact". And in her ultimate core the Prajñaparamita is described as for ever elusive, not possessed by anyone, but absorbing all.

A great number of feminine deities were introduced after A.D.400. Feminine Buddhas were, it is true, never thought of, but the Prajñaparamita now became a celestial Bodhisattva, and others were added as time went on. The most famous and beloved of these are the Taras, "saviouresses" who are the mothers of the world, born of the power of Avalokitesvaras vow and understanding", who protect, reassure and "fulfil all our hopes". More specialized are the functions of the personifications of magical spells, like the "five Protectresses", among whom "the Great Pea Hen" is the most outstanding, or of Hariti who gives children. A whole complicated pantheon has further been elaborated in connection with certain aspects of advanced mystical meditation, and it comprises such figures as Cundā, Vasudharā, Ushṇīshavijayā, Vajravarāhī, and so on. The practitioners of the magic arts have a special devotion for the "Queens of sacred lore" and for the Dakinis, or "sky-walkers". After A.D. 700 one section of the Tantra further added consorts of the Buddhas and Bodhisattvas, called *Vidyās* or *Prajñās*, corresponding to the Śaktis of Śivaism and to the "Ennoia" and "Sophia" of Gnosticism. The cult of these Vidyas is often accompanied by an erotic ritual, which was derived from the age-old customs of non-Aryan populations, and which most Buddhists rejected as unseemly.

We must now say a few words about *magic*. Many people are astonished by the preoccupation of the later Mahayana with magic, and condemn it as a degeneration. I can see nothing astonishing in it, and prefer to regard it as a sign of vitality, and of a catholicity which tries to be all things to all men. Historically speaking, the spiritual and the magical, though essentially different, are everywhere inextricably intertwined. A spirituality which tries to do without magic becomes too diluted, too much cut off from the vital and living forces of the world, to bring the spiritual side of man to maturity. Protestantism is almost the only religion to cut out all magic. After first destroying the centres of spiritual contemplation, it has lately lost much of its capacity for restraining and influencing the conduct of individuals and of societies.

The Buddhists, in their turn, had never been without a belief in the occult, in magic and in miracles. But as for the dangers from evil spirits, no special measures were at first required to deal with them, apart perhaps from an occasional recourse to spells. A scrupulous observance of the rules of moral conduct as well as perseverance in meditation were sufficient to ward off dangers and secure help. But as the spiritual potency of the Dharma waned, and as history was felt to become more and more adverse, greater efforts were held to be required. First of all there was, from about A.D. 300 onwards, a great multiplication of spells (*mantras*) of all kinds, also called *dhāraṇīs* because they "uphold" or "sustain" the religious life. Then, after A.D. 500, all the customary methods of magic were resorted to, rituals, magical circles and diagrams, ritual gestures, even astrology. Buddhist magic does not differ from ordinary magic in any way, and all the methods employed have their parallels in numerous cultures, as the reader can verify from H. Webster's standard work on *Magic* (1948).

These magical procedures were introduced principally to guard the spiritual life of the élite. But as the Mahayana was also a popular religion, it was only natural that they should as well be used to give to the unspiritual multitude that which it desired. Already in the third century we are told of the virtue of pronouncing the name of Avalokitesvara, which by itself dispels countless sufferings and troubles. For instance, when a caravan is in danger, "if then the whole caravan with one voice invoked Avalokita with the words, 'Homage, homage to the Giver of Safety, the Bodhisattva Avalokitesvara, the great being!', then by the mere act of pronouncing that name the caravan will be delivered" (*Saddharma Puṇḍarīkā*, p. 51). In later centuries the Mahayanists, in order, as we said before (p. 51), to increase their usefulness to ordinary people, mobilized the whole apparatus of their magic to provide them with what they had set their hearts on—abundant harvests, good health, children, wealth and other mundane benefits. Up to then the faithful had relied on Brahmanic rituals for obtaining these things, but now the Buddhist priests entered into competition with them in this field.

At the same time there was a natural reaction against the idea that Bodhisattvas had to go through aeons and aeons to reach Buddhahood, their last goal. For many people an aim so distant could not provide a motive for action, and they would drift into lassitude and despair. More immediate and tangible results had to be found for them to work for. Re-birth after death in some Buddhaland, say that of Amitabha in the West, or of Akshobhya in the East, became the near-term goal of the majority of the believers. Others hoped to be re-born with Maitreya, at a time when in the remote future conditions on earth will again be more promising. Those who are re-born in this way can see the radiant body of the Buddha, whose very sight has the most wonderful consequences:

> To see the Buddha, see the Lord, annuls all ills.
> It helps to win the Buddha's own, the highest gnosis.
> (*Buddhist Texts*, p. 189.)

In our present age, with spirituality observably at a very low ebb, the achievement of enlightenment is by general consent normally out of the question. All we can do now is to lay the foundations for it at a future period by acquiring "merit". "Merit" is that which either guarantees a happier and more comfortable life in the future, or, alternatively, increases the scope of our spiritual opportunities and achievements. Buddhists regard our material environment as a reflex of our *karma*, or merit, and the living conditions of beings are determined by their spiritual maturity. We live in a world we deserve to live in—an awesome thought! The Bodhisattvas, by the force of their meritorious *karma*, are capable of realizing, or bringing to perfection, a "Pure Land", and by the merit of our deeds we can be transported into that more auspicious realm where, slowly matured and purified, we will in due course become Buddhas also. Faith and devotion were held to be particulary productive of merit, and great things were expected from doing worship (*pūjā*) to the Buddhas and Bodhisattvas, and bestowing flowers, perfumes, lamps, etc., upon their shrines.

The magicians went still further in their reaction against the long wait imposed upon Bodhisattvas, and claimed that magical methods could furnish an easy and quick way to Buddhahood, not in the course of three endless aeons, but miraculously in this very life, in "the course of one single thought". This theory was put forward at the very time when the Chinese Ch'an masters came to speak of a "sudden Enlightenment", and this coincidence shows that it met the needs of the Buddhists of that age.

Both the mythological and the ontological innovations of the Mahayana paved the way for the wholesale absorption of magical practices and beliefs. Once the Buddhist pantheon had been widened by the inclusion of new Buddhas and Bodhisattvas, the door was open to any number of new mythological figures. After A.D. 600, thousands of personifications of occult forces were at different times named, described and cultivated. Later on the Tibetans attempted to classify the resulting deities, and arranged them in ten classes, beginning with the Buddhas, and ending with godlings who inhabit mountains and rivers, with fairies, sprites, fiends, demons and ghosts. In view of the increasing sense of adversity greater and greater stress was laid on the "Protectors of the Dharma", also called "Kings of the sacred lore" (*vidyārājā*), who, though inherently benevolent, assume a terrifying appearance to protect the faithful.

The ontological thesis of the identity of Nirvana and Samsara, of the sameness of the Absolute with the phenomenal world was easily capable of the kind of cosmic interpretation which is the philosophical basis of all magic. The Absolute, the philosophical principle behind the world, is identical with the principle of religious salvation, with Buddhahood or a personal Buddha. The Supreme Buddha pervades the entire universe, and is present in everything. Each thought, sound and action is in its true essence an activity of his saving grace. As a manifestation of the Absolute this very world contains all the mysteries of reality, and its hidden forces can be used for salvation. As a reflex of the Non-dual, it must everywhere mirror, manifest and reveal this all-comprehensive unity. If all things are fundamentally identical in one Pure Spirit, all cosmic phenomena can be conceived of as closely linked together by many invisible threads, each word, action and thought as somehow connected with the eternal Ground of the world.

The magic is this unity, as it were, in action. If Thought is the only reality, and everything material an expression of spiritual forces, then the thoughts condensed in the *mantras* could easily have power over material things. The Emptiness, in its turn, being nothing particular in itself, offers no resistance to being transformed by *mantras* into the particular form of a god or goddess, in whose powers the magician can share by identification. As long as one's own self is no longer in the way, and if one is acquainted with the secret lore of the Sages, one can without difficulty transform oneself into the One, or any of its manifestations.

This ends our survey of the Mahayana. In India a synthesis of all its diverse elements was effected in the Buddhist universities under the Pala dynasty (750–1150). Then, after about

A.D. 1200, Buddhism, and with it the Mahayana, disappeared from India, not without first having left a deep imprint on Hinduism. By then Pala Buddhism had migrated to Tibet, which became its citadel for another 750 years.

The Meditation on Death

If we can believe Buddhaghosa (III 57–60), two only among the forty meditational practices are always and under all circumstances beneficial—the development of friendliness, and the recollection of death. "As a result of the recollection of death one reflects on the fact that one is sure to die, gives up the search for what is unworthy, and steadily increases one's agitation until one has lost all sluggishness". This agrees fairly well with Plato when he says in his Phaidon (64A) that they are the "true votaries of knowledge" who "practise nothing else but how to die or to meet death". Few things indeed are as salutary to a Buddhist as to meditate on death, the inevitable sequel of a life governed by craving and ignorance.

The Meditation, as outlined by Buddhaghosa, considers death from eight points of view. My translation has been made from H. C. Warren's edition of the *Visuddhimagga* (1950), and gives the bulk of Buddhaghosa's argument, i.e. no. 3–17 and 25–41 of chap. VIII. After the translation I give some hints about the way in which his instructions are best carried out, and show how this can be turned into an interesting and fruitful exercise for the contemporary Western student of the Dharma.

Buddhaghosa on the Recollection of Death

In "the recollection of death", the word "death" refers to the cutting off of the life-force which lasts for the length of one existence. Whoso wants to develop it, should in seclusion and solitude wisely set up attention with the words: "Death will take place, the life-force will be cut off", or (simply), "Death, death". But if somebody takes up an unwise attitude (to this problem of death), then sorrow will arise in him when he recalls the death of a loved person, like the grief of a mother when she thinks of the death of the dear child whom she has borne; and joy will arise when he recalls the death of an unloved person, like the rejoicing of a foe who thinks of an enemy's death; and when he recalls the death of an indifferent person, no perturbation will arise in him, just as the man who all day long burns corpses looks on dead bodies without perturbation; when, finally, he recalls his own death, violent trembling arises in him, as in a frightened man who sees before him a murderer with his sword drawn. And all this is the result of a lack in mindfulness, (reasonable) perturbation, and cognition.

Therefore the Yogin should look upon beings killed or dead here and there, and advert to the death of beings who died after having first seen prosperity. To this (observation) he should apply mindfulness, perturbation and cognition, and set up attention with the words, "Death will take place", and so on. When he proceeds thus, he proceeds wisely, i.e. he proceeds expediently. For only if someone proceeds in this way will his hindrances be impeded, will mindfulness be established with death for its object, and will some degree of concentration be achieved.[1]

If this is not enough (to produce access), he should recall death from the following eight points of view:

1. As a murderer, standing in front of him.
2. From the (inevitable) loss of (all) achievement.
3. By inference.
4. Because one's body is shared with many others.
5. From the weakness of the stuff of life.
6. From the absence of signs.
7. Because the life-span is limited.
8. From the shortness of the moment.

1. "As a murderer standing in front of him" means, "as if a murderer were standing in front of him". One should recall that death stands in front of us just like a murderer, who confronts us with his drawn sword raised to our neck, intending to cut off our head. And why? Because death comes together with birth, and deprives us of life.

a) As a budding mushroom shoots upwards carrying soil on its head, so beings from their birth onwards carry decay and death along with them. For death has come together with birth, because everyone who is born must certainly die. Therefore this living being, from the time of his birth onwards, moves in the direction of death, without turning back even for a moment;

[1] Literally: "will the subject of meditation attain to access." See page 97.

b) just as the sun, once it has arisen, goes forward in the direction of its setting, and does not turn back for a moment on the path it traverses in that direction; *c*) or as a mountain stream rapidly tears down on its way, flows and rushes along, without turning back even for a moment. To one who goes along like that, death is always near; *d*) just as brooks get extinguished when dried up by the summer heat, *e*) as fruits are bound to fall from a tree early one day when their stalks have been rotted away by the early morning mists; *f*) as earthenware breaks when hit with a hammer; *g*) and as dewdrops are dispersed when touched by the rays of the sun. Thus death, like a murderer with a drawn sword, has come together with birth. Like the murderer who has raised his sword to our neck, so it deprives us of life. And there is no chance that it might desist.

2. "BY THE FAILURE OF ACHIEVEMENT", which means: Here in this world achievement prospers only so long as it is not overwhelmed by failure. And there is no single achievement that stands out as having transcended the (threat of) failure.

Moreover, all health ends in sickness, all youth in old age, all life in death; wherever one may dwell in the world, one is afflicted by birth, overtaken by old age, oppressed by sickness, struck down by death. Through realizing that the achievements of life thus end in the failure of death, he should recollect death from the failure of achievement.

3. "BY INFERENCE", means that one draws an inference for oneself from others. And it is with seven kinds of person that one should compare oneself: those great in fame, great in merit, great in might, great in magical power, great in wisdom, Pratyekabuddhas, and fully enlightened Buddhas.

In what manner? This death has assuredly befallen even those (kings) like Mahasammata, Mandhatu, Mahasudassana, Dalhanemin and Nimippabhuti, who possessed great fame, a great retinue, and who abounded in treasures and might. How then could it be that it will not befall also me?

> "The greatly famous, noble kings,
> Like Mahasammata and others,
> They all fell down before the might of death.
> What need is there to speak of men like us?"

(And so for the other kinds of distinction.)

In this way he draws from others, who have achieved great

fame, and so on, an inference as to himself, i.e. that death is common to himself and to them. When he recalls that, "as for those distinguished beings so also for me death will take place", then the subject of meditation attains to access.

4. "BECAUSE ONE'S BODY IS SHARED WITH MANY OTHERS:" This body is the common property of many. It is shared by the eighty classes of parasitic animals, and it incurs death as a result of their turbulence. Likewise it belongs to the many hundreds of diseases which arise within it, as well as to the outside occasions of death, such as snakes, scorpions, and so on.

For just as, flying from all directions, arrows, spears, lances, stones, and so on, fall on a target placed at the cross roads, so on the body also all kinds of misfortune are bound to descend. And through the onslaught of these misfortunes it incurs death. Hence the Lord has said: "Here, monks, a monk, when the day is over and night comes round, thinks to himself: many are, to be sure, for me the occasions of death: a snake, or a scorpion, or a centipede may bite me; thereby I may lose my life, and that may act as an obstacle (to my spiritual progress). Or I may stumble and fall, or the food I have eaten may upset me, or the bile may trouble me, or the phlegm, or the winds which cut like knives; and thereby I may lose my life, and that may act as an obstacle" (*Anguttara* III, 306).

5. "FROM THE WEAKNESS OF THE STUFF OF LIFE:" This life-force is without strength and feeble. For the life of beings is bound up with *a*) breathing in and out, *b*) the postures, *c*) heat and cold, *d*) the (four) great primaries, and *e*) with food.

a) It goes on only as long as it can obtain an even functioning of breathing in and out; as soon, however, as air issues from the nose without re-entering, or enters without going out again, one is considered dead. *b*) Again, it goes on only as long as it can obtain an even functioning of the four postures; but through the preponderance of one or the other of these the vital activities are cut off. *c*) Again, it goes on as long as it can obtain the even functioning of heat and cold; but it fails when oppressed by excessive heat or cold. *d*) Again, it goes on as long as it can obtain the even functioning of the (four) great primaries; but through the disturbance of one or the other of them (i.e.) of the solid, fluid, etc., element, the life of even a strong person is extinguished, be it by the stiffening of his body, or because his body has become wet and putrid from dysentery, and so on, or because it is overcome by a high temperature, or because his sinews are torn. *e*) Again, life goes on only as long as one obtains solid food, at suitable times; when one cannot get food, it gets extinguished.

6. "FROM THE ABSENCE OF SIGNS", because one cannot determine (the time of death, etc.). "From the absence of a definite limit", that is the meaning. For one says with regard to the death of beings:

a) Life's duration, *b*) sickness, *c*) time,
d) the place where the body is cast off, *e*) the future destiny.
These are five things about this animate world,
Which never can be known for certain, for no sign exists.

a) There is no sign (i.e. no clear indication) of the duration of life, because one cannot determine that so long will one live, and no longer. For beings may die in the first embryonic state, or in the second, third, or fourth, or after one month, or two, three, four, five or ten months, at the time when they issue from the womb, and further still at any time within or beyond one hundred years.

b) There is also no sign of the (fatal) sickness, insofar as one cannot determine that beings will die of this or that sickness, and no other; for beings may die from a disease of the eyes, or the ears, or any other.

c) There is also no sign of the time, insofar as one cannot determine that one will have to die just at this time of day and no other; for beings may die in the morning, or at midday, or at any other time.

d) There is also no sign as to the laying down of the body; for, when one is dying, one cannot determine that the body should be laid down just here and not anywhere else. For the body of those born within a village may fall away outside the village; and those born outside a village may perish inside one; those born on land may perish in water, those born in water may perish on land; and so this might be expanded in various ways.

e) There is also no sign of the future destiny, insofar as one cannot determine that one who has deceased there will be reborn here. For those who have deceased in the world of the gods may be reborn among men, and those deceased in the world of men may be reborn in the world of the gods, or anywhere else. In this way the world revolves round the five kinds of rebirth like an ox yoked to an oil-pressing mill.

7. "BECAUSE THE LIFE-SPAN IS LIMITED." Brief is the life of men at present; he lives long who lives for a hundred years, or a little more. Hence the Lord has said: "Short, oh monks, is the life-span of men, transient, having its sequel elsewhere; one should do what is wholesome, one should lead a holy life, no one who is born can escape death; he lives long who lives for a hundred years, or a little more.

Short is the life of men, the good must scorn it,
And act as if their turban were ablaze.
For death is surely bound to come" (*Samyutta* I, 108).

Furthermore, the whole Araka-Sutta (*Anguttara* IV, 136–8) with its seven similes should be considered in detail: (i.e. Life is fleeting, and passes away quickly, *a*) like dewdrops on the tips of blades of grass, which soon dry up when the sun rises; *b*) or like the bubbles which rain causes in water, and which burst soon; *c*) or like the line made by a stick in water, which vanishes soon; *d*) or like a mountain brook, which does not stand still for a moment; *e*) or like a gob of spittle spat out with ease; *f*) or like a lump of meat thrown into a hot iron pot, which does not last long; *g*) or like a cow about to be slaughtered; each time she raises her foot she comes nearer to death).

Furthermore, He said: "If, oh monks, a monk develops the recollection of death in such a way that he thinks—'may I just live for one day and night—for one day—for as long as it takes to eat an alms-meal—for as long as it takes to chew and swallow four or five lumps of food—and I will then attend to the Lord's religion, and much surely will still be done by me'—then such monks are said to lead heedless lives, and they develop in a sluggish way the recollection of death which aims at the extinction of the outflows. But if, oh monks, a monk develops the recollection of death in such a way that he thinks—'may I just live for so long as it takes to chew and swallow one lump of food—were I to live just long enough to breathe in after breathing out, or to breathe out after breathing in'—then such monks are said to lead watchful lives, and they develop keenly the recollection of death which aims at the extinction of the outflows" (*Anguttara* III, 305–6). And the span of life is brief like a mere swallowing of four or five lumps of food, and it cannot be trusted.

8. "FROM THE SHORTNESS OF THE MOMENT." In ultimate reality beings live only for an exceedingly brief moment, for it (life) lasts just as long as one single moment of thought. Just as a cart-wheel, whether it rolls along or stands still, always rests on one single spot of the rim; just so the life of beings lasts for one single moment of thought. As soon as that thought has ceased, the being also is said to have ceased. As it has been said: "In the past thought-moment one has lived, but one does not live and one will not live in it; in the future thought-moment one has not lived, but one does live, and one will live; in the present thought-moment one has not lived, but one does live, and one will not live in it.

Our life and our whole personality,
All our joys and all our pains,
Are bound up with one single thought,
And rapidly that moment passes.
And those skandhas which are stopped,
For one who's dying, or one remaining here,
They all alike have gone away,
And are no longer reproduced.
Nothing is born from what is unproduced;
One lives by that which is at present there.
When thought breaks up, then all the world is dead.
So't is when final truth the concept guides".

(*Niddesa* I, 42.)

Result: When he recollects (death) from one or the other of these eight points of view, his mind by repeated attention becomes practised therein, mindfulness with death for its object is established, the hindrances are impeded, the Jhana-limbs become manifest. But, because of the intrinsic nature of the object and the agitation it produces, the Jhana only reaches access and not full ecstasy.

Benefits: And the monk who is devoted to this recollection of death is always watchful, he feels disgust for all forms of becoming, he forsakes the hankering after life, he disapproves of evil, he does not hoard up many things, and with regard to the necessities of life he is free from the taint of stinginess. He gains familiarity with the notion of impermanence, and, when he follows that up, also the notions of ill and not-self will stand out to him. At the hour of death, beings who have not developed the recollection of death, feel fear, fright and bewilderment, as if they were suddenly attacked by wild beasts, ghosts, snakes, robbers or murderers. He, on the contrary, dies without fear and bewilderment. If in this very life he does not win deathlessness, he is, on the dissolution of his body, bound for a happy destiny.

Commentary

Four stages can be distinguished in the assimilation of a Buddhist text on meditation. It must first of all 1. Be well memorized. 2. Then understood in all its details. 3. To some extent be Westernized; and finally 4. Be made into a matter of concrete, personal experience.

1. First of all it cannot be said too clearly that there can be no progress at all without the patience to learn the salient points of the meditation by heart. There are eight main items to be remembered, to which we must add thirty-one subsidiary points (7 at 1, 7 at 3, 5 at 5, 5 at 6, 7 at 7), and later on (at (4)) I will show that to these another eighteen can be usefully added. This brings the total up to fifty-eight. Many of our contemporaries are unwilling or unable to memorise anything whatsoever, and so they fall by the wayside already at this elementary stage. Their spiritual training will have to resort to other methods. Those, on the other hand, who are able to memorise will soon come to appreciate the advantages of repetitive meditations which go over the same points again and again. They will, incidentally, find that a string of beads is a great aid to their memory, and that it reduces the chances of floundering into a state of bewildered confusion.

Attention to their logical connections helps to recall the sequence of the eight main points. The meditation starts with the injunction to think that "death will take place". This is a fruitful thing to do because generally we are so unwilling to think of death, and on the contrary cover it up with all sorts of euphemisms and fancy ideas, do not like to take it seriously or to reckon with it, and so in the end "We are amazed that death, that tyrant grim, should think of us, who never thought of him". Buddhaghosa's first point, "as a murderer standing in front of him", then tries to make clear that, whatever may be the occasions of death, its cause is an inherent part of the constitution of this precious I. With the act of birth, with re-conception, death became quite inevitable. At birth we have irrevocably jumped off into a condition which is heading for death. Of each one of us it can be said that "he bears the seed of ruin in himself". Points 2 to 7 are then concerned with effecting a close and indissoluble fusion between the idea of "I" on the one hand, and that of "death" on the other. It has often been said that the average person, although he knows better, never really believes that he himself will die. "To himself everyone is an immortal", as psychologists put it. In some illogical way the idea of death is all the time kept away from, and outside the sacred precincts of the intimate self. At point 2 the student is therefore bidden to reflect on the contents of this self of his, and to see that none of them has gone beyond its opposite—apart from Nirvana, his true "Buddha-self", which is, however, not really a part of himself in the same sense in which the other things are. There remains, however, the more or less subconscious narcissistic tendency, rooted in the "vain-glory of life", by which each person regards himself as somebody quite special and unique. This is counteracted by point 3. If men so much greater than you have succumbed to death, "what need is there to speak of men like us?" And as for the power of this "I" over the organism, it is very small indeed. The very area of the body has to be shared with many strangers (point 4), and the stuff it is made of is at the mercy of countless uncontrollable factors which it has little power to resist (point 5). A little bit of air missing, a little bit of blood gone, a small hole in the skin, a little poison in the blood or bowels, a bulky object falling on the head—any of these things suffices to bring irreparable ruin to this inglorious object, the body. So small indeed is our control over the conditions of our continued existence that (point 6) we do not even know when, where, or how we shall die. This is not because we do not want to know, since we habitually fill up the gaps in our knowledge with ruminations that can give neither certainty nor security. And in any case, if we look at the span of life accorded to this body in its proper perspective—on the background of human history, or the history of the earth, or the length of an aeon—it is seen (point 7) to be exceedingly brief. The middle-aged, it is true, find it easier to appreciate this point than the young, to whom time passes more slowly and who sometimes feel that they have a whole eternity before them. As point 1 set the basic theme, the relation between self and death, and as point 2 to 7 elaborated it, so now point 8 leaves the ego quite behind, discards the illusion of a permanent self altogether, and views the actual facts from the standpoint of ultimate truth. Dying, like becoming, or like coming to birth, is really a continuous process, going on steadily all the time. We die all the time, from moment to moment, and what is really there is a perpetual succession of extremely shortlived events. Death is not to be regarded as a unique catastrophe which happens when one existence comes to an end, but it takes place all the time within that existence. In this way, when they are considered in their logical interconnections, Buddhaghosa's eight points are easy to remember.

2. It is desirable that all the words which occur in the description of a meditation should be clearly understood. Otherwise the mind is apt to become uneasy, and unwilling to concentrate on the task in hand. Luckily Buddhaghosa is here fairly straightforward, and in my experience I have found only eleven words which are liable to cause difficulty. I will now explain them one by one.

In the preamble it is said that we should feel "*perturbation*" about death. People who pay no attention to the hierarchy of the stages of the spiritual life wonder how that can be so. They think that the sage should be indifferent to death, and not perturbed by it. The answer is that he should end up by being indifferent, but that he must go through much perturbation to get to that state.

"... It is because
Then thou didst fear, that now thou dost not fear."

The anxiety, to be finally overcome, must first be intensified. And if the disciple is told to be "perturbed", that does not only mean that he should know how afraid he really is and face this animal fear of his, but also that in his spirit he should be shocked at finding himself in such a perilous and thoroughly ignominious condition, where eagerly each one makes his own pile, only to lose it through death again and again. It is held to be unreasonable not to be disturbed by the contemplation of this recurring futility.

The second difficult word, "*access*", refers to the mechanism of Jhana. If one does not understand it, it is best to just skip this expression, as fairly irrelevant to his particular meditation, and that applies equally to the phrase at the end (under "Result"), which speaks of the "*hindrances being impeded*", and of the "*Jhana-limbs becoming manifest*".

At point 4 we meet with the "*eighty classes of parasitic animals*", literally the "eighty families of worms". Elsewhere we read that, as a lump of foam is full of holes and breaches, so is this body, and in it live the eighty families of worms, it is their "birthplace, nursing home, cemetery and lavatory". In the works of the Sarvastivadine we are, in addition, given the names of these "eighty families", but even that does not help us to identify them in terms of the current lore about the subhuman inhabitants of our body. I sometimes think that they must be some kind of mythological vermin, and I feel that the intention of the authors of this phrase is sufficiently obscure to be safely discarded. We may think of leucocytes, bacteria and viruses instead. And we can add that this body is a part of the processes of nature, the sun's energy, the nitrogen cycle, and so on.

"For dust thou art, and unto dust thou shalt return".

"Whate'er thou lovest, man, that too, become thou must,—
God, if thou lovest God; dust, if thou lovest dust."

Likewise, at point 5b it is not easy to grasp the full import of what is said on the "*four postures*". A man is obviously dead when he gets stuck with one of them, i.e., if he stays put either lying down, or sitting, or standing, or walking. But it is rather hard to visualize this for all the postures, though perhaps that does not matter. More intractable still is the equation of "*the tearing of the sinews*" at 5e with the element of air. Indian physiology in this case differs radically from our own. In the distribution of physiological processes the action of the sinews, which are confused with the nerves, is assigned to the element "air" or "wind". I cannot say that I have ever really understood this, and it is perhaps best to either ignore it, or adapt it to our own conceptions.

At 6a we must remember that Buddhaghosa with "*ten months*" is still at the pre-natal state, because he means *lunar* months. "*The five kinds of rebirth*" are among gods, men, inhabitants of the hells, hungry ghosts and animals.

At 7, to act "*as if their turban were ablaze*", means to act with some sense of urgency. A man with a burning headgear does not dawdle or hesitate, but gets rid of it as fast as he can. So should we deal with the world and its ills. The "*extinction of the outflows*" is a synonym of "Arhatship", and its exact connotation does not matter here. Finally, the verse at 8 is admittedly full of unresolved difficulties in the original, and while I have done my best with it, I am still unsatisfied with the result.

3. The Westernizing, or de-Orientalizing, must, I think, already begin with the very definition of death. Buddhaghosa defines death as "the cutting asunder of the bond by which the life-faculty holds together all that is included in one existence". This is quite correct in itself, but the term "life-faculty" conveys little to us at present. Buddhaghosa's definition must be replaced with something nearer to our own modes of thinking. This is how I myself think of it: "If a shock is the sudden annihilation of a part of what we think belongs to us, then death is the greatest shock of all. The craving bursts apart from its objects, our grasping activities are forcibly separated from that which they have grasped, and the craving, deprived of the fruits of a lifetime, is left by itself, hanging in the air, as it were. Death means that craving is once more parted from its wealth, forced to give it up, and to let it go, because the third constituent in us has remained unrealized—the emptiness which is form, the real home and resting-place of our spirit. We die because we missed that possibility. It is therefore right that we should not only fear death, but also be ashamed of it, as the silent witness to the fact that we have failed to arrive at our true destiny. Death is the price the individual pays for the separation and isolation which is born of ignorance, and at the same time it is the supreme lesson in renunciation". Thus from the very beginning the problem of death is put into its proper perspective, and the subject of meditation made clear. Others will, of course, prefer other formulations.

Secondly, it is, I think, helpful to strengthen our grasp of the various points by recalling their poetical expression in European literature.

At 1, for instance, we have:

"Our term of life depends not on our deed;
Before our birth our funeral was decreed."

At 1g we may think of Coleridge's:

"She passed away like morning dew
Before the sun was high;
So brief her time, she scarcely knew
The meaning of a sigh."

At 2 there is the famous:

"The boast of heraldry, the pomp of power,
And all that beauty, all that wealth e'er gave,
Awaits alike th'inevitable hour.
The paths of glory lead but to the grave."

Or: "Naked to earth was I brought
Naked to earth I descend.
What do I labour for nought,
Seeing the naked end."

Or at 3, we are not likely to be greatly moved by the death of such unknown entities as Mahasammata, and others. European examples are likely to be more impressive:

"Imperious Caesar, dead and turn'd to clay,
Might stop a hole to keep the wind away:
O, that the earth, which kept the world in awe,
Should patch a wall to expel the winter's flaw."

Or, there is the moving, though slightly sentimental, ditty:

"This quiet dust was Gentlemen and Ladies,
And Lads and Girls;
Was laughter and ability and sighing,
And frocks and curls."

At 6 we have:

"Leaves have their time to fall,
And flowers to wither at the North-wind's breath,
And stars to set—but all
Thou hast all seasons for thine own, O Death."

And so one could go on for quite a time.

4. Now I proceed to my fourth point. To be fruitful, meditations of this kind should at each stage be fused with the concrete and individual experiences of the person who practises them. In articles destined for the general public it is naturally impossible to say much about this side of the matter, because the experiences in question are particular to each person. While their detailed description might be an interesting contribution to the author's biography, it would in no way teach others what they should either think or do. In front of large and indiscriminate audiences meditation can be discussed only in general terms. The concrete details must be reserved for small groups of specially chosen people whose individual circumstances are sufficiently familiar to be taken into account.

I therefore pass on to two further additions to Buddhaghosa's meditations, which greatly assist this process of concretizing the meditation and which should precede his first point, following directly on the definition of death.

1. It helps to prepare the mind for the meditations to come if we first of all survey the constituents of our personality, and divide them into two groups, (A) those which are affected by death and (B) those which are not. (A) As to the first, death obviously means not only the loss and dissolution of this body of ours, but it carries away much more besides. One should therefore make a full inventory of all that we lose through it, under the following six headings: 1. Body; 2. Possessions; 3. Achievements; 4. Privileges; 5. Defences; 6. Hopes and plans. These items should then be analysed into their constituent parts, and the loss of each one of these should be felt as keenly as if it were actually taking place. The six headings are, on the whole, self-explanatory. By 4) "privileges" I mean all those features of our present existence which compare favourably with the conditions of life say among destitute slum dwellers, the blind and the crippled, among insects, or animals destined for "scientific" research. As to 5) "defences"—with much sweat and perturbation, after much trial and error, I have now that I am in my fifties, at last learned to find my way about in the part of the world where I live, have to some extent understood the rules of the game, and evolved fairly effective methods of dealing with the recurrent difficulties of this particular environment—and therefore I would hate to

find myself all unprepared again in quite unfamiliar surroundings, repeating the bewildered dismay of my childhood. And, finally 6), our "hopes and plans" continually urge us to wish for the postponement of our death. Death may be inevitable, but it would nevertheless be rather galling if it were to come upon us just before we have completed this or that task, visited this or that place, seen this or that person, and so on.

(B) As distinct from these six items, all equally doomed to destruction by death, two others survive it. They are: 1. Our karmic potentialities. 2. The spark of transcendental reality in our hearts.

These also would deserve closer consideration.

As to the first, none of us is without some meritorious karma, and the "privileges" we spoke about are our temporary rewards for the good deeds of our past. Nevertheless, the recollection of his karma must fill almost everyone, to a greater or lesser extent, with misgivings about the future, and our hearts are bound to become heavy when we think of our debts to the world which are still unpaid, and which surely will have to be paid at some future date. As to the second, we must remember that, however improbable it may seem, we are all potential Buddhas, and at this stage the meditation on death may very well branch out into a meditation on Nirvana, and the "Buddha-self within us". But these are huge topics, and would deserve separate treatment. So I now proceed to my second point.

2. The subsidiary fears which are associated with death should next be called up and considered. "One cannot look directly at either the sun or death", as La Rochefoucauld has said. But one can look at the emotions which the idea of death incurs. As long as they feel quite safe and happily alive, people are apt to imagine that they are even-minded about death, and in times of stress and worry they may even look forward to it. When, however, actually faced with the immediate prospect of death, they easily come under the sway of the frantic "will to live" which nature seems to have imparted to all living creatures. Their mood changes, a kind of panic comes over them, and they cannot help feeling that it is always just a bit too early just now. This fear is partly instinctual, but in part it is due to subsidiary ideas associated with death, ideas which are very numerous, and greatly vary from person to person.

A comprehensive list would fill many pages. A bare dozen will suffice here.

There is 1) the pain of dying, a very important point, which each one should elaborate further in his own way. Then there is 2) the fear that, faced with death, the body may be quite out of hand, either from panic, or as a result of the drugs with which our hospitals at present ease our transition to another world. There are 3) often strong, largely unconscious, associations with violence, assault and mutilation. More universal is 4) the sense of guilt, already mentioned before. The account is not yet settled, punishment is sure to come after death, and evil thoughts and deeds, matured, will lead to a rebirth even more unpleasant than the present one. This is a man's fear of being "sent to his account, with all his imperfections on his head". 5) Since the emotions have a logic of their own, this fear may very well alternate with its opposite, arising from the thought that there may be nothing at all after death. This may, on the one side, be a source of relief, so eloquently described by Lucretius, but on the other hand our mind strongly resists the idea of its total annihilation. Also, if one's whole life had been planned on the assumption of its continuation after death, one could not help feeling rather foolish if there were nothing to come at all. 6) A quite irrational set of fears centres round the shadow world of ghosts, the dread of "loss of soul", and suchlike. It does not seem unreasonable to assume that death is followed by a state where our disembodied desires, deprived of their physical basis, their objects, and their home in our habits and defences, fuse with the occult forces which exist all around us, and confront us, frightening us with magical dread. This is what the Egyptians thought, this is what the Tibetan Book of the Dead teaches, and it is instructive and interesting to see that Newman in his "Dream of Gerontius" should have independently come to the same conclusion. 7) In addition it is also said that, for a moment divested of all our encumbrances, we shall be raised just for an instant to the glory of the supreme light, and come face to face with the emptiness of the Absolute. Reflection on this prospect may lead either to a fear of the glare of the divine light as such, or to a fear of the inadequacy which we are bound to reveal in face of it, with the result that, rejecting it, we rush away into a new body. 8) Turning to more mundane matters, we may find that our deeprooted attachment to our body may involve us in quite a number of fears, like that of being buried alive, or a narcissistic aversion to being eaten by worms, and so on. This, by an easy transition, leads to point 9)—death as a blow to self-conceit: "Death is such a waste of me." Also its levelling effect may not be appreciated by the more haughty and fastidious—"Death calls me to the crowd of common men." In any case we are at death exposed to an extreme of impotence and frustration—whatever we may have achieved in this life, it avails us not. Among further, fairly constant, associations with death we may mention 10) that with cold, or with darkness—"to lie in cold obstructions and to rot", "the deep damp vault, the darkness and the worm". Furthermore 11) death can be conceived as a perilous leap in the dark, and there is the fear of falling headlong into space, through a dark tunnel, analogous to what the more sensitive feel under gas. Finally, 12) there are the conditions of existence among the dead. Certainty about them is, of course, impossible, and when we compare the conflicting accounts of the different authorities we may very well wonder whether anybody knows anything about them. On the other hand, believers in rebirth are, perhaps foolishly, disinclined to suspend their judgment entirely, and they decide with the eye of faith that one of the many accounts is more probable than the others. The author of this article is a believer in the Bardo state, an interval in which, after decease, invested with a "mind-made body", we seek for a new abode. He cannot feel very reassured by what he reads about it. Sure to reject the chance of redemption offered to him at the first stage, he will be exposed once again to the unearthly terrors, the "fearful narrow passage-way", of the latter half of the Bardo state. As the *Tibetan Book of the Dead* (p. 165) informs us, after the fifteenth day we miss our old body, and seek for a new one. "Wherefore finding no place for thyself to enter into, thou wilt be dissatisfied and have the sensationof being squeezed into crack and crevices, amidst rocks and boulders." To some people this is more than mere literature. In my youth, long before I had read Evans-Wentz, they formed the frequent topic of bad nightmares, perhaps in memory of what I had to go through before I was born. It would, I feel, be most unpleasant to have all that all over again.

This brings me to the end of the two salutary considerations which should precede Buddhaghosa's eight points. These eight points do not, of course, by themselves exhaust the meditational possibilities offered by the topic of death. They may be followed by others, according to the aspirant's personal choice. I will be content to mention just three possibilities.

There could be, as point 9, the thought that by death we only lose troublesome disguises, and that "it is the meaner part that dies". "There is no death, what seems so is transition." "Nothing is dead but that which wished to die. Nothing is dead but wretchedness and pain." One must, however, take care that this line of approach does not act as a bromide. As point 10, we may reflect that we have had many bodies. As point 11, that the best preparation for death is to "die by inches", in one's own lifetime, and that the practice of renunciation is really the only effective preparation of death. Nor ought we finally, as point 12, to forget the wonderful koans and farewell songs of the Japanese, about which D. T. Suzuki has written so beautifully. Even in Europe we find similar sayings, which may act as a flint from which to strike the spark of insight. Our scientific humanists, for instance, are usually as stupid on the subject of death as they are clever on other things. But when Harriet Martineau remarked that "I see no reason why the existence of Harriet Martineau should be perpetuated", then this saying is surely worthy of a Buddhist of the best period.

THE LOTUS OF THE GOOD LAW

Chapter 5: On Plants

Thereupon the Lord addressed the Ven. Mahakasyapa and the other elders and great disciples, and spoke these words: "Well said, Mahakasyapa, well said! You did well to enumerate a Tathagata's virtues and qualities. There are many others in addition to those you have mentioned—without measure or number. Even by enumerating them for innumerable aeons one could not easily come to the end of them. The Tathagata, Kasyapa, is the lord[1] of Dharma, He is the king of all dharmas, their master and sovereign. Any dharma which the Tathagata lays down, wherever it may be, that is just so. The Tathagata lays down all dharmas properly,[2] He lays them down with His Tathagata-cognition, and in such a way that all those dharmas in the end lead to the stage of those who know all. For the Tathagata is able to survey the destination and objective reality of all dharmas. The Tathagata, the Arhat, the fully enlightened Buddha has won the sovereignty over the objective reality of all dharmas, He is determined to know all dharmas, He has reached supreme perfection in the cognition of all dharmas, in their skilful handling and philosophical explanation, He makes manifest the cognition of the all-knowing, imparts and establishes it.

"His activities can be compared to those of a huge thundercloud, full of rain, which soars up in this great trichiliocosm, above all the grasses, shrubs, plants and thickets of various kinds and appearance, above all the multitudes of plants with different names, whether they grow on flat ground, on hills or in valleys in the mountains. Covering the entire great trichiliocosm, such a cloud would release its rain everywhere at the

[1] Or: proprietor, owner; *svāmin*.

[2] Skilfully, aptly; *yuktyā*.

same time. All the young and tender stalks, twigs, leaves and foliage, all the grasses, shrubs, plants and thickets, as well as the forest trees and forest giants absorb the watery element from the rain which that great thundercloud has released, each one according to its own strength and within its own domain. As a result of the rain, all of one essence,[1] which the great thunder-cloud has so abundantly released, they shoot forth from their respective seeds, grow, increase and multiply, generate flowers and fruits, and will receive, each severally, their appropriate names. Rooted in one and the same soil all those multitudes of plants are moistened and saturated by this fluid which is of one essence throughout.

"Just so the Tathagata, the Arhat, the fully enlightened Buddha appears in the world. As the great thunder-cloud soars up, so the Tathagata, once He has appeared, makes the entire world, with its gods, men and asuras, resound with the sound of His voice. As the great thunder-cloud overspreads the entire great trichiliocosm, so the Tathagata lifts up His voice in front of the world with its gods, men and asuras, and utters these words: "I am a Tathagata, o ye gods and men, an Arhat, a fully enlightened Buddha! Having crossed over I help others across; freed I free others; comforted I comfort others; gone to final Nirvana I help others to win it. By my right wisdom I wisely know both this and the other world as they really are, for I know all, see all. Come to Me, ye gods and men, so that you may hear the Dharma! I am He who makes known the Path, who indicates the Path, who knows the Path, who has heard of the Path, who is fully conversant with the Path." Thereupon innumerable living beings come to hear the Dharma from the Tathagata. And the Tathagata takes cognizance of the full variety of their capacities and energies, some more considerable than others, provides them with manifold discourses on Dharma, and gives them many an exposition of Dharma, copious, diversified, delightful, satisfying, elating, conducive to their welfare and ease. As a result of these expositions those beings become happy in this life, and after death they are reborn in favourable conditions where they enjoy abundant pleasures and hear the Dharma. On hearing that Dharma they become free from the

[1] Lit. "taste."

hindrances[1] and progressively practise the dharmas of the all-knowing, each one according to his power, range and strength.

"As the great thunder-cloud, on having covered the entire trichiliocosm, releases the rain which, the same everywhere, refreshes all the grasses, shrubs, plants and thickets, each of them absorbing the water according to its power, range and strength, and thereby reaching its own full specific size; just so, whatever Dharma the Tathagata may teach, all that Dharma has one single taste, i.e. the taste of deliverance, dispassion and cessation, and it final aim is the gnosis of the all-knowing. But those being who hear, bear in mind and practise the Dharma taught by the Tathagata do not know, perceive or understand themselves by themselves. The Tathagata alone can cognize those beings in such a way that He knows who, in which manner and of what kind they are, on what, in which manner and whereby they reflect and meditate, and what in which manner and whereby they attain. The Tathagata alone sees all this directly and intuitively, and He alone sees exactly on which stage each of these beings finds himself—corresponding to the gradations of the various plants, some mean, some middling, some supreme. Having known the Dharma as having one single taste, i.e. the taste of deliverance, the taste of the Blessed Rest, as having Nirvana for its final aim, as the state of those who are in permanent Parinirvana, as having only one single level,[2] as situated in space—I do not, because of my tender regard for the dispositions[3] of beings, precipitately[4] reveal the gnosis of the all-knowing. You are surprised, Kasyapa, you are astonished that you cannot fathom the Tathagata's secret hints![5] They are in fact very hard to discern."

[1] The "hindrances" are sense-desire, ill-will, sloth and torpor, excitedness and sense of guilt, doubt.

[2] I.e. the Buddha-level.

[3] *Adhimukti*, resolve. It is of the essence of all those who seek or exercise "power", that they wish to disregard and override the wishes of others, whereas as a "guide" the Tathagata carefully respects their dignity.

[4] Or: inconsiderately, hastily, forcibly, doing violence to others; *na sahasaiva*.

[5] *Sandhābhāshita*, as in *Diamond Sutra*, chap. 6, for which see my *Buddhist Wisdom Books*, pp. 35–6. In other words, if the reader believes he has understood this section at once and without much effort, he is most probably mistaken.

Thereupon the Lord, so as to more fully explain this topic, uttered on that occasion the following verses:[1]

1. "In the world I arose as the king of the Dharma who crushes becoming;
   Dharma I teach, but careful to take account of the varying dispositions of beings.
2. Capable of sustained thought, the great heroes[2] guard my teachings for many years.
   Keep their secret message to themselves, and tell no one about it.
3. For hard to understand is this gnosis. Foolish people who precipitately hear of it
   Will understand and doubt it, will run away from it and go astray.
4. According to My listeners' range and strength I speak.
   Their views I straighten out with many various kinds of expositions.
5. It is like a great cloud[3] which rises above the whole world,
   Covers up everything and overshadows the earth;
6. Chockfull of water, wreathed with lightning,
   It resounds with thunder, and refreshes all creatures.
7. The sun's rays it wards off, the atmosphere it cools down,
   Descending within hand's reach it everywhere releases its fluid.

[1] The previously translated section of the *Lotus of the Good Law* was in prose, and written in fairly accurate Sanskrit. These verses, however, use a dialect which cannot always be construed with full certainty, and in doubtful cases I have followed the Tibetan translation.

[2] This is an epithet of the Bodhisattvas.

[3] This simile is not peculiar to the "Mahayana". It is mentioned, for instance, by Buddhaghosa when he says, "The Enlightened One is like a great rain-cloud; the True Idea is like a downpour of rain; and the Community, in which the dust of defilement has been laid, is like the countryside in which the dust has been laid by the fall of rain." *The Illustrator of Ultimate Meaning*, part I, trs. Bhikkhu Ñāṇamoli, 1960, p. 15.

8. By releasing an abundant mass of water, the same everywhere,
Which flows forth from its every part, it refreshes this earth.

9. And whatever on this earth the vegetation may be—
Grasses, shrubs, thickets, forest trees and forest giants,

10. All kinds of corn and all that is verdantly green,
And all that grows on hills, in valleys or in bowers—

11. That cloud gives life anew to all those grasses, shrubs and thickets,
Refreshes the thirsty earth, and waters its vegetation.

12. And that rain, all of one essence, which the cloud has released,
The grasses and the shrubs absorb it according to their strength and reach.

13. Also the trees—large, small or medium—
Absorb the rain as their vigour and capacity dictates.
And so they grow just as their hearts do prompt them.

14. Of all the plants on which the cloud has shed its rain
The trunk and stalks and bark will grow,
And so the twigs, the branches, leaves and flowers and fruits.

15. Each one perpetuates itself in its own way,
Depending on its strength, its range and on the special nature of its seed;
The rain, however, which came down had had one single essence only.

16. Just so, O Kashyapa, the Buddha also
Arises in this world just like a rain-cloud.
And once the World's Saviour has arisen, then He speaks,
And shows the true course to all living beings.

17. And so it is that, honoured by the world, the Seer, so great, announces:
"The Tathagata I am, the best of men, a Jina,[1]
Arisen in the world just like a rain-cloud.

[1] Lit. "Conqueror," "Victor," an epithet of the Buddha.

18. I shall refresh all living beings,
Whose bodies wither away, who cling to the triple world,
Who wither away in pain—at ease I will place them,
Both pleasures I will give them and the final Rest.

19. Listen to Me, ye hosts of gods and men,
Come nearer, so that you may see Me closely!
The Tathagata I am, the Lord unvanquished,
Born in this world to save[1] (the beings in it).

20. To countless beings I teach a Dharma pure and very fine.
One single fact alone it shows[2]—deliverance and the final Rest.

21. I preach the Dharma with one single message.[3]
Enlightenment is always its foundation.[4]
For this is the same (for all), there can be no inequality about it,
Nor can it lead to greed or enmity in anyone.

22. Free from partiality I feel no love or hate for any person.
To all creatures I proclaim one and the same Dharma; as to one so to the others.[5]

23. This Dharma I proclaim without ever doing anything else,
Whether I walk, stand, sit, or lie Me down.
Once I have mounted the pulpit.
No tiredness takes ever hold of Me.

[1] Lit. "ferry across"; *saṃtāraṇa, bsgral-ba.*

[2] *Ekā ca tasyo samatā tathatvam; de-yi mñam-pa ñid daṅ yaṅ-dag gcig.*

[3] Lit. "voice"; *svara, dbyaṅs.* An adequate translation seems impossible. The sentence refers to the doctrine of the Mahasanghikas according to which the Buddha by one single sound reveals the entire range of the dharmic world. He speaks one word only and all beings hear the Dharma in a fashion adapted to their own nature, and as capable of removing the defilements peculiar to each one of them. By one single sound the Buddha can proclaim the entire Dharma, and his listeners will understand its meaning, be it gross or subtle, according to their own particular aptitude. Another well-known Mahasanghika doctrine is stated in verse 23.

[4] *Bodhiṃ nidānaṃ kariyāna nityam; rtag-tu byaṅ-chub phyir ni shugs-par yaṅ.*

[5] *yathaika-sattvasya tathā parasya; sems-can gcig bshin 'gro-ba gshan-la ste.*

24. This entire world I refresh like a cloud which releases its rain evenly for all.
Equal is my attitude[1] to noble and mean, to moral and immoral men,

25. Whether their life be depraved or their conduct be good,
Whether their views be false and unsound, or right and pure.

26. I preach the Dharma to men of superior or inferior intellect,
And even to those whose faculties are quite dull.
Setting aside all tiredness,
I rain down the rain of the Dharma in the right way.

27. Those who listen to Me, each according to his strength,
Find themselves on a great many levels:
Amongst gods, men or ghosts,
Among Indras, Brahmas or universal monarchs."

28. Now listen closely, for I shall reveal
What corresponds to plants of different size,
The small, the middling and the larger ones.

29. The small plants correspond to men
Who wisely know the dharmas without outflows,
Who dwell in their attainment of Nirvana, and possess
Six kinds of superknowledge[2] and the triple lore.[3]

30. The middling plants again do correspond to men
Who dwell in mountain caves, and long to win
Enlightenment peculiar to Pratyekabuddhas;
Their intellect is moderately purified.

31. But the supreme plants correspond to persons
Who strive to win the state of those who are the mightiest of men,[4]
Want to become Buddhas, saviours of men and gods,
And with this aim practise vigour and meditation.

[1] *Buddhi, blo.*

[2] The six kinds of superknowledge are: psychic power, heavenly ear, cognition of others' thought, recollection of past lives, heavenly eye, cognition of the extinction of outflows.

[3] The "triple lore" consists of the last three of the six superknowledges.

[4] "The mightiest of men" is, of course, the Buddha.

32. The forest trees here correspond to those of the Sugata's[1] sons
Who have set out,[2] who practise lovingkindness, and who, calm
And free from doubts know that one day they will be like the mightiest of men.

33. But forest giants correspond to those
Who turn the wheel which no one can turn back,
Who can work wonders firmly in their own way,
And by whom countless living beings are set free.

34. Nevertheless, the Jina always teaches the same Dharma
Just as one and the same rain is released by a cloud everywhere.
The difference lies in the spiritual capacities[3] of those who are addressed,
Which correspond to the different sizes of plants on the face of the earth.

35. This parable may teach you the Tathagata's skills—
He teaches but one single Dharma,
But different are His formulations like so many drops of rain.

36. When I rain down the rain of Dharma,
Then all this world is well refreshed.
Each one according to their power take to heart
This well-taught Dharma, one in taste.

37. As, when it rains, the grasses and small plants,
And likewise plants of middling size,
The forest trees and forest giants,
Are all made splendid in the regions ten;

38. So this Dharma, to the world always beneficial, can refresh it in its entirety;
The world refreshed, its plants will burst forth into blossoms.

[1] The Buddha is called Su-gata, "Well-Gone" because by the Noble eightfold path he has gone to Nirvana. For a more detailed explanation see Buddhaghosa, *The Path of Purification*, trsl. Bhikkhu Ñāṇamoli, 1956, 215–6, and E. Lamotte, *Le traité de la grande vertu de sagesse*, I, 1944, 131–2.

[2] I.e. on the path of a Bodhisattva.

[3] *Abhijñā*, usually trsl. as "superknowledges".

39. There are some plants which grow to medium size.
They are like those by whom this well-taught Dharma is accomplished
When they are Arhats well established in the extinction of the outflows,
Or Pratyekabuddhas who practise in woody thickets.

40. The many Bodhisattvas, mindful and courageous,
Who again and again, deliberately and of set purpose, seek rebirth[1] everywhere in the triple world,
While all the time they pursue this supreme enlightenment,
They continue to grow for a long time as forest trees do.

41. But those with miraculous powers, adepts in the trances,
Who feel[2] joyous zest when hearing of Emptiness,
And who emit many thousands of rays,
They are in this context called the forest giants.

42. In this way, Kashyapa, the demonstration of Dharma
Has been released, like rain from a cloud, as the same everywhere;
Through it, as the manifold plants are made to grow
Endless flowers are produced among men.

43. (First) I reveal dharma(s) as self-conditioned;[3]
And in due time I also show the Buddha-enlightenment.
This is My supreme skill in means
And also that of all the leaders of the world.

44. In this way I have taught true reality in its ultimate sense.
Those Disciples in fact never enter the final Rest.[4]
Having gone on a pilgrimage to the supreme enlightenment
All these Disciples shall become Buddhas!"

[1] *Gatiṃ-gatāḥ; rtogs-par khoṅ-du chud-pa.*

[2] Lit "generate."

[3] *Svapratyayaṃ dharma*; but the Tibetan has *raṅ-gis rig-pa'i chos-rnams*, i.e. I reveal "dharmas as self-known." I do not quite understand this passage. There may be some allusion to a *pratyaya-buddah* = Pratyekabuddha. cf. Edgerton 375–6.

[4] The idea here seems to be that no Arhat is in fact ever content with Arhatship, but that, once he has attained it, he is bound to move forward until he reaches Buddhahood. This teaching accords with verse 21c, but does not agree very well with the usual assumption that there are three distinct vehicles and goals—Arhatship, Pratyekabuddhahood and Buddahood.

Moreover, Kashyapa, in his disciplining of beings the Tathagata is impartial, and not at all partial. Just as the light of the sun and the moon shines upon all the world in its entirety—on those who act well and those who act badly, on those who stand high and those who stand low, on those who smell well and those who smell badly—everywhere the light shines down impartially, without any partiality; just so the light of the thought that contains the cognition of the all-knowing which is shed by the Tathagatas shines upon beings reborn in all the five places of rebirth, and the demonstration of the good Dharma proceeds impartially, whether beings are disposed to follow the great vehicle, or the vehicle of the Pratyekabuddhas, or the vehicle of the Disciples. There is no deficiency or excess in the light emitted by the Tathagata's cognition, and it always conduces to the full achievement of both merit and cognition. There are not three vehicles, Kashyapa, but only beings who follow different courses of action. In that sense does one conceive of the three vehicles.

Mahakaśyapa: If, O Lord, there are no three vehicles, for what reason has one at the present period formed the conception of Disciples, Pratyekabuddhas and Bodhisattvas?

The Lord: A potter makes many vessels out of the same clay. Some of them hold sugar, others ghee, others curd and milk, and others again impure waste matter. There is no difference in the clay, but only in the substances which are put into the resulting pots. Just so, Kashyapa, there is just this one single Buddha-vehicle, and a second or third vehicle does not exist.

Mahakaśyapa: But if, O Lord, those beings who have found their way out of the triple world have different dispositions, will their Nirvana be one, two or three?

The Lord: Nirvana results from understanding the sameness of all dharmas. Hence there is but one Nirvana, not two or three. I will now give you a simile, which should clarify the problem for you. A blind-born man may well say, "there are no handsome and ugly shapes, and there are no men who can see them; there are no such things as the sun and the moon, as the asterisms and planets, and there are no men who can see them." Other people, however, will say to this blind-born person that "there are handsome and ugly shapes, and there are men who can see them; there are such things as the sun and moon, as the asterisms and planets, and there are men who can see them." But that blind-born man would not believe, nor accept what they say.

Now a physician who knows all diseases would look at that blind-born man and think to himself: "This man's disease has arisen from a bad deed he did in his past. All diseases that there are can be traced to four possible causes—the wind, the bile, the phlegm, and a disorder of the humours." The physician further reflects again and again how he can find a means to cure this disease, and he thinks to himself: "The usual drugs cannot cure this disease. But in the Himalaya, the king of mountains, there are four herbs, i.e. the first called 'Possessed-of-all-sorts-of-colours-and-flavours,' the second 'freeing-from-all-illness,' the third 'destroying-all-poisons,' and the fourth 'bestowing-ease-on-those-who-stand-in-the-right-place'." And the physician, feeling compassion for that blind-born man, contrives by some device to travel to the Himalaya, the king of mountains. There he climbs up, down and across in his search for the four herbs, which he finds in the end. Some of these he gives to the patient after chewing them with his teeth, others after pounding, others after boiling them together with other substances, others after mixing them with unboiled drugs, others by piercing the body with a lancet, others by scorching them in fire, and others again by mixing them up with various substances in drink or food, etc. Through these devices the blind-born man regains his sight, and can see all forms, inside and outside, far and near, the light of the sun and moon, the asterisms and the planets. He will then say: "How foolish of me that I formerly did not believe what they told me, nor accept what they said! Now I can see everything, am delivered from my blindness, and have regained my sight. There is no one superior to me."

But at that very moment seers endowed with the five superknowledges—skilled in the heavenly eye, the heavenly ear, the cognition of others' thought, in the cognition of the recollection of past lives and in psychic power, as well as in the determination to win the deliverances—will say to that man: "All that you have done, my dear man, is that you have just recovered your sight! But still you do not know anything at all! So why be so conceited? You have no wisdom, and are not really a well-informed person." And they will further say to him: "When you sit inside your house, you neither see nor know the forms which are outside it, nor do you know which beings have friendly and which have hostile thoughts. At a distance of five miles you cannot discern what someone says, nor can you hear or appreciate the sound of a drum, conch shell and the like. You cannot walk even as far as a league without lifting up your feet. You have grown in the belly of your mother, and have been born from it, but you do not remember that fact. How then can you call yourself a well-informed person, and how can you say that you see everything? What you do is to mistake darkness for light, and light for darkness."

Thereupon that man would ask those seers: "Through what device, or by doing what good deeds, could I acquire this wisdom, or how could I with your favour acquire those good qualities?"

And the seers answer: "If you wish to gain them, just live in the remote forest or in mountain caves, sit down, meditate on the Dharma and forsake your defilements! When you are endowed with the virtues which result from the ascetic practices you will acquire the superknowledges."

Having caught their meaning, that man takes up the homeless life. Dwelling in the remote forest he becomes singleminded, forsakes his craving for the world, and wins the five superknowledges. Thereupon he reflects: "When I acted differently in the past, no good accrued to me. Now I can go whither my mind prompts me, but formerly I had little wisdom and experience, and was quite blind."

This, Kashyapa, is the simile by which I intend to communicate my message. And this is the meaning of the parable: "The man who is born-blind refers to the beings who are in the six places of rebirth which constitute birth-and-death. They do not know the good Dharma and are apt to augment the dark gloom of their defilements. Blinded by ignorance they heap up the karma-formations, conditioned by the karma-formations there arises name-and-form, and so on, and so there originates all this huge mass of ill.

Blinded by ignorance beings thus stay within birth-and-death. But the Tathagata who has escaped from the triple world has generated compassion within himself. His compassion is like that of a father for his dear and only son, he appears in the triple world and sees beings there being whirled around on the wheel of birth-and-death, and that without knowing that there is an escape from it. And the Lord when he has seen these beings with the eye of wisdom, cognizes as follows: "These beings, having done wholesome deeds in the past, have not much hate but intense greed, or alternatively not much greed but intense hate; some have little wisdom and others are well-informed; some are mature in their purity and others have wrong views." In his skill in means the Tathagata then shows three vehicles to these beings.

Furthermore, the seers with the five superknowledges and the pure spiritual vision are the Bodhisattvas who will in due course fully know the utmost, right and perfect enlightenment, after they have produced the thought of enlightenment and have acquired the patient acquiescence in dharmas which fail to be produced.

The great physician is equivalent to the Tathagata. To the man born blind may be likened the beings blinded by their delusion. Wind, bile and phlegm correspond to greed, hate and delusion, and the sixty-two false views (correspond to the diseases caused by a disorder of the humours). The four herbs correspond to the doors of Emptiness, the Signless and Wishless, and to Nirvana. To the extent that the medicinal substances are applied, the diseases are cured. Just so, when they have entered the doors to deliverance, i.e. Emptiness, the Signless and the Wishless, beings stop ignorance. The stopping of ignorance leads to the stopping of the karma-formations, and of this entire huge mass of ill. The thought (of the one who has been thus set free) abides no longer in what is wholesome or evil.

The blind man who regains his sight corresponds to those who belong to the vehicle of the Disciples or Pratyekabuddhas. They cut through the bonds which tie them to birth-and-death, they are freed from the bonds of the defilements, they are released from the triple world and from the places of rebirth. As a result someone who belongs to the vehicle of the Disciples may think and speak as follows: "There are no more dharmas which I must fully know. Because I have reached Nirvana."

The Tathagata, however, will demonstrate to him Dharma as

follows: "Since you have not attained all dharmas, how can you have won Nirvana?"

The Lord then encourages him to win enlightenment. The thought of enlightenment arises in him, and in consequence he no longer abides in birth-and-death nor does he attain Nirvana. Having understood, he sees this triple world in the ten directions as empty, as an illusory magical creation, as a mock show, as a dream, a mirage or an echo. He sees that all dharmas are not produced or stopped, not bound or freed, not dark or bright. And while he sees the deep dharmas in this manner, he sees, as if he were not seeing, the whole triple world filled with beings of various dispositions and intentions.

Thereupon the Lord, so as to more fully explain this topic, uttered on that occasion the following verses:

45. "The light of sun and moon falls alike on all men,
Be they virtuous or evil, and there is never too little for some, or too much for others.[1]

46. In exactly the same way the light of the Tathagata's wisdom
Disciplines all beings, and nowhere is it either deficient or excessive.

47. A potter makes many clay vessels out of the same clay;
Some may hold sugar, others ghee, others milk, others water,

48. Others impure waste matter, and others again curdled milk.
But the clay which the potter uses for these vessels is all of one kind,

49. And the vessels are distinguished only by what is put into them.
Just so beings are basically non-different, but vary in their inclinations,

50. And that is why the Tathagatas speak of a diversity of vehicles, although the Buddha-vehicle be the only true one.
Those who remain unaware of the wheel of birth-and-death cannot become aware of the Blessed Rest.

[1] This is how both Kern and I understand *prabhāyā nona-pūrṇatā*. The statement is, however, open to doubt, and the Tibetan translates rather freely and ambiguously by *de-la skye shiṅ 'bri-ba med*, perhaps "and it does not increase or decrease".

51. But those who are aware that all dharmas are empty and devoid of a self,
    They cognize the enlightenment of the fully enlightened Lords as it is in real truth.
52. Those of medium wisdom are called Pratyekabuddhas.
    And those who lack the cognition of the Void are termed Disciples.
53. But a fully enlightened Buddha is one who has understood all dharmas
    Constantly, through hundreds of devices, he demonstrates Dharma to living beings.[1]
54. A man, born blind, who cannot see the sun, moon, planets or stars,
    May say that there are no visible shapes at all anywhere.
55. A great physician may then feel compassion for him,
    Go to the Himalaya, travelling up, down and across its mountains,
56. And fetch from them four herbs, "Possessed-of-all-sorts of-colours-and-flavours"
    And the other three, which he thereupon proceeds to apply.
57. Some he gives to the blind-born man after chewing them with his teeth,
    Others after pounding them, others by putting them into his body with the point of a needle.
58. On having regained his sight he can now see the sun, moon, planets and stars,
    And he realizes that it was from sheer ignorance that he spoke as he did before.
59. Just so beings, greatly ignorant, wander about here and there, like people born blind;
    It is because they ignore the wheel of conditioned production that they tread the track of ill.
60. But then in this world which is deluded by ignorance, the supreme all-knowing one appears.
    The Tathagata, the great physician, full of compassion.
61. A Teacher, skilled in means, he demonstrates the good Dharma:
    To those most advanced he shows the supreme enlightenment of a Buddha;

[1] Tib. omits this line.

62. To those of medium wisdom the Leader reveals a medium enlightenment;
Another enlightenment again he recommends to those who are just afraid of birth-and-death.[1]
63. Disciples, who have escaped from the triple world, and who are given to discrimination.
May believe that they have attained Nirvana, the immaculate and serene.
64. But now I reveal to them that this is not what is meant by Nirvana.[2]
For it is through the full understanding of all dharmas that the deathless Nirvana must be attained.
65. The great Seers, out of their compassionate hearts, will in fact say to them:
"Deluded you are, and mistaken to think that you have won gnosis!
66. "When you are inside your room, enclosed by walls,
You do not know what takes place outside—so tiny is your mental power!
67. "When you are inside your room, you do not know
What people outside are doing or not doing—so tiny is your mental power!
68. "You cannot hear a sound five miles away,
How much less one that is still further afar!
69. "Whether others are well or badly disposed towards you,
That you cannot know; how can you be so conceited?
70. "When you have to walk for only a mile, you cannot do so without a beaten track;
And what happened to you in your mother's womb, all that you have quite forgotten.
71. "Without the five kinds of superknowledge,[3] no one can be called omniscient.
It would be mere delusion to call yourself omniscient when you know none of all this.[4]

[1] These are the "Disciples" of the next verse.
[2] Tib. omits this line.
[3] They correspond to vv. 66–70, and overcome the limitations described there. For a description see E. Conze, *Buddhist Scriptures*, 1959, 121–133.
[4] Tib.: You are deluded and ignorant if you call yourself omniscient.

72. "If you wish to win omniscience, you must aspire to the superknowledges.
And then, in the remote forest, you must reflect on the pure Dharma,
And through that you will gain the superknowledges."[1]

73. When he has grasped the meaning (of this advice), he will go to the remote forest, reflect there in deep concentration,
And will then attain the five superknowledges, before long endowed with their virtues.

74. Thus to all those Disciples who have formed the notion that they have attained Nirvana
The Jina teaches that theirs is a temporary repose, and not the final Nirvana.

75. He adds that this method[2] has been introduced as a device of the Buddhas;
But that in actual fact outside all-knowledge there is no (final) Nirvana, and that one should exert oneself on behalf of that.

76. The infinite cognition of the three periods of time, as well as the six salutary perfections,
Emptiness, the Signless, the shedding of plans for the future,[3]

77. The thought of enlightenment, and all the other dharmas which lead to Nirvana.
(Be they with outflows, or without outflows and tranquil, though all like empty space),[4]

[1] I do not quite understand verse 72.

[2] *Naya, tshul. Naya,* from the root *nī*, means "that which leads to something". Here it refers to the procedures by which the "Disciples" win their inferior form of enlightenment, and also to the theoretical presuppositions underlying them.

[3] This corresponds to what is often translated as "the Wishless". I have described these three "doors to deliverance" in some detail in my *Buddhist Thought in India*, 1962, pp. 59–69, and have treated them there as an essential constituent of the "archaic Buddhism" which preceded the division into "Hinayana" and "Mahayana". Apparently Professor Lamotte has independently come to the same conclusion when he says that "les trois *samādhi* offrent aux deux Véhicules le meilleur terrain de rapprochement" (*L'enseignement de Vimalakīrti*, 1962, p. 148).

[4] Tib. omits this line.

78. The four stations of Brahma[1] and the (four) means of conversion[2]—
All that the great Seers have proclaimed so that beings be trained.
79. And someone who discerns dharmas as in their own-being like a dream or illusion,
Without core like a plaintain tree, or similar to an echo,
80. And who knows that the entire triple world, without exception, has such an own-being,
And that it is neither bound nor freed, he does not discern Nirvana (as separate from the triple world).
81. Since all dharmas are the same, empty, essentially without multiplicity,
He does not look towards them, and he does not perceive any separate dharma,
82. But, greatly wise, he sees nothing but the Dharma-body.
There is no triad of vehicles, but only one.
83. All dharmas are the same, all the same, always quite the same.
When that has been cognized, Nirvana, the deathless and serene, has been understood."

[1] I.e. unlimited friendliness, compassion, sympathetic joy and evenmindedness.

[2] These are well explained in Har Dayal, *The Bodhisattva Doctrine*, 1932, pp. 251–9.

The Development of Prajñāpāramitā Thought

Many people in the West, and among them the author of this article, first heard of the *Prajñāpāramitā* through the writings of D. T. Suzuki, especially his *Manual of Zen Buddhism*, (1935) and his *Essays in Zen Buddhism*, vol. III, 1934, pp. 187–288. In my own case the good news wrought quite a revolution in my thinking, and has induced me to devote the last twenty-five years to the study of these Scriptures. It is therefore only natural that I should be delighted to be asked to contribute to the volume issued in commemoration of my honoured teacher's ninetieth birthday.

This essay adopts the historical approach which comes natural to scholars reared in the West. One must admit, of course, that it tends to subject spiritual truth to historical relativity, and its application to Christian documents has done little to strengthen the faith of earnest believers. At the same time, while we may well agree that the Spirit itself has no history, there may be no great harm in tracing the historical development of the actual documents with which we are confronted.

The conclusions here briefly presented can be no more than provisional suggestions. Knowing almost no Chinese, I could make no use of the early Chinese documents (*T* 221–227), but had to confine myself to the Sanskrit and Tibetan sources. Others will, I hope, be stimulated to do better than I have done. Another difficulty which has for long deterred me from writing on this subject lay in the uncertainties about the dating of the various documents. But since I have found that Prof. R. Hikata[1] and myself have independently come to practically the same conclusions, this is no longer a serious obstacle. What perturbs me more is that at present we have no clear idea of the circumstances under which these Sūtras were composed. Who

[1] An Introductory Essay on Prajñāpāramitā Literature, in his edition of the *Suvikrāntavikrāmiparipṛcchā*, 1958.

wrote them, or why, how, or for whom they were written—all that is lost in the fog of the past.

One must, I think, distinguish nine steps in the development of *Prajñāpāramitā* thought, and for the convenience of the reader I list them here at the very outset:

I. The initial formulation represented by the first two chapters of *Rgs.*[1] II. Chapters 3–28 of *Rgs.* III. Incorporation of matter from the Abhidharma. IV. Concessions to the Buddhism of Faith. V. The last third of the Large *Prajñāpāramitā*. VI. The short Sūtras. VII. Yogācārin commentaries. VIII, IX. The Tantra and Ch'an.

I. The first formulation of *Prajñāpāramitā* doctrine is contained in the first two chapters of the *Ratnaguṇasaṃcayagāthā*, which may well go back to 100 B.C. These Chapters (A) define four new key terms, (B) develop certain ideas of the Hīnayāna tradition, and (C) indicate the source of the new teaching.

I. A. The new key-terms are, first ***bodhisattva*** (I v. 16) and ***mahāsattva*** (I vv. 17–20), by which the incipient Mahāyāna proclaimed its allegiance to a new type of saint, different from the "Arhats" of the preceding period, and then ***bodhiyāna*** (I vv. 21–23), by which a new goal was proclaimed, nothing less than the full enlightenment of a Buddha; ***sarvajñatām ca parigṛhṇāti śikṣamāṇo***, as it is said in II 8.

The fourth is the ***prajñavarapāramitāya caryā***, which is mentioned eleven times in the forty-one verses of these two chapters. Though remarkably inconspicuous in the ancient formula of the Eightfold Path, ***prajñā*** had in orthodox post-Aśokan Buddhism become the foremost virtue. This text now promises us the culmination of that ***prajñā***. Here already, at this early

[1] A note on my quotations from the texts:
A = *Aṣṭasāhasrikā*, ed. R. Mitra, 1888, but as printed in Wogihara (1932–5).
AA = *Abhisamayālaṅkāra*, ed. Th. Stcherbatsky and E. Obermiller, 1929, and trsl. E. Conze, 1954.
Ad = *Aṣṭādaśasāhasrikā*, quoted by the folios of the Gilgit MS. now in New Delhi and Rome.
P = *Pañcaviṃśatisāhasrikā*, ed. N. Dutt, 1934, and Cambridge MS. Add. 1628.
Rgs = *Ratnaguṇasaṃcayagāthā*, ed. E. Obermiller, 1937; reprinted 1960.
Ś = *Śatasāhasrikā*, ed. P. Ghosha, 1902–13 and the Cambridge MSS.

stage, the *Prajñāpāramitā* is designated in I v. 15 as *Jināna mātā*, "the mother of the Jinas". If the Buddha died about 480 B.C., it would have taken about four hundred years until he was provided with a spiritual "mother" in the shape of the *Prajñāpāramitā*. That is approximately the same time which elapsed before the Council of Ephesus in 431 proclaimed the Virgin Mary, the *sedes sapientiae*, as the "Mother of God". The Christian dogma was formulated in the city in which the traditions about the Great Mother, which had simmered for millenia in Asia Minor, had an important organizational centre. Prof. E. O. James has recently reminded us that "under the shadow of the great temple dedicated to the Magna Mater since 330 B.C., the title 'God-bearer' hardly could fail to be upheld."[1] If, as I believe, the *Prajñāpāramitā* originated in the South of India[2], it would represent an irruption into Buddhism of the devotion to the Mother-Goddess current in the more matriarchal Dravidian society in which it originated. This oldest religion of mankind was evolved in the caves of the Palaeolithic and by allying itself with it Buddhism became a truly Catholic religion, capable of spreading throughout Asia, far beyond the confines of India.

I. B. What then are the actual teachings of this *Prajñāpāramitā* when it first appeared on the scene? If we except verses 16–23, the remainder of the two chapters, with the doubtful exception of *tathatā* (II v. 2), contain no new terms. Relying more on selection than on open innovation they give essentially a simple re-statement of what for the sake of convenience we may call "archaic Buddhism". Three topics dominate the argument:

1. The all-important problem of the *self*. Quite at the beginning we have a reference to the "Wanderer Śreṇika."[3] Śreṇika

[1] *The Cult of the Mother Goddess*, 1959, p. 207.

[2] E. Lamotte (Sur la formation du Mahāyāna, in *Asiatica*, 1954) has argued for a North-Western origin, but I regard his case as unproved, and must refer to my *The Prajñāpāramitā Literature* (1960) for my counter-arguments.

[3] v. 7. *atha Śreṇikasya abhutī parivrājakasya jñānopalambhu na hi skandhavibhāvanā ca.*

This is slightly more intelligible in the Tibetan: *ji-ltar kun-tu rgyu-ba phreṅ-caṅ śes-pa-yis dmigs med phuṅ-po rnam-par 'jig-pa 'byuṅ-ba ltar.*

Vatsagotra was a non-Buddhist ascetic whose conversations with the Buddha form a section of the *Samyuktāgama* of the Sarvāstivādins. On one occasion[1] he raised the question of the "true self", which he identified with the Tathāgata. The Buddha told him that the Tathāgata cannot be found in the skandhas, nor outside them, nor in their absence. In a supreme act of faith Śreṇika was willing to accept the Tathāgata in spite of his inability to relate Him to anything that is known empirically. Śreṇika's *jñāna* was, however, as the prose text of *A* I 9 puts it, only a *prādeśika-jñāna*, a knowledge with a limited scope, i.e. as Haribhadra explains, it stopped short at the understanding of *pudgalanairātmya*, whereas the Bodhisattva can extend his insight to all dharmas. And so the *Ratnaguṇa* draws the Mahāyānistic conclusion: "Just so the Bodhisattva, when he comprehends the dharmas as he should, Does not retire into Blessed Rest. In Wisdom then he dwells."[2]

"Blessed Rest," *nirvṛti* is the Nirvāṇa which excludes the world of suffering. The Bodhisattva should not get absorbed in it, because then he would separate himself, or his self, from the skandhas which are the basis of suffering, and act against his insight which showed him, in the words of *A* I 9, that Buddhahood, or the cognition of the all-knowing, is not inside the skandhas, nor outside them, nor both inside and outside, nor other than the skandhas.

And quite at the end, at II 12, the ultimate unreality of the self is asserted in the memorable words:

"If for aeons countless as the sands of the Ganges
The Leader himself would continue to pronounce the word 'being',
Still, pure from the very start, no being could ever result from his speaking."

2. Furthermore the text describes three aspects of the attitude which the wise man should adopt towards all the phenomena he may encounter:

a) He should be *aniketacārī*, I vv. 6, 10, II 3. This term which for a long time had designated the monk's non-attachment to

[1] *Samyuktāgama* no. 105, *T* pp. 31c–32.

[2] *yo bodhisattvo parijānati eva dharmān na ca nirvṛtiṃ spṛśati so viharāti prajñāṃ.*

possessions and social ties, now acquires an ontological meaning. Nowhere in the five skandhas do the wise find a place to rest on (*sthānu*), and with regard to all dharmas they are *asthita, asthitaka* (II 1 sq.) and *aparigṛhīta*. To "course without a home" means "not to course in" any of the skandhas, "his thoughts directed to non-production" (*anupādadhī*).[1] To rid himself of all attachments, that is indeed the essence of a Bodhisattva's life, and to be rid of them that of a Buddha's enlightenment.[2]

b) He should practise *non-apprehension* (*anupalabdhi*). As it is said at I 5:

"No wisdom can we get hold of, no highest perfection.
No Bodhisattva, no thought of enlightenment either.
When told of this, if not bewildered and in no way anxious
A Bodhisattva courses in the Well-Gone's wisdom."

Fictitious things, like the "self" or a "person," had often been characterized by the phrase that they "cannot be apprehended", "cannot be got at", *nopalabhyante*,[3] but here this characterization is extended to the very machinery of salvation.

c) All phenomena should be treated as *illusory*, as *māyā*. That the skandhas (I v. 14) and beings (I v. 19) are illusory had often been said in the past. The novelty lay in now (II v. 5) extending this concept to the transcendental world, and saying that the fruits of the holy life, whether won by Arhats, Pratyekabuddhas or fully enlightened Buddhas, and that Nirvāṇa itself "are mere illusions, mere dreams". In *Rgs* this is regarded as so startling that it is backed up by the assertion, "so has the Tathāgata taught us"[4] and the prose text of *A* II 40, when it describes the astonishment of the *devaputrā* at this message, does not conceal that we have here to deal with a rather shocking departure from accepted ideas.

[1] This "non-production" is in itself, of course, not a new idea, since the *anutpādajñāna* is well known to form a regular part of the stock of Hīnayāna teaching.

[2] *sarvatra sangakṣaya icchati saṅgacchedī bodhiṃ spṛśiṣyati Jināna asaṅgabbūtāṃ tasmād dhi nāma labhate ayu bodhisattvo.* I 16; cf. I 20.

[3] So also at *Rgs* I 22–3.

[4] *nirvāṇu yo adhigato vidupaṇḍitehi sarve ta māyaja nirdiṣṭu Tathāgatena.*

3. Thirdly, we find an interpretation, or rather re-interpretation of the higher stages of the Path.

a) A monistic conclusion is drawn from the formula of the first formless *dhyāna*.

"When freed from the notion of multiple things, he courses in peace,
Then that is his practice of wisdom, the highest perfection."[1]

Here *nānātvasaṃjñāvigato* clearly alludes to *iha sarvaśo rūpasaṃjñānāṃ samatikrāmāt, pratighasaṃjñānām astaṅgamāt, nānātvasaṃjñānām amanasikārād, anantam ākāśam ity ākāśānantyāyatanam upasampadya viharati.* The implicit inference seems to be that on the higher stages of wisdom a Bodhisattva should never fall below the level of the insight attained in the first formless *dhyāna*. It also underlies the comparisons at II 9–10 of wisdom, of objective supports (*ārambaṇa*) and of beings with space, which is "without a break or crack,"[2] and which in its essential original nature (*prakṛti*) is *anantapārā* (*pha mtha' med*), or "boundless". It is important that these doctrines derive not from metaphysical speculations, but from Yogic insights. Of the four formless *dhyānas* the *Prajñāpāramitā* makes most use of the first and third, whereas the second and fourth, which concern not the object but the subject, seem to have made almost no impression, and to have inspired Yogācāra thought.

b) The Hīnayāna provided a ready-made starting point for the Mahāyāna doctrine of emptiness with its teaching about the three *samādhis*, or doors to deliverance. Emptiness, the Signless and the Wishless there marked mystic states which take place at a certain stage of the Path. In our two chapters the third of these is not mentioned, and in fact all *Prajñāpāramitā* texts show little, if any, interest in *apraṇihita*. But *śūnya* and *ānimitta* occur jointly as *samādhis* in I 9–10, and all the *Rgs* does it to imply that the insight gained in them should be a permanent feature of a Bodhisattva's ontological beliefs. We must leave it at that here, because the relationship between the three kinds of *śūnyatā*—revealed respectively by *samādhi*, by *prajñā* and by *prajñāpāramitā*—is as yet little explored and

[1] *nānātvasaṃjñāvigato upaśāntacārī eṣā sa prajñavarapāramitāya caryā*. I. v. 14.

[2] *ākāśadhātusama tasya na cāsti bhedaḥ*. II 9.

any discussion of these rarified issues will take up too much space.

c) At the end of the journey we come to Nirvāṇa, the meaning of which is explained in I v. 22:

"Thus transcending the world, he eludes our apprehensions.
'He goes to Nirvāṇa' but no one can say where he went to.
A fire's extinguished, but where, do we ask, has it gone to?
Likewise, how can we find him who has found the Rest of the Blessed?"[1]

Every student of Buddhism will at once see that there is nothing original about this, and that we have to do with just a variation of one of the best-known passages of the *Suttanipāta* (vv. 1074, 1076).

To sum up: The purpose of what I call "the oldest *Prajñāpāramitā*" is to guard spirituality against all the current misunderstandings which try to fix it, to pin it down, in accordance with the remark of my old friend Charles du Bos who once said that "le spirituel est un élément, au sens premier du terme, mais un élément insaisissable en lui-même, qui n'est jamais identifié, appréhendé que dans ses manifestations". This agrees well with those Indian Buddhists who compared the Emptiness-doctrine to salt, in that it is useful to flavour the dish, but eaten separately in large lumps it is really not much use. Those who wish to adhere to the definition of the spiritual as the completely undefinable will, of course, have to contend all the time against the onrush of anxiety in their minds,[2] and it is therefore not surprising that the *Prajñāpāramitā* should so often insist that the absence of anxiety is the sign which indicates that one can actually bear this doctrine.[3]

I. C. Finally a few words about the source of this teaching. It is widely believed at present that almost anybody can arrive at the truth by the mere light of nature, if only he "thinks for

[1] *na ca labhyate ya vrajate diśa āruhitvā, nirvāṇa ukta gamanaṃ gati nopalabdih, yatha agninirvṛtu na tasya gatipracāro, so tena nirvṛti pravucyati kāraṇena.*

The second line runs in Tibetan: mya ṅan 'das-par 'gro-bar gsuṅs-pa 'gro mi dmigs

[2] I have tried to show the connection in some detail in my book on *Buddhism*, 1951, pp. 22–3, 137.

[3] E.g. *Rgs* I 5: *evaṃ śruṇitva na ca muhyati nāsti trāso, so bodhisattvo carate Sugātana prajñām.* Also I 8, 15, 20, 28, II 4, 6.

himself". That was not the opinion of the Buddhists of this period, who were convinced that only the words of an omniscient, superhuman being could introduce some truth into this world of ignorance and delusion. If there are four possible sources of knowledge—perception, reason, spiritual intuition and revelation—then the Sūtra assumes that all worth-while knowledge is due to revelation, *sarvo ayaṃ puruṣakāru Tathāgatasya* (I v. 3), with the spiritual intuition of the saints as a subsidiary and subordinate source (I v. 4).

There was, of course, the difficulty that the historical Buddha had not actually preached these texts. In our two chapters this is ignored, but later on it became necessary to think out a new Buddhology and introduce some kind of "direct transmission from mind to mind". It would lead too far to show how this design was effected by the doctrine of the *dharmakāya* which figures in *A* IV 94, 99, XVII 338 and XXXI 513, but it may be worth pointing out that none of these passages is paralleled in the earlier verse version of *Rgs.*

II. The second stage of *Prajñāpāramitā* thought is represented by chapters 3–28 of *Rgs.*, and those parts of *A* which correspond to them. They are either (A) further developments of the thoughts outlined above, or (B) a series of monographs.

II. A. The further developments are represented by chaps. 7–10, chap. 12 pp. 253–6, chap. 13–15, 18–19, 22–28. They add, little to the ideas of chaps. 1–2, and it would be tedious to go over them in detail.

II. B. The Monographs concern the following topics:

1. A description of Suchness (chap. 16) and 2. of the Tathagata's omniscience (chap. 12, pp. 256–276). 3. The question of merit. chaps. 3–5. 4. Dedication and jubilation (chap. 6). 5. Mara's deeds (chaps. 11, 21). 6. The attributes of an irreversible Bodhisattva (chaps. 17; 20, pp. 380 sq). 7. Skill in means, chap. 20, pp. 370–9.

Only the first two deal with the theoretical side of the doctrine. 1. Chapter 16 is an eloquent exposition of the meaning of "Suchness", which is one of the accepted synonyms of Emptiness. 2. The description of the Tathagata's omniscience is a real *tour de force*, and constitutes one of the most difficult parts of the Sūtra. It is not easy to get to the bottom of it. Its absence in *Rgs.* suggests that it may have been added later, unless, of course, it resisted summing up in verse.

While these two additions try to make the unintelligible slightly more intelligible, the remaining ones aim at making the impracticable more practicable. For we should never forget that the *Prajñāpāramitā* proclaims an extremely otherworldly and world-denying doctrine. Whoever denies the world too much is in danger of being denied by it, and his survival is in doubt. The Christians had at about the same time to grapple with exactly the same problem. They had ushered into the world an almost excessively spiritual and intangible system of beliefs, as a perusal of Paul's epistle to the Galatians will show to any one. How could something as ethereal as that maintain itself in a hostile world? The Christians tried to solve the problem by the formation of a Church, which could act as a social force of its own, which was destined to take over many of the administrative functions of the Roman Empire, and which greatly increased its internal coherence by the elaboration of a rigid dogma couched in the terms of Greek philosophy. For obvious reasons the adherents of the *Prajñāpāramitā* could not countenance such methods of keeping their feet on the earth. They took no cognizance of social forces, made no attempt to manipulate them, but placed their entire trust in the immutable karmic laws which would give those endowed with the requisite merit access to this sublime teaching.

3. "Merit" (*puṇya*) is the motive force which propels us towards enlightenment, and in order to strive fruitfully we are bound to wish to amass it. The *Rgs.*, as well as *A* and all subsequent *Prajñāpāramitā* writings devote a great deal of space to the merit to be derived from Perfect Wisdom, and in manifold variations it is placed above the merit gained by all other pious acts. To some extent these lengthy and fulsome assertions about the meritoriousness of learning, studying, writing, etc. the *Prajñāpāramitā* are fairly effective propagandistic devices to assure its perpetuation. They reach their height in the "transmission" of this Sūtra to Ānanda (*A* xxviii, 460–464a), which does not yet form part of *Rgs.*, and which declares that, if Ānanda were to forget any other part of the Buddha's sayings, "that would be a slight offence against Me. But if you should forget one verse of the *Prajñāpāramitā*, or merely a part of one, that would be a very serious offence against Me, and would

greatly displease Me" (*A* 460–1).

It is, however, at once obvious that in so extravagantly praising the merit to be derived from Perfect Wisdom, the authors were, by appealing to the acquisitive instincts of mankind, in danger of sinning against the very spirit of the *Prajñāpāramitā*. To hoard "merit" is surely better than to hoard money, titles and honours, but it is still hoarding. "And as contrary to the ways of the entire world has this Dharma been demonstrated. It teaches you not to seize on dharmas, but the world is wont to grasp at anything" (*A* xv 305). Or, as the *Rgs.* puts it (XV 8):

"For beings delight in a place to settle in (*ālayarato*) and are eager for sense-objects (*viṣayābhilāṣī*),
Bent on grasping (*grahe*), unintelligent and quite blinded.
The Dharma should be attained as nothing to settle in (*anālayu*) and as nothing to grasp (*anāgrahu*).
Its conflict with the world is manifest."

The *Prajñāpāramitā* offers two measures designed to eliminate the danger of treating spiritual gains as if they were worldly possessions: Firstly, a consideration of the ontological character of the merit shows that it cannot possibly grow or increase,[1] and that, since it is like everything else empty, only a fool would want to grasp at it or to appropriate it. Secondly 4. a positive counter-measure is recommended, the Dedication of all personal merit to the great task of leading all beings to the supreme enlightenment.[2]

5. The world is quite obviously not made for self-effacement and self-extinction, and offers the greatest obstacles to those who pursue objects such as these. Ordinary people recognize the saint by his halo, spiritual people by the hell of a time he has on earth and the amount of indifference, rejection and hostility he has had to endure. "Whatever is very precious, that provokes much hostility. Because it is so superior, being hard to get and of great value. One should therefore expect that as a rule many obstacles will arise to this Perfection of Wisdom" (*A* xi 250). The *Prajñāpāramitā* goes to some lengths to explain the difficulties of the elect as the result of Māra's deeds and to bolster up their morale by pointing out that Māra has power over them

[1] E.g. *A* xviii 348–351 = *Rgs* xviii 7–8; xxii 405–9, not in *Rgs*.
[2] Also at *A* iii 80–81, vii 172, viii 190–1, xv 292–3, xvi 312, xix 328, etc.

only thanks to their own imperfections, and consoles them by the assertion (*Rgs*. xi 10) that while

"Māra will be zealous to cause obstacles,
The Buddhas in the ten directions will be intent on helping."

6. One foe, however, is infinitely worse than even Māra the Evil One, and that is Impermanence which, once realized, may sap the will of even the strongest. The Buddhists of this period longed as much as everyone else for a permanent achievement which can no more be lost. This longing crystallized itself in the concept of an "irreversible Bodhisattva", which aroused a quite extraordinary interest in the first centuries of the Christian era. The authors of the *Prajñāpāramitā* also contributed to this much debated problem and enumerated a number of attributes[1] of irreversible Bodhisattvas. In addition they made a few attempts to define the practices which would insure a Bodhisattva against the future loss of what he has attained, and also stressed the fact that the Perfection of Wisdom and the *dharmadhātu* are inexhaustible and indestructible.[2]

7. This leaves the seventh, and by far the most difficult problem—"skill in means." How can a Bodhisattva tone down, without at the same time losing, his gnostic insight and his transic exaltation[3] to such an extent that he maintains contact with the world as it falsely appears to be and with the essentially illusory beings whom he is pledged to save? It is well known from the *Daśabhūmika* that skill in means is a virtue even more exalted than perfect wisdom, and its explanation will therefore be correspondingly even more difficult. Apart from some occasional remarks[4] the *Aṣṭa* devotes its twentieth chapter to this subject. The three similes of pp. 371–375 (=*Rgs* xx 2–10) are quite easy to follow, but the remainder of the chapter is rather obscure, and *Rgs* sums it up in two brief verses (xx 1, 21) and shows its conviction that the problem should be clarified by metaphor rather than abstract reasoning when it adds

[1] *Rgs* xvii 7: *avivartiyāna imi liṅga prajānitavya. A* speaks of the *ākārā liṅgāni nimittāni* of the *avinivartanīya-bodhisattva.*

[2] E.g. *Rgs* xxviii.

[3] The transic aspect is stressed in *Rgs* xx 1: *asamāhito karuṇa prekṣati sattvadhātum atrāntare na parihāyati buddhadharme.*

[4] iii 58, 75, xi 243, xiv 287, xvi 310, xix 356, xxv 427.

another five similes (xx 11–20) not found in *A*. This was only a first attempt at coming to grips with "skill in means", and we must agree with Hikata[1] that most of the later elaborations of the *Prajñāpāramitā* which we have assigned to the Fifth phase deal essentially with the various aspects of *upāyakauśalya*.

These are the chief additions made in the second phase of *Prajñāpāramitā* thought, arranged in what I conceive to be their logical order.

III. Our third stage is represented by those parts of the Large *Prajñāpāramitā*—whether in 18,000, in 25,000 or in 100,000 *ślokas*,—which correspond to the first twenty-eight chapters of *A*. The text was now tremendously enlarged by the incorporation of matter from the *Abhidharma*. This took two forms, A. Abhidharma lists were incessantly repeated, and did much to swell the bulk of the Sūtra; and B. some of the items in these lists were defined.

III. A. The *lists* serve as a basis for meditational drill. The book which is devoted to the splendour of the "Mother of the Buddhas" now incorporates into itself the contents of an older form of literature, the *mātṛkā*, which were likewise preoccupied with both "wisdom" and the concept of motherhood. For *mātṛkā* means, among other things, "mother", and Przyluski translates the Chinese equivalent in the *A-yu-wang-king* as "sagesse-mère." It was probably towards the end of Aśoka's reign[2] that the adherents of a comparatively late concern with *prajñā* composed a literature of numerical summaries, or *mātṛkās*. Later on the rationalists in the Buddhist community developed them into works on Abhidharma, whereas the mystics absorbed them into the *Prajñāpāramitā*. Both the *Vinaya* of the Mūlasarvāstivādins and the *Aśokāvadāna* give the following definition of the *mātṛkāpiṭaka*:[3] It clarifies the distinguishing points of that which ought to be known (*jñeya*). It comprises the four applications of mindfulness, the four right efforts, the four roads to psychic power, the five dominants, the five powers, the seven limbs of enlightenment, the eight limbs of the path, the four analytical knowledges, the

[1] l. c. xxxi.
[2] A. Migot, *Un grand disciple du Buddha, Śāriputra*, BEFEO XLVI, 1954, pp. 538–41.
[3] Ibid. p. 524.

araṇasamādhi and the *praṇidhānasamādhi*.[1] This is precisely the list which, with many additions towards the end, takes up so much space in the Large *Prajñāpāramitā* Sūtras.

III. B. We now turn to the *definitions*. They cover: 1. The 16–20 kinds of emptiness (*P* 195–8). 2. The 112 kinds of meditative practices[2] (*P* 198–203). 3. The twenty-one practices of the path (*P* 203–212). 4. The forty-three *dhāraṇīs*[3] (*P* 212–214). 5. The Ten Stages (*P* 214–225). They are probably later than chaps. 3–28 of the *Aṣṭa* and were arbitrarily inserted into the text at the point where *A* I 22 asks, "what is that great vehicle?"[4]

Of these, nos. 1 and 5 have been truly assimilated to the *Prajñāpāramitā* teaching. As concerns no. 1, no theoretical development of the concept of emptiness is intended. When it is said to be the result of dharmas "being neither permanent nor destroyed",[5] this is only a repetition of the old saying common to all schools, which represents Buddhism as the "middle way" between the two extremes of Eternalism and Annihilationism. What the passage[6] actually does is to make emptiness ready for meditation by dividing it into a number of varieties—in *Ś* originally 16 and later on 20, 17 in *Ad* f. 263b, 18 in *P*, and occasionally we hear of aberrant lists of 7[7] and 14.[8] Similar

[1] J. Przyluski, *Le concile the Rājagṛha*, 1926, p. 45. This gives 43 items (see note 3). In *Lalitavistara* 127 the alphabet is called *mātṛkā*.

[2] The number varies in the different sources. In Dutt's edition of the revised P there are 112; the New Delhi MS. of the original *P* gives 117, whereas the Tibetan translation of *Ś* has 162.

[3] It is not easy to decide whether the correct number is 43 or 42. The *Gaṇḍavyūha* and Kumārajīva have 42, and S. Lévi (*Mémorial S. Lévi*, 1932, pp. 355–63) and F. W. Thomas (Miscellanea Academica Berolinensia, 1950, p. 204) assume this is to be the original number. This is to some extent confirmed by *P* 536b, duplicated by *Ad* f. 282r, which speaks of 42 *akṣaras*, though not explicitly in connection with the Arapacana. On the other hand, the number is clearly 43 in Yüan-tsang, in Ghoshe's edition of *Ś* and, most important of all, in the New Delhi MS. of *P*. Sanskrit has 48 letters, Pali normally 41, though *Mogallānavyākaraṇa* (Colombo 1890) gives 43.

[4] The *Daśasāhasrikā* has collected many of these definitions into the first and second chapters.

[5] *Akūṭasṭhāvināśitāmupādāya*.

[6] Suzuki saw its importance and explains it in *EZB* III 222–8. This should be compared with Haribhadra pp. 96–6.

[7] *S* i 137, though the corresponding passage of New Delhi *P* gives 10.

[8] Ad LXIII 248b.

lists occur, with quite different explanations, in *Sandhinirmocanasūtra* (VIII 29), *Madhyāntavibhāgaṭīkā* pp. 52–59 and *Laṅkāvatārasūtra* p. 74, but their relation to the *Prajñāpāramitā* lists is not easy to explain. The growth and historical development of all these categories awaits further study.

No. 5 constitutes one of the most impressive sections of the Large Sūtra. *A*, in its later parts (xxvi 435) knew of four stages of a Bodhisattva's career. Now ten *bhūmis* are systematically expounded, and our Sūtra stands halfway between the chaos of the *Mahāvastu* and the architectonic elaborateness of the *Daśabhūmika*. This account of the *bhūmis* was probably specially written for the *Prajñāpāramitā*, and is consonant with its spirit. The decisive *bhūmi* is the seventh, on which the *prajñāpāramitā* is realized.[1] In the rest of the Sūtra this treatment of the *bhūmis* is, however, really ignored, no use is made of it and a quite different, essentially Hīnayāna, list is frequently enumerated. That is however, nowhere defined, and later scholastics had some difficulties in squaring it with the Mahāyāna list.[2]

No. 3 is a mere list of standard formulas annexed from other traditions, and most of the terms and definitions are shared with the Hīnāyana schools. Finally, nos. 4 and 2, the *dhāraṇīs* and *samādhis*, concern the *occult* side of this teaching. The A-ra-pa-ca-na was a peculiar arrangement of the letters of the Sanskrit alphabet, which is attested for the *Dharmaguptavinaya*,[3] occurs also in the *Gaṇḍavyūha* (chap. 45) and in Tantric times was personified in the well-known figure of Arapacana Mañjuśrī. The *Prajñāpāramitā* used it to summarize certain of its specific teachings, just as the *Lalitavistara* (127–8) employed the ordinary Sanskrit alphabet for the illustration of Old Wisdom Buddhism, and the *Gaṇḍavyūha* the Arapacana for that of the philosophy of the Avataṃsaka.

The list of *samādhis* likewise seems to have been appropriated from some outside source, although we have no clue at present to what that was. Their explanation is to some extent adjusted

[1] In *Daśabhūmika* and *Bodhisattvabhūmi* the *prajnāpāramitā* is assigned to the sixth *bhūmi*.

[2] See my *Marginal Notes to the Abhisamayālaṅkāra*. Liebenthal Festschrift, Sino-Indian Studies, V 3–4, 1957, pp. 26–31.

[3] *T* 1428 xi. cf. JAs 1915, 1, p. 440.

to the special viewpoint of *Prajñāpāramitā* thinking, but at the same time the treatment of the *samādhis* is couched in an esoteric phraseology which we do not understand very well and which is not otherwise found in this Sūtra. Examples are *mudrā, mudrita, dhvaja, raśmimukha, balavyūha, samādhimaṇḍala, jñānaketu, cāritravatī, śubhapuṣpitaśuddhi, ākārābhinirhāra, sarvasamādhīnāṃ saṃketarutāni, jvalanolkā*. The whole passage remains a kind of foreign body, and none of the *samādhis* in this list is ever mentioned again, except of course in the numerous enumerations of lists.

IV. As a next step, two items concerning the Buddhism of Faith were added on. They are (A) the reference to *Akṣobhya*[1] and (B) the *avadāna* of Sadāprarudita.[2] These were certainly later than chaps. 3–28 of *Rgs*, and in all probability later than the Abhidharma insertions just discussed.

A. Short though they are, the references to Aksobhya are nevertheless important, and we have here to deal with a deep undercurrent in *Prajñāpāramitā* thought, which came to the fore in the Tantra four or five centuries later. The Tantric system of the Five Jinas associates the *Prajñāpāramitā* with the "family" of the Buddha Akṣobhya. In two *sādhanās* of the *Sādhanamālā* (nos. 153, 151) it is stated that he should be shown on the headdress, or crown, of the images representing her. Buddhist Scriptures are medicines, antidotes to specific ills and ailments, and their whole purpose is to counteract certain faults that hold us back. Three types of human beings are usually distinguished, according to whether they are dominated by greed, hate or delusion. Now it is well known that the Vajrayāna associates Akṣobhya with the hate-family, and equally that many sources[3] regard wisdom (*prajñā*) as the specific antidote to hate. The *Prajñāpāramitā* Sūtras seem to be specially addressed to people of the hate-type, and designed to help them to sublimate their hate. "As hate leads to the rejection of beings, so wisdom to that of all conditioned things." So Buddhaghosa. It is the aim and purpose of hatred to smash that which offends. While "nihilism" is by no means the last word

[1] *A* xix 366–7, xxvii 450–2, xxviii 464a, 465, 474; also *P* 91.

[2] *A* xxx, xxxi, xxxiii 527.

[3] E.g. *Visuddhimagga*, ed. H. C. Warren, 1950, ch. III 76. Saṅgharakṣa *Yogācārabhūmi*, 191a.

of the *Prajñāpāramitā*, the thorough emotional and intellectual annihilation of the world is an important step on the way towards winning the gnosis of Perfect Wisdom. In the ontology of the *Prajñāpāramitā* the entire world, all entities, whatever they are, are completely smashed and done away with, not only ground to powder, but reduced to nothingness.[1] This is a great triumph of universal hate. If one's own self is included in the general annihilation, it is at the same time also a triumph of the spirit.

That is one side of the introduction of Akṣobhya. The second lies in that the *Prajñāpāramitā* deliberately supplements its abstractions with the personifications of mythology. Likewise Nāgārjuna was not only a great logician and philosopher, but one of the "Patriarchs" of the "Pure Land" school as well. These men realized that a religion is bound to become emaciated if defined in terms acceptable only to highbrows and intellectuals. As Mahāyānists they aimed at universality, and therefore sought ways and means of making their philosophy to some extent meaningful also to the masses of the people. While society was still primarily agricultural, it could be assumed that the virtue of the masses lay in faith, and that a wisdom doctrine meant for the élite had to be supplemented by one offering objects of faith to the ordinary people. This method no longer works well with the urbanized masses and no one has yet found a way of making the traditional religions attractive to the industrial worker or the clerk in his office. But before 1850 no religion could establish itself firmly in society without re-stating its doctrines in terms of Faith also. About A.D. 150 that faith was directed to Akṣobhya, and two centuries later links were forged with Avalokiteśvara, as in the *Hṛdaya* and *Svalpākṣara*.

B. The story of Sadāprarudita is concerned with the problem of how one should search (*paryeṣṭavyā*) for the perfection of wisdom. What are the moral and spiritual qualifications which a person must have in order to grasp and realize these sublime teachings? The answer, as exemplified by the conduct

[1] As M. Eckhart has it: Das ist ein offenbares Zeichen dass ein Mensch den Geist der Weisheit hat, wenn er alle Dinge achtet als ein lauteres Nichts—nicht als einen Pfuhl, nicht als ein Sandkorn—als ein lauteres Nichts.

of Sadāprarudita, is that complete self-sacrifice must precede any deeper understanding of this doctrine. Later on, in the *Suvikrāntavikrāmiparipṛcchā* the same problem is discussed slightly more systematically, and in two beautiful passages[1] we are told what kind of people are fit and worthy to learn about *Prajñāpāramitā*. Not many such people can obviously be found among us, and in this phase *Prajñāpāramitā* thought was clearly rather pessimistic on this subject. In the later parts of the *Aṣṭa* the only persons who are named as actually dwelling in perfect wisdom are the Bodhisattvas Ratnaketu, Śikhin and Gandhahastin who all reside in the Buddhafield of Akṣobhya. Likewise it is said of Sadāprarudita, the "Ever-Weeping", that "at present he leads the holy life with the Tathāgata Bhīṣmagarjitanirghoṣasvara", i.e. wherever he may be—perhaps, according to the *Saddharmapuṇḍarīka* (p. 318) in the world-system *Mahāsaṃbhava*—he is in any case not on this earth.

V. Finally a substantial section was added to the Large Sūtra which deals almost exclusively with one of the facets of "Skill in means." Why, if everything is one vast emptiness, if there is no person, no object, no thought, no goal, no anything, should anyone strive for perfect enlightenment through a practice of virtue and a knowledge of dharmas? Hundreds of times Subhūti is made to ask the self-same question, and hundreds of times the Buddha answers it. The problem was obviously felt to be a most intractable one, and in the *Śatasāhasrikā* 413 leaves are devoted to it. The apparent conflict between the ontology of the *Prajñāpāramitā* and the practical needs of the struggle for enlightenment presented a serious difficulty because experience shows that the *Prajñāpāramitā* teachings are liable to degenerate into a complete nihilism as far as the practical side of the spiritual life is concerned. Three examples will suffice:

The first comes from India, and consists in the well-known quotation from the *Sarvadharmavaipulyasaṃgrahasūtra* in *Sikṣāsamuccaya*:[2] "As to the complete accomplishment (*samudāgama*) of the six perfections which the Bodhisattvas

[1] I 4b–6a, II 19b–24a. Translated in my *Selected Sayings from the Perfection of Wisdom*, 1955, pp. 27–31.

[2] P. 97. Bendall-Rouse's translation pp. 98–9 is, I think, misleading, and so I have re-translated the passage.

must have so as to win full enlightenment, these deluded people will say 'a Bodhisattva should train in the perfection of wisdom, and not the other perfections'; so they will disparage (*dūṣayitavya*) the other perfections. Was the king of Kāśi acting unwisely (*duṣprajña*) when he gave his own flesh to the hawk to save the dove? Have I in any way been injured (*apakṛta*) by the roots of merit bound up with the six perfections which I have heaped up during my long practice (*caryā*) as a Bodhisattva? . . . But these deluded people will say, 'enlightenment comes from one method (*naya*) only, i.e. that of Emptiness'. How can they be quite pure in their practices (*caryāsu*)?'' The second example comes from the debates which accompanied the Council of Lhasa, or Bsam-yas, of ca. 790. At that time Kamalaśīla and the Indian *paṇḍits* believed, rightly or wrongly, that the Ch'an interpretation of *Prajñāpāramitā* excluded the necessity for making any special effort. At present we witness a similar phenomenon in Europe and North America in those circles which have been stirred by Suzuki's presentation of Zen. While in the U.S.A. the Beatniks seems to regard it as advocating a life of undisciplined whimsy, in Europe many Zen followers rejoice at this teaching because it seems to create a vacuum in which their own egotism can operate without let or hindrance.

It has thus often been thought that in attempting to safeguard the spiritual intent of all religious striving, the *Prajñāpāramitā* takes away the motive for doing any striving at all. Apparently it was not easy to prove these nihilistic conclusions to be unjustified. If the paradox could have been resolved by a few cogent arguments, they would have been given. By lavishing so many words on it, the authors of the *Prajñāpāramitā* showed by implication that no verbal answer is possible. The living rhythm of the spiritual life, lived from day to day, alone can teach what words fail to convey.

We have now roughly defined the main theme of the last third of the Large *Prajñāpāramitā*. In connection with it we are given a number of lengthy treatises which discuss all the six perfections and their possible combinations in great detail. The discussion throughout this part proceeds on a very advanced level, and frequently employs terms which we understand only imperfectly. This last flowering of *Prajñāpāramitā* thought also gives a number of useful definitions, e.g. of the three kinds of omniscience, of the Buddha, of enlightenment, of Perfect Wisdom, of *prapañca*, of the major and minor marks of a Buddha's body, and so on.

VI. This concludes our discussion of the Large *Prajñāpāramitā*. The really creative period, which we surmised to have begun in 100 B.C., ceased, on the evidence of the Chinese translations, two hundred and fifty years later. It now remained to produce what we may call "portable editions" of this vast document, which was too extensive to be memorized, and too obscure to be copied out correctly for long.[1] Short Sūtras in 25, 300, 500, 700 and 1250 *ślokas* aimed at providing handy summaries of its contents, and we must now ask ourselves whether they are mere abbreviations of the Large Sūtra, or propound original ideas of their own.

Generally speaking, these documents of the fourth to seventh centuries follow the doctrines outlined in the Large Sūtra. The differences mainly concern such external points as the kind of Abhidharmic teaching which is subjected to the new analysis. The version in 500 *ślokas* alludes to many Abhidharma categories unnoticed in the Large *Prajñāpāramitā* and the lists adopted in the version in 1250 *ślokas* are somewhat at variance with those of the Large Sūtra. There are, as far as I can see, only three differences worth commenting upon:

1. During the third phase already the *Prajñāpāramitā* had resorted to the enunciation of plain contradictions[2] as a means of expressing the inexpressible. For if nothing can be said, one way of saying it is to make two contradictory pronouncements at the same time. Now, in the fifth phase, self-contradictory statements become more frequent, bolder and more dramatic. In the *Saptaśatikā* we are assured[3] that the self is the Buddha, that "an undisciplined monk" means "an Arhat whose outflows have dried up", and that "the five deadly sins" are a synonym for "enlightenment". In the *Vajracchedikā* the formula which identifies a term with its contradictory opposite is re-stated in varying forms no fewer than thirty-five

[1] Already the Gilgit MSS of the *Pañcaviṃśatisāhasrikā* and *Aṣṭādaśasāhasrikā* are full of mistakes, as is shown in my Rome edition of chapters 55–69 of *Ad*.

[2] E.g. *Ś* iii 495–502, and *P* 136–38.

[3] 221, 228–9, 231–2.

times.[1] And the bulk of the *Hṛdaya* is occupied with piling one contradiction on top of the other.

2. The later Sūtras show a few distinct Yogācārin influences, which were absent in the older documents. These accretions are not really surprising, because the *Prajñāpāramitā* could live only as long as it absorbed everything that was really alive in Buddhism.

a) There is first the adoption of the exegetical method known as *saṃdhābhāṣya*. In the Scriptures of the Theravadins *sandhāya* (*bhāsitam*, or *vuttam*) means "in reference to". Some scholars have claimed that this is the meaning also in *Vajracchedikā* chap. 6, but that is more than unlikely. "With reference to" demands something to which it refers, and in the Pali *sandhāya* is always preceded by a word in the accusative, such as *etaṃ, taṃ, yaṃ, vacanaṃ, rūpakāyadassanaṃ*, etc.[2] This is not the case in the *Vajracchedikā* passage. The context likewise is perfectly unambiguous. There is nothing esoteric or profound in this parable of the raft as such, which is quite easy to understand and almost self-evident as told in *Majjhimanikāya* I p. 135. But the *Vajracchedikā* gives a twist to it, lays bare its hidden intention, as the Yogācārins were wont to do. "On the face of it, the word 'dharmas' in this saying of the Buddha means 'virtues', and so have Buddhaghosa, Woodward and I. B. Horner (BT no. 77) understood it. By taking 'dharmas' not as a moral, but as a metaphysical term, meaning 'entities', our Sūtra here discloses the 'hidden meaning' of the simile."[3] After its isolated use in the *Vajracchedikā*, the term *saṃdhāya* becomes a fairly regular feature in the *Saptaśatikā*[4] and *Suvikrāntavikrāmiparipṛcchā*,[5] which can be dated about A.D. 450 and 500.

b) There is further the term *cittāvaraṇa* in the *Hṛdaya*. The distinction between *karmāvaraṇa, kleśāvaraṇa* and *jñeyāvaraṇa* is common to all Mahāyānists. But to speak of *cittāvaraṇa* gives sense only within the context of the Yogācārin system, as an

[1] For the references see my edition of *The Vajracchedikā*, 1957, p. 12.

[2] *MN* I p. 503, *Udāna cy* p. 26, 243, *Jātaka* I 203, *Udāna cy* pp. 238, 318, 311. At *Samyutta Cy* (to I 224) and *Jātaka Cy* II 386 the meaning of *sandhāya* is fairly definitely given as *paṭicca*.

[3] E. Conze, *Buddhist Wisdom Books*, 1958, p. 35.

[4] 214, 225–6, 229, 240.

[5] I 10a, 13b, 14a, 19a, iv 55a.–Also *Pañcaśatikā* (undated) 172b–173a.

over-all term for all coverings which obscure the pure subject. The term is attested elsewhere in Asaṅga's verse-commentary to *Vajracchedikā*, v. 42, and in the title of the Tantric Āryadeva's *Cittāvaraṇaviśuddhiprakaraṇa*. Its Yogācārin connotation is further underlined by the variant readings of this *Hṛdaya* passage. Three Chinese transcripts have *cittālambaṇam* and six Nepalese manuscripts *cittārambaṇamātratvāt*.

c) Two specific Yogācārin doçtrines were worked into the revised *Pañcaviṃśatisāhasrikā*, which may well belong to the fifth century. They are 1. The doctrine of the four bodies of the Buddha.[1] 2. The three kinds of own-being.[2] We have also one short Sūtra (*T* 247) which, claiming to give the "direct meaning" of the *Prajñāpāramitā*, includes an enumeration of the ten *vikalpas* of Yogācārin tradition.

3. The later Sūtras show a greater awareness of the pressure of the social environment which Buddhists felt to be increasingly adverse to their ideals. In the very brief span of the *Vajracchedikā* we hear four times[3] of "the last time, the last epoch, the last five hundred years, the time of the collapse of the good doctrine". Since we do not know which date is here assumed for the Nirvāṇa, we can unfortunately not use this for dating the Sūtra. It is, however, noteworthy that there is no such preoccupation with prophecies of gloom in the earlier parts of the *Aṣṭa*. The "last days" are, it is true, mentioned at x 225, where it is said that when they come round the *Prajñāpāramitā* will be studied in the North, but this is a late addition, and absent from *Rgs*.

The Buddhists reacted to their sense of social oppression by soliciting the blessings of heaven and mobilizing, by means of *mantras*, etc., the forces of the invisible world for their succour. The *Hṛdaya* already contains a *mantra* which is connected with the *Prajñāpāramitā*[4] and which is claimed to be *sarvaduḥkhapraśamanaḥ*. After A.D. 500 a number of short Sūtras

[1] *P* 532a6–523b6.

[2] *P* 578a5–583b5.

[3] Chap. 6, 14b, 16b, 21b.

[4] The reading *prajñāparamitāyam ukto* is difficult because, as also Suzuki (*EZB* III 199) has observed, no such *mantra* exists anywhere in the *Prajñāpāramitā*. Matters might be mended by reading with some of of the documents *prajñāpāramitā*(*yā*) *yukto*. The Tibetan has the Genetive and not the Locative case.

were composed[1] which multiply the *mantras* and *dhāraṇīs* at the disposal of the follower of Perfect Wisdom, and Vajrapāni, once mentioned in *A* (xvii 333) now acquires a greater importance than he had before.

Next, stage VII is marked by the production of *systematizing commentaries*. There had, of course, been commentaries before that time, especially the *Mahāprajñāpāramitopadeśa*. But they had been the work of Mādhyamikas who had been content with bringing out the actual meaning of the Sūtra, did little violence to the existing text and confined themselves to explaining just what it said. Now the influence of the Yogācārins produced a new type of commentary which tried to superimpose on the Sūtra some scheme alien to it. These Yogācārin commentaries have been preserved to us in some profusion, because they met the needs of the great Buddhist monasteries of Bihar and Orissa at the time when Buddhism came to Tibet.

The difficulty lay, I think, in this: For a long time some Buddhists had sought emancipation more through *prajñā*, others more through *dhyāna*.[2] This dichotomy is at the basis also of the division between Mādhyamikas and Yogācārins. The Mādhyamika approach was perfectly adjusted to that of the *Prajñāpāramitā*, and no commentatorial juggling was needed to effect reconciliation. The *Mādhyamikakārikā* and the *Prajñāpāramitā* expound exactly the same doctrine, the one to *tīrthikas* and Hīnayānists, the other to Mahāyāna believers. Both use the sharp sword of wisdom to cut through all phenomena and show them all to be equally devoid of own-being, just one emptiness. The standpoint of the Yogācārins is not so much in conflict as incongruous with this. Following to its logical conclusion the traditional *dhyānic* method of withdrawal from all external objects, they attempt to realize the ultimate subject which can never be an object. This is not at all the method of the *Prajñāpāramitā* which by contrast drives to its logical conclusion the traditional method of *dharmapravicaya*, or dharmic analysis.

It was now the fate of the *Prajñāpāramitā* texts to fall into the hands of the Yogācārins, to whom they presented as much

[1] For the details see my *Tantric Prajñāpāramitā Texts*, Sino-Indian Studies, V 2, 1956, pp. 100–122.

[2] See E. Conze, *Buddhism*, 1951, pp. 161–2.

an embarrassment as an inspiration. The Sūtras had been composed on the principle that "the Spirit bloweth where it listeth". Wide open to any suggestion, they meander from subject to subject, and whatever connection there may be between them, it is rarely a logical one. The Yogācārins, working in the fourth century and later, tried to find a hidden *system* behind all these meanderings. Asaṅga and Vasubandhu demonstrated that the *Vajracchedikā* is not as incoherent as it looks, revealed the links between the apparently disconnected arguments, and distributed its subject matter under seven topics.[1] Next we have Dignāga's *Prajñāpāramitāpiṇḍārtha*[2] which claims (in vv. 6, 22, 58) a special connection with the *Aṣṭasāhasrikā*, although the bulk of it (vv. 5–54) is based on passages of the Large *Prajñāpāramitā* which do not occur in it. Here the teaching is arranged under thirty-two subjects. But the most systematic treatment is the first and most influential of these, the *Abhisamayālaṅkāra*, attributed to Maitreya, which reveals the deeper, hidden and indirect meaning as distinct from the plain and obvious sense, and which turns the *Pañcaviṃśatisāhasrikā* into a very elaborate system, with fixed categories, a consecutive argument and manifold divisions and subdivisions. Valuable for the study of the letter of the *Prajñāpāramitā*, it nevertheless seems to some extent to conflict with its spirit.

It had been the exasperating and rather self-contradictory task of the *Prajñāpāramitā* Sūtras to say something about the spiritual world without saying anything definite. As Subhuti once put it to the puzzled Gods, "There is nothing to understand, nothing at all to understand! For nothing in particular has been indicated, nothing in particular explained" (*A* II 38). The *Prajñāpāramitā* had offered an elusive series of subtle allusions, which at times are not unlike what is known as "free association" in modern psychology, and its presentation of the subject is the sign of a mind inwardly free, not unduly concerned with definite facts or achievements, not unduly pre-occupied with self-justification or self-protection. The Yogācārin commentators once more confined the celestial phoenix within a golden cage. Just as five hundred years ago the mindful

[1] The material in G. Tucci, *MBT* I, 1956.
[2] Ed. G. Tucci, *JRAS* 1947, pp. 56–9.

meditations of the monks who watched the rise and fall of dharmas had hardened into a fixed Abhidharmic system which provoked the reaction of the *Prajñāpāramitā*, so now again the prison walls of a fixed scholastic system enclosed the fleeting intuitions of the *Prajñāpāramitā*. The freedom of the spirit was once again in danger.

After A.D. 500 it re-asserted itself in the third creative outburst of the Buddhist spirit, which is represented by the Tantra and by Ch'an. They are both parts of the same process and their similarities become more and more apparent. Their violent reaction against the deadening effects of a successful and flourishing ecclesiastical system equally affected the three departments of Buddhist endeavour, i.e. Morality, Meditation and Wisdom. The antinomianism of the Tantra seems directed chiefly against the third and fifth precept, although the others were not entirely neglected. The same antinomianism is perhaps more subdued in Chinese Ch'an, but in Japanese Zen it openly defies the first precept. As for meditation, the traditional methods were almost entirely discarded, and replaced by new ones, quite unheard of so far. The presentation of Wisdom likewise took entirely new forms.

VIII. The *Adhyardhaśatikā*, the one truly Tantric exposition of the *Prajñāpāramitā*, represents an entirely new departure. It employs a literary form which it calls *prajñāpāramitānaya*, foreshadowed to some extent in the "litanies" of the later parts of *A* (chap. 29 sq.). The best I can do here is to quote one of these *nayas* (no. XII) in a rather faltering translation which reveals not only my own ignorance, but also the irrational nature of these utterances:

"Thereupon the Lord Vairocana, the Tathāgata, again demonstrated this method of the perfection of wisdom, called the power which sustains all beings (*sarvasattvādhiṣṭhānam*):

"All beings are embryonic Tathāgatas (*tathāgatagarbhāḥ*), because they all have the self-nature (*ātmatā*) of Samantabhadra, the great Bodhisattva; thunderbolts in embryo (*vajragarbhāḥ*) are all beings, because they are consecrated with the Thunderbolt-womb (*vajragarbhābhiṣiktatayā*); Dharma in embryo are all beings, because all speech comes to pass (? *sarvavākpravartanatayā*; *ṅag thams-cad rab-tu 'byuṅ-bas*);

Karma is potentially present (*karmagarbhāḥ*) in all beings, because all beings exert themselves in doing deeds."

"Thereupon the outside adamantine families raised a clamour, and (to them) this quintessence (*sñiṅ-po*) was offered and the meaning of this Dharmahood was explained in greater detail. Thereupon the great adamantine Ruler of his own offered this very same quintessence. *Trī*. Thereupon all the heavenly Mothers paid homage to the Lord, and of their own offered this very same quintessence (of the doctrine) called 'the religious observance of the accomplishment of the gathering, taking up and examining all harmonious sayings'. *Bhyoḥ*. Thereupon, beginning with the Bees (? *sbraṅ-rtsir byed-pa la sogs-pa*) the three Brothers (*miṅ-po*) paid homage to the Lord, and, speaking harmoniously (*tshig 'thun-par*), of their own offered this very same quintessence. *Svā*. Thereupon the four Sisters paid homage to the Lord, and of their own offered this very same quintessence. *Hā*."

Whatever this may mean, it is clear that it is replete with terms which have no rational standing or meaning at all, but which give sense only within a ritual system which aimed at achieving harmony with the cosmic rhythm. The *Prajñāpāramitā* thus has been absorbed, but transmuted out of all recognition.

IX. And so it was in Ch'an. The influence of the *Prajñāpāramitā* on Ch'an thinking, and the interpretation of *Prajñāpāramitā* texts by the Ch'an masters would deserve a more detailed investigation. The space allotted to me is now exhausted, and it would in any case not be seemly for me to make self-confident remarks about Zen in an article dedicated to D. T. Suzuki. All that I could do here was to sketch out briefly the changes which *Prajñāpāramitā* thinking underwent in the course of seven or eight centuries, and to suggest some of the reasons which may have prompted this development. A better knowledge of the vast and still largely unexplored material will enable future scholars to fill in the details, and to correct my perspective wherever necessary.

The Prajñāpāramitā-hṛdaya Sūtra

The *Prajñāpāramitā-hṛdaya sūtra* is a religious document of the first importance. It carried *Yüan-tsang* through the Gobi desert,[1] was reproduced, in writing, on stones, in recitation throughout Asia from Kabul to Nara,[2] and formed one of the main inspirations of the Zen school, occupying in Buddhist mysticism about the same place that the "*Mystical Theology*"[3] of *Pseudo-Dionysius Areopagita* occupied in Christian. Unlike other very short *Prajñāpāramitā-sūtras*, the *Hṛdaya* is of great philosophical interest. The *Svalpākṣarā*,[4] and other abbreviations, were designed to bring the benefits of *Prajñāpāramitā* within the reach of those unable to either study or understand it.[5] The *Hṛdaya* alone can be said to have gone really to the heart of the doctrine. The historical analysis of its sources can contribute to the understanding of this *sūtra*, by restoring its components parts to their context within the larger *Prajñāpāramitā sūtras*.

I

The text of the *Hṛdaya* even *in extenso* is short. The editions of *Max Müller*, *D. T. Suzuki*, and *Shaku Hannya* obscure the progress of the argument, and the manuscripts and the *Chinese* translations throw light on the history and meaning of this *sūtra*. The *Hṛdaya*, as is well known, is transmitted in a longer form (about twenty-five ślokas), and a shorter form (about fourteen ślokas). The introduction and end of the longer form are here left unnumbered, while, to facilitate reference, I have

[1] Hwui Li, *The Life of Hiuen-tsiang, trsl. Beal*, 1914, pp. 21–2.

[2] Cf. e.g. M. W. de Visser, *Ancient Buddhism in Japan*, 1928, 1935.

[3] *Mystical Theology*, iii, chaps 4 and 5, in particular, afford a striking parallel to Section IV of the *Hṛdaya*.

[4] Ed. E. Conze, Sino-Indian Studies V 3 (1956), pp. 113–5.

[5] *SiS* p. 113: *deśayatu bhagavān prajñāpāramitāṁ svalpākṣarāṁ mahāpuṇyāṁ yasyāḥ śravaṇa-mātṛena sarva-sattvāh sarva-karmāvaraṇāni kṣapayiṣyanti*, etc.

introduced numbered subdivisions in the short version of the *sūtra.*

I. [1]Oṃ namo Bhagavatyai Ārya-prajñāpāramitāyai!

(Evaṃ mayā śrutam ekasmin samaye. Bhagavān Rājagṛhe viharati sma Gṛdhrakūṭa-parvate, mahatā bhikṣu-saṃghena sārdhaṃ mahatā ca bodhisattva-saṃghena.[a)] tena khalu punaḥ[b)] samayena Bhagavān[c)] gambhīra-avabhāsaṃ nāma dharmaparyāyaṃ bhāṣitvā[c)] samādhiṃ samāpannaḥ. tena[d)] ca[e)] samayena[d)] Ārya-avalokiteśvaro bodhisattvo mahāsattvo gambhīrāyāṃ prajñāpāramitāyāṃ[f)] caryāṃ caramāṇa[g)] evaṃ vyavalokayati sma:[h)] pañca-skandhās tāṃś ca svabhāva-śūnyān vyavalokayati[h)]. atha[i)]-āyuṣmāñc Chāriputro buddha-anubhāvena Ārya-avalokiteśvaraṃ[k)] bodhisattvaṃ mahāsattvam[l)] etad avocat:[m)] yaḥ kaścit kūlaputro vā kuladuhitā vā[m)] asyāṃ[n)] gambhīrāyāṃ prajñāpāramitāyāṃ caryāṃ[o)] cartukāmas tena[p)] kathaṃ śikṣitavyam?[q)] [r)]evam ukta Ārya-avalokiteśvaro[k)] bodhisattvo mahāsattvo āyuṣmantaṃ Sāri-

[1] So N^{bceim} C^{e} Ti.—C^{d}: śrī-ārya-°—N^{h}: ārya-śrī-°—N^{a} omits Bhagavatyai.—N^{d}: Bhagavate ārya-śrī-°—J^{a}: Oṃ namaḥ sarva-jñāyaḥ.

a) C^{ae}: gaṇena.

b) so $N^{abcdeim}$ C^{ad}

c)–c) so N^{ab} C^{ade}.—N^{c}: gambhīrāyāṃ prajñāpāramitāyām avabhāsaṃ nāma dharmaparyāyaḥ.—N^{e}: gambhīrāyāṃ pravara-bhāṣan-nāma @@.—J^{b}: gambhīrāvasaṃbodhaṃ nāma.—N^{m}: gambhīrāvabhāṣan nāma.—N^{l}: gambhīrabhāvaṃ nāma samādhiṃ samāpannaḥ.—Ti.om: bhāsitvā.

d)–d) tasmin samaye N^{deim}.

e) so J^{b} C^{e}.—N^{abc}: khalu punaḥ.—C^{d}: punaḥ.

f) C^{ade}: gambhīrāvabhāsaṁ nāma dharmaparyāyaṃ.—C^{e} om.gambh-° to evam, i.e. vyavalokayati follows on dharmaparyāyam.

g) $N^{abcdeim}$ om.

h)–h) so J^{b}.—om.N^{m} C^{ade}.—N^{abi}: pañca-skandhān svabhāva-śūnyān vyavalokayati sma.—N^{c}: pañca-skandhā svabhāva-sūnyā vyāvalokitavyā.

i) C^{ade}: atha khalv.

k) Avalok-° C^{e}.

l) om. J^{b}; N^{a}?

m)–m) $N^{ce?}$: ye kecit kulaputrā vā kuladuhitā vā.

n) so N^{abc} C^{ade}.

o) °-tāyā cartu-° C^{ad}.

p) so N^{abc} C^{ade}.—N^{de}: cartukāmena.

q) N^{del}: vyavalokitavyam.

r)–r) : N^{del}: Avalokiteśvara āha:

putram etad avocat[r)]: yaḥ kaścic Chāriputra[s)] kulaputro vā kuladuhitā vā asyāṃ[t)] gambhīrāyāṃ prajñāpāramitāyāṃ caryāṃ[u)w)] cartukāmas tenaivaṃ[w)] vyavalokitavyam[v)].)

The short text condenses this into:

II. [2]Ārya-avalokiteśvaro [3]bodhisattvo [4]gambhīrāṃ prajñāpāramitācaryāṃ [5]caramāṇo [6]vyavalokayati sma: [7]pañcaskandhās [8]tāṃś ca svabhāva-śūnyān paśyati sma.

III. [9]iha Śāriputra [10]rūpaṃ śūnyatā śūnyataiva rūpaṃ [11]rūpān na pṛthak śūnyatā [12]śūnyatāyā na pṛthag rūpaṃ [13]yad rūpaṃ sā śūnyatā [14]yā śūnyatā tad rūpaṃ. [15]evam eva [16]vedanā-saṃjñā-saṃskāra-vijñānam.

[s)] N^{e}om.—N^{l} om: kaścic Chāriputra.

[t)] So N^{bc} C^{ade}.—om.N^{l}

[u)] cm. N^{e} C^{ade}.

[v)] D^{ade}: śikṣitavyaṃ yaduta.—N^{d} repeats after vyavalokitavyam: evam ukta, to: vyavalokitavyam.

[w)-w)] N^{i}: cartukāmena.

N^{m}: iha-Āryāvalokiteśvara kulaputrena vā . . . gambhīrāyāṃ prajñāpāramitāyāṃ cartukāmena tenaivaṃ vyavalokitavyam[v)].—N^{l}: iha . . . cartukāmena kathaṃ vy-°, see q).

[2] atha-Ārya- C^{g}.

[6] C^{b}: vyavalokayate.

[7-8] om.N.^{e}—N^{bc}: pañca-skandhān svabhāva-śūnyān vyavalokitavyam.—N^{k} (begins): vyavalokitavyam.—7–9: om. N^{di}.

[8] J^{b} Ti: samanupaśyati.—C^{g}: sma iti.—C^{ae}: svabhāva-śūnyāḥ. kathaṃ pañca-skandhāḥ svabhāva-śūnyāḥ?

[9] iha om. N^{k} ChT.—om. N^{bcek} C^{ae} J^{b} Ti.

[10] om $ChT^{1,2,5,6,7}$.—rūpaṃ sūnyaṃ N^{bcekim} C^{b}.—rūpam eva C^{e}.

[11-12] na rūpaṃ pṛthak śūnyatāyāḥ nāpi śūnyatā pṛthag rūpāt C^{ae}.—na rūpāt pṛthak N^{k}.

[13-14] om. $N^{bcdekim}$ C^{e} Ti.

[15-16] om.N^{b}.—15) evam N^{im} C^{e}.

[16] N^{cikm}: vijñānāni śūnyāni.—Ti:rnam-par śes-rnams stoṅ-pa'o.—N^{de}: vijñānāni śūnyatā.—C^{e}: vijñānāni.—J^{b}: vijñānaṃ ca sūnyatā.

[11-16] Instead, N^{b} has: na rūpāt pṛthak śūnyatā na sūnyatāyā pṛthag rūpaṃ. vedanā śūnyā śūnyataiva vedanā. na vedanāyā pṛthak etc., in extenso for all the five skandhas. After 16: ChT 1, 2, 5, 6 add 度一切苦厄. ChT 1 further adds the equivalent of P 39: Śāriputra yā rūpasya śūnyatā na sā rūpayati, yā vedanāyā śūnyatā na sā vedayati; etc.

IV. [17]iha Śāriputra [18]sarva-dharmāḥ śūnyatālakṣaṇā [19]anutpannā aniruddhā [20]amalā avimalā [21]anūnā aparipūrṇāḥ.

V. [22]tasmāc Chāriputra [23]śūnyatāyāṃ [24]na rūpaṃ na vedanā na saṃjñā na saṃskārāḥ na vijñānam, [25]na cakṣuḥ-śrotra-ghrāṇa-jihvā-kāya-manāṃsi [26]na rūpa-śabda-gandha-rasa-spraṣṭavya-dharmāḥ [27]na cakṣur-dhātur [28]yāvan na [29]manovijñāna-dhātuḥ [30]na-avidyā [31]na-avidyā-kṣayo [32]yāvan na [33]jarāmaraṇaṃ na jarāmaraṇakṣayo [34]na duḥkha-samudaya-nirodha-mārgā [35]na jñānaṃ [36]na prāptir na-aprāptiḥ.

[17] For iha $N^{abcdikm}$ C^{ae} J^{b} have: evaṃ.—om. ChT.—N^{ab}: evaṃ bhadanta.—Ti: śā-ri'i-bu de-lta bas-na (=śāriputra tasmāt tarhi).

[18] N^{abk}: svābhāva-śūnyāḥ alakṣaṇāḥ.—N^{de} :śūnyāḥ svalakṣaṇāḥ.—C^{ade}: svabhāva-śūnyatālakṣaṇā.—Ti: stoṅ-pā ñid de, mtshan-ñid med-pa (=śūnyatā-alakṣaṇā).

[19] C^{ade} add: ajātā.—after aniruddhā N^{e} adds: acyutāḥ acalāḥ.—N^{im}: acalāḥ avimalāḥ acyutāḥ.

[21] J^{a}: nonā?—C^{c}: nonā.—J^{b}: anonā.—N^{e}: anyonyāḥ.—N^{b}: anyatā.—N^{m}: anyonāḥ.—J^{a}: na paripūrṇā?—$B^{ab?dikm}$ C^{ade} J^{b}: asaṃpurṇāḥ; Ti: gaṅ-ba med-pa'o.—N^{e} C^{cg}: na saṃpūrṇāḥ.—After 21. ChT 1 adds, as P40: (yā śūnyatā) nātītā nānāgatā na pratyutpannā, etc.

[22] $N^{abdeikm}$ C^{ade} Ti: tasmāt tarhi.—N^{c}: evaṃ bhadanta.—C^{cg}: om. Śāriputra.

[23] N^{c}: śunyāyām.

[25-26] $N^{abceikm}$ C^{ae} J^{b}: na cakṣur na śrotraṃ, etc. to: na dharma.

[27-29] C^{a} gives a list of all the dhātus.—N^{ab}: na caksurdhātuḥ na rūpadhātuḥ na cakṣurvijñānadhātuḥ; na śrotravijñānadhātuḥ, etc. all to: na manovijñānadhātuḥ.—C^{e}, Ti: na cakṣurdhātu na manodhātu na manovijñānadhātu yāvan.

[28] evaṃ yāvan na.

[29] N^{im}: dharmadhātuḥ yāvan na.

[30] na vidyā ,add in $J^{a}C^{c}$.—$N^{abceikm}$ C^{eg} $ChT^{1,2,5,6}$ Ti om. na vidyā.—N^{abeikm} om. na-avidyā.

[31] na vidyākṣayo add in J^{a}.—N^{abcek} C^{aceg} J^{b} $ChT^{1,2,5,6}$ Ti: om. na vidyākṣayo.—C^{ae} J^{b} give for nāvidyākṣayo: na kṣayo, C^{c} na-akṣayo.

[33] N^{cikm} om. na. jarāmaraṇaṃ.

[30-33] N^{ab}: na-avidyākṣayo na saṃskārakṣayo, etc. all to :na jarāmaraṇakṣayo.

[34] N^{bceikm} C^{e}: na duḥkha(ṃ) na samudaya, etc.—After 34: $N^{abck?}$ add: na-amārgaḥ.—$N^{abck?}$ C^{ad} add: na rūpaṃ.

[35] N^{k} adds: na-ajñānaṃ.

[36] So N^{bek} C^{ade} J^{b} ChT 8, Ti.—J^{a}: na prāptitvaṃ.—N^{cdim} $ChT^{1,2,5,6}$: na prāptiḥ.—ChT 9: na prāptitvaṃ ca na-aprāptiḥ.—C^{b} na prāptir na-abhisamaya.

VI. [37]tasmāc Chāriputra [38]aprāptitvād bodhisattvo [39]prajñāpāramitām āśritya [40]viharaty acittāvaraṇaḥ. [41]cittāvaraṇa-nāstitvād [42]atrasto [43]viparyāsa-atikrānto. [44]niṣṭhā-nirvāṇaḥ.

VII. [45]tryadhva-vyavasthitāḥ [46]sarva-buddhāḥ [47]prajñāpāramitām āśritya- [48]anuttarāṃ samyaksambodhim [49]abhisambuddhāḥ.

VIII. [50]tasmāj jñātavyam [51]prajñāpāramitā [52]mahā-mantro [53]mahā-vidyā-mantro [54]'nuttara-mantro [55]'samasama-mantraḥ [56]sarva-duḥkha-praśamanaḥ [57]satyam amithyatvāt.

37 tasmāt tarhi Śāriputra: N^{abcdeikm} C^{ade} Ti.—Sāriputra also in ChT^{8,9} •—J^{a} C^{c} ChT^{1,2,5,6} omit 37.

38 N$^{ab?c?d?eim}$ C^{g} Ti: aprāptitvāt.—J^{b}: aprāptitvena.—C^{b}: aprāptitva.—J^{a} om. aprāptitvāt.—C^{d}: aprāpti-yāvat.—C^{a}: aprāptitāprāptiryāvavat.—C^{e}: na prāptirna-aprāptir yāvat; this is Feer's correction for what I read as: aprāptitāprāptir-yāvat.—bodhisattvasya J^{a}.—C^{b} J^{b}: bodhisattvānām.—N$^{bcea?}$: bodhisattvā mahāsattvā.—N^{k}: bodhisattvo mahāsattvaḥ.—N^{m}: bodhisattvaḥ.—C^{c}: bodhisattva.—C^{g} N^{l} bodhisattvā.—Ti: byaṅ-chub sems-dpa' rnams.—C^{e} om. bodhisattvo.

39 47 C^{g}: niśritya.

40 J^{a}: viharati cittavaraṇa. cittāvaraṇa.—Kokio's first copy: vaharaty citvavaraṇah, which he corrects to: viharani citnavaraṇaḥ.—J^{b}: viharati cittavaraṇaḥ. cittav-°.—C^{c}: viharya cita/avarṇa cita/a (varṇa-nā) stitva.—C^{g}: viharatya cityāvaraṇa.—N^{b}: viharanti.—Suzuki: viharato.—C^{ae}: viharañś.—N^{m}: viharati/nacittāraṃvana-mātratvād anuttarāyāṃ samyaksambodhau paryāsātikrāntāṃtāniṣṭhā—N^{l}: °-āyāḥ . . . ṣa? māsāntikrānmo . . .—acittāvaraṇaḥ om. N^{abcde} C^{ae} Ti.

41 C^{ade}: cittālambanaṃ.—N$^{abcd?ek}$: cittāraṃbaṇa-mātratvāt.—Ti: sems-la sgrib-pa med ciṅ.

42 N$^{abcek?}$: anuttrastā.

44 J^{a}: tiṣṭha?—N^{abcdikm} C^{ae}: niṣṭhā.—N^{e} om. niṣṭhā.—C^{ae}: nirvāṇaṃ prāpnoti.—N^{abcdeim} Ti: nirvāṇa prāptāḥ.—N^{k}: nirvāṇa? prāptaḥ.

45-49 C^{ae}: tryadhva-vyavasthitair api samyaksambuddhair . . .—bodhiḥ prāptā.—N^{abceikm}: . . . sarva-buddhair api . . . abhisambuddhā.

50 N^{ac}: tasmāt tarhi Sāriputra, etc.—N^{e}: tasmāt tarhi kulaputra, etc.—V^{ae}: etasmāj, etc.—N^{dim} Ti: tasmāt tarhi jñātavyam.

52 om. ChT^{1}.—ChT^{2,5,6,7} 呪 神 大 是 .—N^{cdei} C^{e} Ti om. mahā.

53 N^{a}: sahā?—C^{ae}: vidyā-mantro (-aḥ).—N^{e}: mahā-mantraḥ.—After

54 N^{a} adds: asamā-mantraḥ.—om. N^{m}.

52 -yukto mantraḥ N^{m}.

54 C^{g} om.

55 N^{e}: asamā-mantraḥ.—om. N^{l}.

56 N$^{a?cdeikm}$ C^{age} J^{b} Ti: sarva-duḥkha-praśamano mantraḥ.

57 C^{ac}: samyaktvaṃ na mithyatvaṃ.—N^{c}: samyaktva amithyātvā.

[58]prajñāpāramitāyām ukto mantraḥ. [59]tadyathā [60]oṃ gate gate pāragate pārasaṃgate bodhi svāhā.

(Evaṃ Śāriputra[a)] gambhīrāyāṃ prajñāpāramitāyāṃ caryāyāṃ śikṣitavyaṃ bodhisattvena[a)b)]. Atha khalu Bhagavān[c)] tasmāt[d)] samādher vyutthāya-Ārya-avalokiteśvarāya[da)] bodhisattvāya mahāsattvāya[e)] sādhukāram adāt. sādhu sādhu kulaputra, evam etat kulaputra[f)] evam etad[g)], gambhīrāyāṃ prajñāpāramitāyāṃ caryāṃ cartavyaṃ[g)] yathā tvayā nirdiṣṭam[h)] anumodyate sarva-[i)] Tathāgatair arhadbhiḥ[k)].

idam avocad Bhagavān. āttamanā[l)r)]-āyuṣmāñc Chāriputra[m)] Ārya-avalokiteśvaro bodhisattvo[n)] mahāsattvas[r)] te ca bhikṣavas te ca bodhisattvā mahāsattvāḥ[n)] sā[na)] ca sarvāvatī parṣat sa-deva-mānuṣa-asura-garuḍa[o)]-gandharvaś ca loko Bhagavato bhāṣitam abhyanandann iti.)

[61]ity ārya-[p)q)] prajñāpāramitā-hṛdayaṃ[q)] samāptam.

[58] °-tāyukto N^{l} C^{ae}.—N^{e}: °-tāyāyukto.—N^{c}: °-tāpujāyukta?—om N^{m}.

[a)-a)] C^{ae} Ti: bodhisattvena mahāsattvena prajñāpāramitāyāṃ śikṣitavyaṃ.—N^{el} om. caryāyām.

[b)] N^{cel} add. mahāsattvena.

[c)] C^{ae} add: (t) asyāṃ velāyām.

[d)] N^{del} om. tasmāt.—C^{e}: tasyās.

[da)] Avalok-° C^{e}.

[e)] J^{b}: °-asya °-asya °-asya.—N : °-ena.

[f)] om. N^{ceim}.

[g)-g)] so J^{b}.—C^{ae}: evam evaiṣā prajñāpāramitā.—om. N^{lm}. N^{lm} omits also: caryāṃ cartavyaṃ yathā tvayā.

[h)] N^{ddm} add: tad.

[i)] J^{b} om.

[k)] N^{c} adds: samyaksambuddhaiḥ.—N^{deim} have iti for arhadbhiḥ.—Ti om. arhadbhiḥ.

[l)] J^{b}: ānandamanā.

[m)] C^{ae} om. āyuṣmāñc chāriputra.

[r)-r)] N^{c} om.

[n)-n)] J^{b} om.

[na)] sa C^{e}.

[o)] N^{m} J^{b} C^{e} Ti om.

[p)] so N^{a}.

[q)-q)] N^{c}: prajñāpāramitā-hṛdaya-dhāraṇī pañcaviṃśatikāḥ nāma dhāraṇī.—N^{d}: śrī-prajñāpāramitā-hṛdaya.—N^{e}: pañca-viṃśatikā-prajñāpāramitā-hṛdaya-nāma-dhāraṇī. —N^{f}: pañca-viṃṣatikā prajñāpāramitā-hṛdaya.—N^{h}: śrī-pañcaviṃsatikā prajñāpāramitā-hṛdaya —N^{l}: pañcaviṃśati- prajñāpāramitā.—N^{m}: pañcaviṃśatikā prajñāpāramitā nāma dhāraṇī.—C^{ae}: pañcaviṃśatikā Bhagavatī prajñāpāramitā-hṛdayam.—Ti: Bhagavatī prajñāpāramitā-hṛdaya.

Sources:[1]

Nepalese manuscripts = N.

N[a]: LT. India Office no. 7712 (1). Eighteenth century?

N[b]: LT. Cambridge Add 1485. f. 16–18. A.D. 1677.

N[c]: LT. MS Bodl. 1449 (59) fol. 74v–75v. A.D. 1819

N[d]: LT. RAS, no. 79 V. f. 15–16b. c. 1820.

N[e]: LT. Cambridge Add. 1553. f. 4–7b. Eighteenth century.

N[f]: Calcutta As. Soc. Bengal B 5 (35).

N[g]: Calcutta ASB B 65 (10).

N[h]: fragment, only first 6 lines: Cambridge Add 1164 2 II.

N[i]: LT. Société Asiatique no. 14, fol. 18b, –19b. No. 21.

N[k]: LT. Cambridge Add 1680 ix. Begins at no. 8. ca 1200.

N[l]: Cambr. Add. 1164.2.

N[m]: Bibliothèque Nationale 62, no. 139. ca 1800.

Chinese = C.

C[a]: From a Chinese blockprint, in MM pp. 30–32. Seventeenth century.

C[b]: T 256, transcribed into Chinese characters. Stein Collection no. S 2464. ST. ca 600? ed. T. Matsumoto, *Die Prajñāpāramitā Literatur*, 1932, pp. 44–50.

C[c]: ST. From stone in Mongolia. Before 1,000. ed. Journal of Urusvati, 1932, pp. 73–8.

C[d]: LT. Bell in Peking, now Dairen. Incomplete. Ibid. p. 78.

C[e]: Feer's polyglot edition. Seventeenth century?

C[f]: Stein collection Ch 00330. ca 850.

C[g]: Bibliothèque Nationale 62 no. 139. Pelliot Sogdien. ca 950? In: E. Benveniste, *Textes Sogdiens*, 1940, pp. 142–3.

Japanese = J.

J[a]: MS in Horyūji Temple. ST. A.D. 609.

J[b]: MS brought in ninth century by Yeun, disciple of Kukai. In MM pp. 51–4.

Chinese Translations = ChT.

ST: ChT[1]: Kumārajīva ca 400.—ChT[2]: Yüan-tsang, 649.— LT: ChT[5]: Dharmacandra, 741.—ChT[6]: Prajñā 790.—ChT[7]: Prajñācakra 861.—ChT[8]: Fa-cheng, 856.—ChT[9]: Dānapāla c. 1000.

Tibetan = Ti. LT: Kanjur. ca 750.

Kumārajīva's[2] translation is important, as by far the earliest version of the text which we possess. Below (pp. 159–160) it will be shown to be of great assistance in restoring and tracing out

[1] For further details see JRAS 1948, pp. 48–50 and PPL 71–73.

[2] This translation, strictly speaking, appears not to have been made by *Kumārajīva*, but by one of his disciples. See Matsumoto, *Die Prajñāpāramitā Literatur*, 1932, p. 9, who refers to a Chinese catalogue. In the *Kao-seng-chuan*, a biography compiled in A.D. 519, the *Hṛdaya*, is not mentioned in the list of translations attributed to *Kumārajīva*; cf. J. Nobel, *Stzb. pr. Ak. Wiss.*, 20, 1927.

the argument of the *sūtra* as it is likely to have appeared to its compilers.

While most of the variant readings are of a minor character and self-explanatory, two of them require comment. The textual tradition is particularly unsatisfactory in the two places where, as we shall see, there is a break in the source, and where the pieces are joined together.

The first concerns the passage of the argument from IV to V. The reading adopted here is well supported by the MSS. and gives a smooth transition from IV to V. It seems, however, to have developed only in the course of time. It is not attested by the two oldest documents. *Kumārajīva*, and the Chinese translations up to ChT7 of A.D. 861 seem to have read, [36]*na prāpti*/ [37]*tasmād* [38]*aprāptitvād bodhisattva*(*sya*), etc.[1] The Horyūji MS., written before A.D. 609, gives: [36]*na prāptitvaṁ* [38]*bodhisattvasya*. Something appears to have dropped out here. As far as one can judge from the available evidence, the *sūtra* originally was content to deny in regard to emptiness all the main categories of Buddhist analysis. Later a part of the tradition thought to guard against misunderstanding by denying also the negation of those categories that easily form opposites. Thus *Kumārajīva* and several of the MSS. know nothing of the clause [30]*na vidyā* [31]*na vidyākṣayo*; in no. 34 *na-amārgaḥ* is found only in a few later MSS.; and so with [36]*na-a-prāptiḥ*, which appears in the *Chinese* translations only quite late, after about 850, in ChT8,9.

Obviously the rules of ordinary logic are abrogated in this *sūtra*. Contradictions co-exist in emptiness.[2] By adding "no knowledge", somebody may have wanted to make clear that in the dialectical logic of the *Prajñāpāramitā* a double negation does not make an affirmation. The misconception might arise that "the extinction of ignorance" (= the negation of the negation of knowledge) might be equivalent to a positive entity, named knowledge. The addition, "no knowledge," would

[1] 亦無得。以無所得。

[2] In no. 10 a term (form) is identified with the negation of that term ("emptiness"). Cf. also no. 10 with nos. 23–4. Similarly, *Dionysius Areopagita* in *Myst. Theol.*, i, 2, teaches that with reference to the Absolute there is no opposition (ἀντικείμενα) between affirmation and negation.

guard against that misconception.[1] In the same way, in this kind of logic, one negation is not necessarily like another. *Na mārga* is not the same as *a-mārga*, nor is *na prāpti* the same as *a-prāpti*. *A-prāpti* is, like *prāpti*, one of the seventy-five dharmas of the *Sarvāstivādins*.[2] In emptiness, i.e. in truth, there is no dharma. But while the *a-prāpti* is not a fact, *a-prāptitva*[3] is the basis of the conduct of a bodhisattva, of one who strives for bodhi. This is one of the paradoxes in which the *sūtra* gives expression to the laws of a spiritual life.

The second difficulty concerns the divergence between *cittāvaraṇa* and *cittālambaṇa* in no. 40.[4] When one considers the peculiarities of Sanskrit MSS., the two words do not differ much. We may suppose that originally there was चित्तारम्बण. Now ल and र, and ब and व are constantly interchanged in *Nepalese* MSS., and the म् is represented by an *anusvāra*. This

[1] Although, strictly speaking no. 35 na jñānam would make it superfluous.

[2] In *Nagārjuna's* list of 119 *kuśala-dharmas*, however, only *prāpti* is mentioned. *IHQ*., 1938, p. 317, no. 16.

[3] Cf. *LankS*., p. 307, v. 326–7: *prāptir . . . karma-jā tṛṣṇā-sambhavā*.

[4] In no. 40 the manuscript tradition does not cogently require the reading given in the text. My explanation is now confirmed by the almost exact parallel in the *āvaraṇa-pariccheda* of Vasubandhu's *Madhyānt-avibhāgabhāṣya*, ed. G. M. Nagao, Tokyo 1964, pp. 32–3. Literally translated it reads as follows: "Someone who wants to *attain* enlightenment should first of all produce wholesome roots; thereafter he should *attain* enlightenment through the effect of the power of his wholesome roots. Furthermore, the foundation (*pratiṣṭhā*) of the genesis of these wholesome roots is the thought of enlightenment, and the recipient (*āśraya*, cr. to *āśritya*) of that thought of enlightenment is *the Bodhisattva*. And through his production of the thought of enlightenment and his attainment of the effective power of the wholesome roots *the Bodhisattva*, having forsaken his perverted views (*viparyāsaṃ prahāya*), should produce a state of non-perversion (*aviparyāsa*). Thereupon, having become unperverted on the path of vision, he should forsake all the obstructions (*āvaraṇāni*) on the path of development. Once the obstructions have been forsaken, he should dedicate all the wholesome roots to the supreme enlightenment. Thereafter, through the effect of the power of his dedication, he should not tremble (*na-uttrasitavyam*) at the deep and sublime demonstrations of Dharma. (cf. Sthiramati p. 81. *ko'yam atrāsaḥ? śūnyatāyāṃ gambhīra-udareṣu ca buddhavacanad-harmeṣv adhimuktir abhīrutā*.) Having thus with a fearless (*anuttrasta*) mind seen the virtues of (these) dharmas, he should reveal them in detail to others. Thereafter the Bodhisattva, as a result of that great variety

would give °रंवरण". If the *anusvāra* is dropped, as often happens, a simple juxtaposition would lead to °वरण". Although the reading *cittāvaraṇa* makes sense it is perhaps not the original reading.[1] The normal *Chinese* equivalent for *āvaraṇa* is 障. This occurs only in the seventh and eighth version of the Sūtra, done in 861 and 856 respectively. The earlier versions, 1, 2, 5, and 6, done between 400 and 790, all have 心無罣礙. According to *Soothill*[2] 罣 means: "A snare, an impediment, cause of anxiety, anxious." The sign is related to a meaning "hung up", "suspended", and therefore seems to have more affinity to *ā-LAMB-ana* than to *ā-VAR-ana*.

II

The bulk of the *Hṛdaya*, from Sections I to V, is an instruction

of virtues, gains a power which enables him to quickly attain (*anuprāptavān*; *thob-nas*) the supreme enlightenment as well as the sovereignty over all dharmas." A similar sequence (*anukrama*) is found in Sthiramati's *Madhyāntavibhāgaṭīkā*, ed. S. Yamaguchi, 1934, pp. 87, 24–88, 19, paralleled to some extent by pp. 76, 16–77, 5. A further confirmation is the last sentence of Vasubandhu's commentary (p. 76), which says: *atrāsa-anunnaty-aviparyāsena nirāvaraṇo niryāti*, i.e. "he goes forth (to Nirvana) when he is free from obstructions as a result of the non-perversion which consists in the absence of both fear and pride" (cf. p. 68). On the previous page the *buddha-bhūmisamudāgamaḥ* had been identified with *nirāvaraṇatā*. And finally we have p. 97, 1–3 of Stiramati's *ṭikā*: *tatra prajñāpāramitā lokottara-nirvikalpa-jñānam. tena jñānena krameṇa sarva-āvaraṇa-prahāṇam*. But *Kumārajīva* either read *viharaty acitta*@, or he understood *cittāvaraṇaḥ as citta-a-varaṇaḥ*. M. Müller and A. Wayman (*PhEW*, xi, 1961, 113, "dwells with obscuration of the mental substance") read *viharati cittavaraṇaḥ*. The passage would then mean: "Because he has not attained, the Bodhisattva, based on the perfection of wisdom, dwells with thought obstructed. But only when obstruction is removed does he reach *Nirvāṇa*". The idea that someone could be based on the perfection of wisdom, and yet dwell with thought obstructed, is alien to the larger *Prajñāpāramitā-sūtras*. *A-cittāvaraṇaḥ* would, however, give a meaning well in keeping with the larger *sūtras*, as is shown on p. 164.

[1] The term *cittāvaraṇa* seems to be exceedingly rare. I have so far met it only in two other cases. The first *Tibetan* translation of *Āryadeva's Cittaviśuddhiprakaraṇaṁ* gives, in transliteration and translation, the title as: *cittāvaraṇaviśodhananāma-prakaranaṁ*, cf. *Tōhoku Catalogue*, no. 1804, where *citta-varaṇa* is given as a variant (!). And Asanga's commentary to the *Vajracchedikā* speaks at v. 42 of *cittāvaraṇam*, "obstruction of mind".

[2] *A Dictionary of Chinese Buddhist Terms*, 1937, p. 362b.

in the four Holy Truths, as reinterpreted in the light of the dominant idea of emptiness.[1] In the *Pañcaviṁśatisāhasrikā-prajñāpāramitā* (=P) on pp. 43–7, corresponding to *Śatasāhasrikā-prajñāpāramitā* (=S), pp. 136, 5–141, 13, we find a series of arguments, which *Haribhadra*, or whoever edited that recast version of the *Pañcaviṁśati*, considers as an instruction (*avavāda*) in at least the first three Truths. This passage is the source of the first part of the *Hṛdaya*. It is true that *Haribhadra* lived about A.D. 800–*c*. 800 to 300 years after the elaboration of the *Prajñāpāramitā* texts—and that many of his divisions and interpretations are artificial and far-fetched. But much of his commentary goes back to much earlier times.[2] In any case, in this instance *Haribhadra* merely follows the *kārikā* of *Maitreyanātha*,[3] whose *Abhisamayālaṅkāra* would be about contemporary with the *Hṛdaya*, if both can be assigned to *c*. A.D. 350. Also, the soundness of *Haribhadra's* diagnosis can be demonstrated from independent documents.

In the case of the *Third Truth*, of *nirodha*, the text of the *Pañcaviṁśati* is very similar to Sections III and IV of the *Hṛdaya*:

śūnyatā Śāriputra notpadyate na nirudhyate, na saṃkliśyate na vyavadāyate, na hīyate na vardhate. na-atītā na-anāgatā na pratyutpannā. *yā ca īdṛśī na rūpaṁ na vedanā* . . .; na pṛthivī-dhātur . . .; *na cakṣur* . . .; *na rūpaṁ na śabda* . . .; na cakṣurāyātanaṁ na rūpāyatanaṁ . . .; *na cakṣur-dhātur* . . .; *na-avidyotpādo na-avidyā-nirodhaḥ na saṁskārotpādo* . . .; *na duḥkhaṁ na samudayo na nirodho na mārgo*; *na prāptir* na-abhisamayo.[4] na srotaāpanno na srotaāpatti-phalaṁ . . . na pratyekabuddho na pratyekabodhiḥ; na buddho na bodhiḥ. evaṁ hi Śāriputra bodhisattvo mahāsattvaḥ prajñāpāramitāyāṁ caran yukto yukta iti vaktavyaḥ. (iti nirodha-satyāvavādaḥ.)

The *Hṛdaya* obviously gives an abbreviated version of this

[1] The passage in *Aṣṭa*, ii, 34, *sūnyatāyāṁ Kauśika tiṣṭhatā bodhisattvena mahāsattvena prajñāpāramitāyāṁ sthātavyaṁ*, is given by *Haribhadra* as *catuḥ-satya-ākāra*.

[2] Cf. Bu-ston II, 158.

[3] I.e. *kār* I, 21: *pratipattau ca satyeṣu buddharatn'ādisu triṣu . . . 22 ity avavādo daś'ātmakaḥ*.

[4] *Kumārajīva* in *Taishō Issaikyō*, vii, 223*a*, gives: 亦無智亦無得 for *nāprāptir nābhisamaya*, just as in nos. 35–6 of the *Hṛdaya*.

passage. It is noteworthy that on two occasions our documents preserve more of the original than the current text does. *Kumārajīva* leaves in: *na-atītā na-anāgatā na pratyutpannā*, using literally the same signs as in his translation of the *Pañcaviṁśati* itself.[1] The *Tun Huang* MS. Cb gives *na prāptir na-abhisamaya*. It is possible that *Kumārajīva's* addition suggests that the text about A.D. 400 contained it, while the *Tun Huang* addition may be a mere reminiscence of the numerous occasions on which *prāpti* and *abhisamaya* are coupled in the *Prajñāpāramitā sūtras.*[2]

The truth of stopping, as *Haribhadra* sums up,[3] means that *nirodha* is really emptiness, and therefore devoid of any dharma.

The case is less clear with the *second* truth, of *samudaya*. The *Pañcaviṁśati* passage reads:

sa na rūpam utpāda-dharmi vā nirodha-dharmi vā samanupaśyati . . . na rūpaṁ samkleśa-dharmi vā vyavadāna-dharmi vā samanupaśyati . . . punaraparaṃ Śāriputra bodhisattvo mahāsattvo na rūpam vedanāyāṁ samavasarati[4]-iti samanupaśyati. na vedanā saṁjñāyām samavasaratīti samanupaśyati . . . na vijñānaṁ dharme samavasaratīti samanupaśyati. na dharmaḥ kvacid dharme samavasaratīti samanupaśyati. tat kasya hetoḥ? na hi kaścid dharmaḥ kvacid dharme samavasarati prakṛti-śūnyatām upādāya. tat kasya hetoḥ? tathā hi Śāriputra yā rūpasya śūnyatā na tad rūpam . . . (tat kasya hetoḥ? tathā hi yā rūpa-śūnyatā na sā rūpayati . . . yā . . . vedayati; . . . saṁjānīte . . .; abhisaṃskaroti; . . . vijānāti. tat kasya hetoḥ?) *tathā hi Śāriputra na-anyad rūpam anyā śūnyatā. na-anyā śūnyatā anyad rūpaṁ. rūpam eva śūnyatā*

[1] *Taishō Issaikyō*, vol. viii, p. 223*a*.

[2] E.g. Aṣṭa (= A) VIII, 187, 189; A XV, 303; and A I, 30, which we will show to be the source of a part of Section V.

[3] Ed. *Wogihara*, 1935, p. 32. *nirodhe śūnyatāyām utpāda-nirodha-saṁkleśa-vyavadāna-hāni-vṛddhy-ādi-rahitāyāṃ na rūpaṁ yāvan na-avidyotpādo na-avidyā-nirodho na buddho na bodhir iti.*

[4] Up to this point the *Sāgaramati*, in *Śikṣāsamuccaya*, p. 263, gives a close parallel to this passage. Instead of *samavasarati* the terms *samsṛjyate* and *raṇati* are used there. In *Prasannapadā*, chap. 14, we find the arguments of the *Madhyamika* against the real existence of *samsarga*. The chief point is that *saṁsarga* implies *anyathva* or *pṛthaktva*, and that is not a real fact. Ś: *saha samavasarati* = Lhan-cig kun-tu rgyu shes bya-bar.

śūnyataiva rūpaṁ. na-anyā vedanā anyā śūnyatā . . . iti samudaya-satya-avavādaḥ.

The *Hṛdaya* reproduces only the substance of the last two sentences of this passage. But *Kumārajīva* also gives the sentences marked in ( ), preceding this, and that again literally in the same words as in his translation of the *Pañcaviṁśati.*[1] It is noteworthy that the *Chinese* and *Tibetan* translations, and three of the MSS., remain close to the *Pañcaviṁśati* text in that they have only two clauses, omitting either nos. 10–11 or nos. 13–14.[2]

But how is this argument connected with the truth of origination? As interpreted by the *Prajñāpāramitā*, the truth of origination means[3] that form, etc., considered as the cause of ill, are really identical with[4] emptiness, not separate from it. In other words, in reality there is no origination.[5]

As for the *first truth,* of ill, *Kumārajīva* was well aware that Section I referred to it, as is shown by his addition, "and so we go beyond all suffering and calamity (obstruction)."[6] Anyone familiar with the thought of the *Prajñāpāramitā* knows that the connotations of the term *vyavalokayati* point in the same direction. In *Aṣṭa* xxii, pp. 402–3, for instance, it is explained that a Bodhisattva, endowed with wisdom, "looks down" in the sense that he surveys the sufferings of beings with compassion. In the traditional formula of the first Truth *duḥkha* is

[1] *Taishō Issaikyō,* vol. viii, p. 223*a*.

[2] *Kumārajīva's* 色卽是空, etc., does not translate nos. 13–14, but nos. 10–11. In other places the phrase is also used to render *rūpam eva śūnyatā śūnyataiva rūpaṁ*; e.g. *Taishō Issaikyō,* viii, 221*c*=P 38; 223*a*=P. 45.

[3] *Abhisamayālaṅkārālokā,* p. 32: *samudaye śūnyatā hetu-bhūta-rūpādayor avyatiriktatvena* (=*a-pṛthaktvena*) *rūpādi na saṁudaya-nirodha-saṁkleśa-vyavadāna-dharmi-iti*.

[4] The formula of nos. 13–14 is designed as a parallel to the classical formula of the *satkāyadṛṣṭi*, which is the chief cause of becoming, cf. e.g. *Atthasālinī*, p. 353: *idh'ekacco rūpam attato samanupasyati. yaṁ rūpaṁ so ahaṁ, yo ahaṁ taṁ rūpan ti, rūpañ ca attañ ca advayam samanupasyati.* In Section II of this *sūtra, śūnyatā* takes the place which *ātman* occupies in the *satkāyadṛṣṭi*.

[5] And therefore as in the *Pañcaviṁśati* passage, *utpāda, saṁkleśa, saṁsāra,* which are all synonyms of the world viewed as originated.

[6] There is no trace of this addition in any Sanskrit document, and it may have been made in *Central Asia,* from where *Kumārajīva's* text is said to be derived.

equated with the *pañcopādāna-skandhā*. But what, according to the *Prajñāpāramitā*, is the real fact or truth about the *skandhas*? That they are empty in their own being. Thus, if *duḥkha* = *skandhā*, and if *skandhā* = *svabhāva-śūnyā*, then *duḥkha* = *svabhāva-śūnya*.[1] The compassion of a Bodhisattva, which at first has suffering beings as its objects, continues to grow even when the beings are replaced by objects more true to reality—first a group of *skandhas* or a procession of *dharmas*, and finally by emptiness, or no object at all.[2]

In the section dealing with the *duḥkha-satya*, the *Pañcaviṁśati* expresses this idea more elaborately:

Śāriputra: kathaṁ yujyamāno Bhagavan bodhisattvo mahāsattvaḥ prajñāpāramitāyāṁ yukta iti vaktavyaḥ? *Bhagavān*: iha Śāriputra bodhisattvo mahāsattvo rūpa-śūnyatāyāṁ yukto yukta iti vaktavyaḥ . . . etc., list as in Section IV to jarāmaraṇa-śoka - parideva-duḥkha - daurmanasyopāyāsa-śūnya - tāyāṃ yukto yukta iti vaktavyaḥ. Punaraparaṁ Śāriputra bodhisattvo mahāsattvaḥ prajñāpāramitāyāṁ carann ādhyātma-śūnyatāyāṁ yukto yukta iti vaktavyaḥ . . . yāvat parabhāva-śūnyatāyāṁ yukto yukta iti vaktavyaḥ. evaṁ hi Śāriputra bodhisattvo mahāsattvo prajñāpāramitāyāṁ carann āsu sarvāsu[3] śūnyatāsu yukto yukta iti vaktavyaḥ. sa ābhiḥ[4] śūnyatābhih prajñāpāramitāyāṁ caran na tāvad bodhisattvo mahāsattvo yukta iti vaktavyo 'yukta iti. Tat kasya

[1] In the *Abhidharma*, *śūnya* is one of the four equivalents of *duḥkha*. It is there explained as the negation of *mamagrāha* and *ātmadṛṣṭi*. *AK*., vii, 13. Now, according to the *Abhisamayālaṅkarāloka*, p. 38, the *śrāvakas* contemplate the sixteen modes or aspects of the four Truths as antidotes to *ātma-darśana*, and the Bodhisattvas as antidotes to *dharma-darśana*. Then in the case of the latter *śūnya* would mean *svabhāva-śūnya*, instead of *anātmīya*.

[2] *Sattva-ārambaṇa*, *dharma-ārambaṇa*, *an-ārambaṇa*. *Akṣayamati sūtra* in *Śikṣāsamuccaya*, p. 212, 12 sq.; cf. also *Pitṛputrasamāgama* in *Śikṣāsamuccaya*, 259, 10 sq., *Upāliparipṛcchā* in *Prasannapadā*, xii, 234, the *Pañjika*, pp. 486–93, on *Bodhicāryāvatāra*, ix, 76–8, and *Madhyamakāvatāra*, pp. 9–11, *Muséon*, 1907, pp. 258–60. These passages form the context into which section I of the *Hṛdaya* is to be placed, and taken together they form an illuminating commentary to it.

[3] S: Saptasu, bdun-po 'di-dag-la brtson; Gilgit P: sa ābhi daśabhiḥ śūnyatābhiḥ.

[4] S+ saptabhi, bdun-po.

hetoḥ? tathā hi na sa rūpaṁ . . . yuktam iti vā ayuktam iti vā samanupaśyati. iti duḥkha-satya-avavādaḥ.

The truth of ill thus means[1] that in their essential being the skandhas, considered as a result of craving and as essentially ill, are identical with emptiness. In actual reality, the fact of ill cannot maintain itself against the fact of emptiness.[2]

From the printed text of the *Pañcaviṁśati* it appears that the *fourth truth*, of the Path, is not treated in this passage, and *N. Dutt*[3] is explicit in drawing this conclusion. *Haribhadra*, however, in the *Abhisamayālaṅkārālokā*[4] takes it that the sentences following *iti nirodha-satya-avavādaḥ*[5] do not treat of the *Buddha-ratna*, as the printed text suggests, but of the Path. Section V of the *Hṛdaya* is, however, not based on that passage. The reason may be that the tradition on the attribution of this passage was somewhat confused, and also that the account of the Path given there did not go to the bottom of the question, and lost itself in comparative side-issues. We have to look for the source of Section V elsewhere.

The end of the first chapter of the *Aṣṭasahasrikā*(=A) is devoted to a long argument, which according to *Haribhadra* deals with *niryāṇa*, going forth, on the last three stages of a Bodhisattva's career.[6] The authors of the *Prajñāpāramitā sūtras* seem to have been aware that they deal there with the

[1] *Abhisamayālaṅkārālokā*, p. 32: *duḥkhe phala-bhūta-rūpādi-śūnyatā prajñāpāramitāyos tathatā rūpatvād aikātmyam iti.*

[2] *Madhyamaka-kārikā*, xxiv, 21: *anityam uktaṁ duhkham hi tat svābhāvye na vidyate. Prasannapadā*, xii, p. 234. *tasmāt svabhāvato na santi duḥkhādīnīty avasīyate. atha viparyāsa-mātra-labdhātmasattākāyā duḥkhādi.*

[3] *Aspects of Mahāyāna Buddhism, etc.*, 1930, p. 228, "as the mārga has no place in this interpretation of the āryasatyas, the Prajñāpāramitā omits it."

[4] Ed. *Wogihara*, 1935, p. 32. See: *The Large Sutra on Perfect Wisdom*, I, 1961, pp. 28–9.

[5] I.e. P 47, 8–49, 10.

[6] *Kārikā*, i, 72, 73 . . . *niryāṇaṁ prāpti-laksanaṁ/sarvākārajñatāyāṁ ca niryāṇaṁ mārga-gocaraṁ/niryāṇa-pratipaj jñeyā seyam aṣṭavidhātmikā*. Cf. E. Obermiller, *Analysis of the Abhisamayālaṅkārālokā*, 1936, pp. 185 sq. *Niryāṇa* is, in the *Abhidharma* tradition, one of the four synonyms of *mārga*, cf. *Abhidharmakośa*, vii, 13, p. 32: 4. *nairyāṇika—atyantaṁ niryāṇāya prabhavati* (*Vyākhyā*, p. 626, 26), sortie définitive, parce qu'il faut passer au delà d'une manière définitive. Also *Paṭisambhidamaggā*, i, 118.

very core of their teaching, and each successive version labours to bring out the idea more clearly. The *Śatasāhasrikā* remodels the account of the *Aṣṭa* to a greater extent than it usually does, and the *Pañcaviṁśati*, what is still more unusual, has recast it again, and made some additions of its own.[1]

In its Section V the *Hṛdaya* at first follows step by step the argument of the larger *Prajñāpāramitā sūtras*, which thus provide an excellent commentary to its somewhat cryptic brevity.

1. First, there is no attainment in actual fact. Attainment implies *abhinirvṛtti* and duality, and neither of these exists in reality.[2]

2. Secondly, there is no desire, on the part of the Bodhisattva, for any attainment. The argument begins with a definition of the Bodhisattva, and proceeds to show that he does not *wish* for an attainment.[3]

3. Then follows a discussion on "relying on".[4]

4. Then, corresponding to *Hṛdaya* no. 40, *viharati*, comes the point that *ayaṃ bodhisattvo mahāsattvo viharaty anena prajñāpāramitā-vihāreṇa*.

5. Here the literal correspondence breaks down, and the *Hṛdaya* employs terms not directly used in the larger account. The larger *sūtras* proceed to discuss the dialectics of a bodhisattva's mental activity (*manasikāra*), which, if *Haribhadra's* interpretation[5] can be trusted, is very much akin to what is said

[1] P 265, 6–22, is absent in Ś xiii, and so is P 266, 5–21.—The only other substantial addition to the *Śatas.*, in the printed portion of the *Pañcav.*, is on pp. 149, 14–150, 16, where it is due to a desire to maintain a scheme which cannot be read into the existing *Śatas.* text.

[2] *Haribhadra*, i, 10, 6, *prāpti-niryāṇam* = A I, 24, 16–27, 6 = P 242, 13–256, 9 = S xiii, 1635, 13 sq. MS. Cambridge Add 1630, to fol. 98.

[3] *Haribhadra*, i, 10, 7, *sarvākārajñatā-niryāṇam* = A 27, 7–31, 9 = P 256, 7–263, 17 = Ś MS. fol. 98–137.—P 260: *Subhūti: na-aham anutpannasya dharmasya prāptim icchāmi, na-apy abhisamayaṁ.*

[4] *Haribhadra*, i. 10, 8, *mārga-niryāṇam* for (3) to (5) = A I, 31, 10–32 = P 263, 18–269, 6 = Ś MS fol. 137*b*–144*b*.—*Aṣṭa*, p. 31. *prajñāpāramitaiva sārva-yānikī sarva-dharma-aniśritatayā sarva-dharma-aniśritā pāramitā ca.*

[5] *Aṣṭa*, 31, 18. *Abhisamayālaṅkārāloka*, p. 125: e.g. *nanu manaskāraś cetasa ābhoga ālambane citta-dhārana-karmakaḥ. prajñāpāramitā-vihāraś ca tad-viparita-svabhāva.* Cf. also to A 32, 7, cf. p. 127, 26, *manasikāreṇa aviparyāsa pravṛttatvād.* The trembling is alluded to in *Aṣṭa*, p. 31, 15–16.

in the remainder of Section V. It would take too long to show this in detail.

In any case, the terms used in the second part of Section V are closely connected with *mārga*. That is obviously so with *niṣṭhā* and *nirvāṇa*. It is, however, perhaps worth mentioning that the cognition of the uncovered thought, of the *cittaṁ na-āvaraṇaiḥ samyuktaṁ na visamyuktam*, is placed by the *Abhisamayālaṅkāra* under *mārga-satya*,[1] and that *pratipatti*, the third *ākāra* (mode, aspect) of *mārga*, is defined as *cittasya-aviparyāsa-pratipādana*.[2]

At first sight one would be inclined to think that Section VII, the passage dealing with the perfection of wisdom as a mantra, is a later addition, due to the influence of *Tantrism*. One must, however, bear in mind that we can trace in the *Niddesa* and in the *Pali* commentaries an old tradition, according to which *paññā* is called *mantā*, a term understood there as the feminine of *manto*, *mantra*.[3] Then there is the term *vidyā*. In the *dhamma-cakka-ppavattana-vaggo* of the *Saṁyutta Nikāya*, which, as we will see, embodies some of the traditions forming the background of the *Hṛdaya*, *vijjā* is equated with a knowledge of the four Truths.[4] In other contexts, however, the term shades off into meaning a kind of secret, mysterious lore of magical potency which can be compresssed into a magical formula, a spell. What is really new in *Tantrism* is merely the stress laid on the belief that all the means of salvation can be compressed into the words of a short formula.[5]

The *Śatasahasrikā*, in chap. xix,[6] gives a close parallel to the beginning of Section VII. The only difference is that the term *vidyā* is used instead of *mantra*. The parallel is all the more impressive, in that VII is also in the *Śatas.* coupled with VI, although VI here does not precede but follow it.[7]

[1] P 121, 5–123, 5=S 490, 14–503, 5.

[2] Ed. *Wogihara*, p. 137.

[3] *Niddesa* ii, 497. Dh-A iv, 93. Sn-A 204, 549. Vv-A 262.

[4] *SaṁyN.*, v, p. 430. *yaṁ kho bhikkhu dukkhe ñānaṁ dukkha-samudaye ñānaṁ . . . ayam vuccati bhikhhu vijjā. Ettāvatā ca vijjāgato hoti.*

[5] E.g. *Sādhanamālā*, p. 270. *ayaṃ mantrarājo buddhatvaṃ dadāti, kiṃ punar anyāḥ siddhayaḥ?*

[6] MS. Cambridge Add 1630, fol. 293*b*. Corresponds to A III, 73 sq.

[7] *Kumārajīva*, by omitting no. 52, is again nearer to the presumed original of this passage.

Śakra: mahāvidyeyaṁ bhagavan yad uta prajñāpāramitā. anuttareyaṁ vidyā bhagavan yad uta prajñāpāramitā. asamasameyaṁ vidyā bhagavan yad uta prajñāpāramitā. Tat kasya hetoḥ? tathā hi bhagavan prajñāpāramitā sarveṣāṃ kuśalānāṃ dharmānām āhārayitrī. *Bhagavān*: evam etat Kauśika evam etat. mahāvidyeyam Kauśika . . . yad uta prajñāpāramitā. Tat kasya hetoḥ? tathā hi Kauśika ye te' bhūvann atīte' dhvani tathāgatāḥ . . . te enāṁ vidyām āgamya anuttarāṃ samyaksambodhim abhisambuddhāḥ. ye 'pi te bhaviṣyanty anāgate . . . ye 'pi te etarhi daśadig lokadhātuṣu tathāgatāḥ . . . tiṣṭhanti dhriyante yāpayanti, te 'py enāṁ vidyām āgamya anuttarām samyaksambodhim abhisambuddhāḥ.[1]

This statement according to which the perfection of wisdom is a *vidyā*, and, as it were, the mother of the Tathagatas, occurs with slight variations once more in the same chapter of the *Aṣṭasahasrikā*. The other passage[2] contains the parallel to no. 56 of the *Hṛdaya*.

[1] Here again there is an allusion to the four Truths in that the second part of the quotation is modelled on the classical formula, which, in the *Sacca-Samyutta* (*Samy. N.*, v, pp. 433–4) runs as follows: *ye hi keci bhikkhave atītam addhānam arahanto sammā-sambuddhā yathābhūtam abhisambujjhimsu, sabbe te cattāri ariyasaccāni yathābhūtam abhisambujjhimsu . . . anāgatam addhānam . . . etarhi. . . .*—Each branch of Buddhist thought rephrased this formula according to its needs. The *Mantrayāna*, for instance, in *Saṅ hyaṅ Kamahāyānan*, v. 3, says of the Buddhas of the past, present, and future:

> *taiś ca sarvair imaṁ vajran*
> *jñatvā mantravidhiṃ param*
> *prāptā sarvajñatā vīraih*
> *bodhimūle hy alakṣaṇā.*

The thought itself forms an essential part of the tradition on the first turning of the wheel of the law, cf. e.g. *Lal. Vist.*, xxvi, p. 418 (=*Samy.N.*, v, p. 422): *iti hi bhikṣavo yāvad eva me eṣu caturṣv āryasatyeṣu yoniśo manasikurvato evaṁ triparivartaṁ dvādasākāraṁ jñāna-darśanam utpadyate na tāvad ahaṃ bhikṣavo 'nuttarāṁ samyaksaṁbodhim abhisambuddho'smi iti pratyajñāsiṣaṁ, na ca me jñāna-darsana utpadyate, yataś ca me bhikṣava eṣu caturṣv āryasatyeṣv . . . jñāna-darśan utpannaṁ, akopyā ca me cetovimuktiḥ prajñā-vimuktiś ca sākṣātkṛtā. 'haṃ bhikṣavo 'nuttarāṁ samyaksaṁbodhim abhisaṁbuddho'sm pratyajñāsiṣam.*

[2] The other passage is A III, 54–5 = S xviii, fol. 280*a*–81*b*.

We have thus been able to trace roughly nine-tenths of the *Hṛdaya* to the larger *Prajñāpāramitā* sūtras. We can, I think, draw the conclusion that the *Hṛdaya* was originally intended as a restatement, for beginners,[1] of the four holy Truths,[2] followed by a few remarks on the method of bearing this teaching in mind and on the spiritual advantages of following it.

This analysis permits us to see the *Hṛdaya* in its historical perspective. It is the *dharma-cakra-pravartana-sūtra* of the new dispensation. It is the result of eight hundred years of continuous meditation on the tradition concerning the first turning of the wheel of the law. In the literature of the second turning of the wheel of the law[3] the *Hṛdaya* is meant to occupy the same central and fundamental position which the *dharma-cakra-pravartana-sūtra* occupies in the scriptures of the first turning.[4]

The *Prajñāpāramitā* texts are so elusive to our understanding, because they are full of hidden hints, allusions, and indirect

[1] The connotations of *avavāda* can be gathered from *Sūtrālaṁkāra*, ch. xiv, and from *Buddhaghosa's* definition, *Samantapāsādikā*, v. p. 982: *api ca otiṅṅe vā anotinne vā paṭhama-vacanam ovādo, punapunnam vacanam anusāsanī ti*.

[2] There are other instances of a *Mahāyānistic* reinterpretation of the four Truths. Cf. the *Dhyayitamusti sūtra*, quoted in *Prasannapadā*, p. 298, cf. Prasannapadā, ch. 24. *Lankavatāra sūtra*, p. 299, v. 260, is short enough to be quoted: *cittasya duḥkha satyaṁ samudayo jñānā-gocaraḥ/ dve satye buddhabhūmiśca prajñā yatra pravartate*.

[3] *Aṣṭa*, ix, p. 203, states expressly: *dvitīyaṃ batedaṃ dharmacakrapravartanaṁ Jambūdvīpe paśyāma iti*.

[4] The *Hṛdaya* abounds in allusions to the traditions as laid down in various *dharma-cakra-pravartana sūtras*. In the *dhamma-cakka-* [illegible]*ana vaggo* of *Samyutta Nikāya* (preserved also in *Tibetan* mdo [illegible]nd in *Chinese* T 109), we have first a statement of the four [illegible] followed (p. 426) by a passage on *dhāraṇa* (equivalent to *mantra*), [illegible]rning that no other truth of ill, etc., is possible. The end of the [illegible]milar to *Hṛdaya* no. 57: (p. 430) *idaṁ dukkhan ti bhikkhave* [illegible]*ccam, satyam*) *etam avitatham etan anaññatatham etam* [illegible]o *amithyatvāt*). *Śāriputra's* position in the *Hṛdaya* gains [illegible]tradition common to all schools that *Śāriputra* alone [illegible] the wheel of the law after the *Tathāgata* (e.g. Sn 557; [illegible]: Divy. 394), and from the statement in the *Sacca-* [illegible]*ajjhima Nikāya* 141: *Sāriputto, bhikkhave, pahoti* [illegible]*vena ācikkhitum*, etc. But it would be tedious to [illegible] to follow up this suggestion will find a list of [illegible]*harma-cakra-pravartana-sūtra* in E. Wald- [illegible]54.

references to the pre-existing body of scriptures and traditions circulating in the memory of the Buddhist community at the time. They are more often than not an echo of older sayings. Without the relation to the older sayings they lose most of their point. We at present have to reconstruct laboriously what seemed a matter of course 1,500 years ago.

The Composition of the Aṣṭasāhasrikā Prajñāpāramitā

The *Aṣṭasāhasrikā prajñāpāramitā*, like many other Oriental books, is a collective work which has been subjected to additions and alterations in the course of the centuries, to suit the tastes of successive generations. In this respect it does not differ from the *Mahāvastu*, the *Lalitavistara*, the *Saddharmapuṇḍarīka*, the *Suvarṇaprabhāsa*, etc., which have all been slowly built up over a long period. If the historical investigation of the doctrinal development within the Mahāyāna is to make any progress, we must learn to distinguish between the different layers in these texts. Some work has been done already on the *Saddharmapuṇḍarīka*,[1] the *Samādhirāja*,[2] the *Suvarṇaprabhāsa*,[3] and the *Kāraṇḍavyūha*.[4] Without hoping to exhaust the subject, I intend to point out in this article the most obvious accretions to the basic original text of the *Aṣṭa*. This, in its turn, must have grown gradually, but in the present state of our knowledge we cannot, I think, trace out its growth. In any case, such analytical studies of ancient writings are tedious to compose and unattractive to read, and when carried too far they threaten to shatter and pulverize the very text which they set out to examine, as we have seen in the case of Homer and the New Testament.

In addition to the text of the *Aṣṭa*° itself, we have at our disposal two other sources for the examination of this problem: the early Chinese translations and the *Ratnaguṇasaṃcayagāthā* (=*Rgs*). The earliest Chinese translation, by Chih-lu-chia-ch'an (*Lokakṣema*?) goes back to A.D. 180, and that of Chih-ch'ien to A.D. 225. The chapter headings of these two

[1] By H. Kern and W. Soothill in the Introductions to their translations, 1884 and 1930. There is also a Japanese study by K. Fuse, mentioned in *Bibliographie Bouddhique*, ii, 1929–30, no. 136.

[2] Cf. N. Dutt, *Gilgit Manuscripts*, ii, 1941.

[3] Cf. J. Nobel's edition, 1937.

[4] Cf. M.-Th. de Mallmann, *Introduction a l'étude d'Avalokiteśvara*, 1948, pp. 39–47.

versions seem to suggest that by *c.* A.D. 150 the text to the *Aṣṭa°* was constituted roughly as it is to-day. I have been unable to consult these old translations in any detail, and it must be left to someone else, better qualified, to compare the Chinese versions with our Sanskrit text, and to record the passages which they lack. The *Ratnaguṇasaṃcayagāthā* are a collection of 302 *Gāthās*, in Buddhist Sanskrit, which reproduce a substantial part of the text of the *Aṣṭa°*. It is well known that the early Mahāyāna *Sūtras* generally expound each topic twice, once in prose and once in verse. In the case of the *Aṣṭa°* the verses seem to have been taken out and made into a separate book, which also recurs as chap. 84 of the Tibetan recension of the *Aṣṭādaśasāhasrikā* (=*Ad*). The original text of the *Rgs* seems to have perished. The existing text, printed by E. Obermiller,[1] has been rearranged by Haribhadra (*c.* A.D. 800) so as to make it correspond to the present chapter division of the *Aṣṭa°*. Its value for chronological and historical studies is thereby greatly diminished, and we cannot be certain that Haribhadra did not add, omit, or alter occasional verses.

We have thus three landmarks in the history of the *Aṣṭa°*: 1. The *Abhisamayālaṅkārāloka* of Haribhadra, *c.* 800, which comments on a text identical with our present one, which in its turn is attested by manuscripts from *c.* A.D. 1000 onwards. 2. The text of the earliest Chinese translation, *c.* A.D. 150. 3. The text summarized by the *Gāthās* of *Rgs*. In its present shape the *Rgs* dates from A.D. 800, but large portions of it may well go back to before 50 B.C. I will in this article mainly rely on the internal evidence of the text of the *Aṣṭa°*, supported by the more obvious inferences that can be drawn from *Rgs*.

I

First of all, it is obvious that chaps. 29 to 31 are later than the remainder of the *Aṣṭa°*, both on external and internal grounds. The verses which our *Rgs* gives under chaps. 29 to 31 do not correspond at all to the text of the *Aṣṭa°*. The *Rgs* has filled the gap with a short treatise on the five perfections, beginning with the *dhyāna-pāramitā*. The *Abhisamayālaṅkāra* makes no attempt to fit chaps. 29 to 31 into its scheme. It is true that

[1] ***Bibliotheca Buddhica*, 1937. Reprinted 1960 with Indices.**

Haribhadra's *Āloka* seems to correlate chap. 29 with the end of the fifth, and with the sixth to eighth *abhisamaya.*[1] In actual fact, the correlation is quite superficial, and was obviously never intended by the author of the *Abhisamayālaṅkāra*, which is based on the *Pañcaviṃśatisāhasrikā* (=*P*). The last items of the fifth *abhisamaya*, as well as the sixth to eighth *abhisamaya*, sum up a part of the *Pañcaviṃśati* to which there is no counterpart at all in the *Aṣṭa*°.[2]

Chapter 29 is an independent essay in the form of a litany. Three other litanies have been incorporated into our text of the *Aṣṭa*°, at vii, 170–1, ix, 205–7, and xxxi, 525–6. In *Rgs* none of them is even alluded to. Chapter 29 is absent in all the more extensive recensions of the *Prajñāpāramitā*, i.e. in *S*, *P*, and *Ad*, which in general follow the *Aṣṭa*° fairly closely.

Chapters 30 and 31 give the story, carried on into the first page of chap. 32, of the Bodhisattva *Sadāprarudita* ("Everweeping"), who went out to seek for perfect wisdom, and who was willing to sacrifice everything to gain it. The almost turgid devotionalism of these chapters is very unlike the lucid rationality which marks the sober and highly intellectual discussions between the Lord and his disciples in the first chapter of the *Aṣṭa*°. The story of *Sadāprarudita* serves the purposes of propaganda and edification. Its authors wished to inspire devotion to the perfection of wisdom and to show that inability to understand it is due to the unworthiness of those who are unwilling to make the necessary self-sacrifices.

The somewhat abstract and unfactual text of the *Aṣṭa*° is normally devoid of data which are even roughly datable. At first sight one is tempted to assign chap. 30 to the first century of the Christian era on the basis of a curious passage in chap. 30, p. 507, 12–18, which offers a striking parallel to a passage in the Revelation of St. John (v, 1). I give the two passages one after the other:

Sadāprarudita: kvāsau Kauśika prajñāpāramitā yā bodhisattvānāṃ mahāsattvānām mātā pariṇāyikā?

Śakra āha: eṣā kulaputra-*asya kūṭāgārasya madhye* suvarṇapaṭṭeṣu vilīnena vaiḍūryeṇa *likhitvā* āryeṇa Dharmodgatena

[1] Pp. 893–926.

[2] I.e. folios 465 to 593 of P., or chaps. 53 to 73 of Śatasāhasrikā (=*S*).

bodhisattvena mahāsattvena *saptabhir mudrābhir mudrayitvā* sthāpitā sā na sukarāsmābhis tava darśayitum.

> καὶ εἶδον ἐπὶ τὴν δεξιάν τοῦ καθημένου ἐπὶ τοῦ θρόνου βιβλίον γεγραμμένον ἔσωθεν καὶ ἔξωθεν, κατεσφραγισμένον σφραγῖσιν ἑπτά.

Sadāprarudita : Where is this perfection of wisdom which is the mother and guide of the Bodhisattvas, the great beings?

Śakra: It has, son of good family, been placed by the holy Dharmodgata, the Bodhisattva, the great being, in the middle of this pointed tower, after he had written it on golden tablets with melted Vaidūrya, and sealed it with seven seals. We cannot easily show it to you.

> And I saw lying in the right hand of Him a book written within and without closely sealed with seven seals.

The parallelism between *Aṣṭa*° and Revelation is not confined to this one passage. It extends over the entire context. Not to mention that *sadā prarudita* means "Ever-weeping", and that St. John in v, 4, "weeps bitterly", the reason for introducing the book with the seven seals is the same in both cases. Revelation v, 2, asks who is worthy to open the book and to break its seals. The answer is that it is the Lamb alone, slaughtered in sacrifice (v, 9). In the same way, chaps. 30 and 31 of the *Aṣṭa*° describe in detail how *Sadāprarudita* slaughtered himself in sacrifice, and how thereby he became worthy of the perfection of wisdom.

This parallel is interesting as showing a new connection between Christian and Buddhist scriptures. It does not, however, prove that chap. 30 was composed in the first century of the Christian era, especially since the passage in question is absent in the two oldest Chinese translations.[1] There are as far as I can

[1] I.e. T 224, k. 9, A.D. 180; T 225, k. 6, A.D. 225—It is found first in T 221, k. 20, p. 144b 29, A.D. 290, and then in T 223, k. 27, 420c 23–4; T 227, k. 10, 583c 5, T 220, k. 399, p. 1066a 28; and T 228, k. 25, p. 673a 23.—I owe this information to the kindness of Prof. Lamotte.

see three possibilities: either the *Aṣṭa°* borrowed from Revelation, or Revelation borrowed from the *Aṣṭa°*, or both borrow from a common source, i.e. a tradition current in mystical circles in the Mediterranean. Although the term *mudrā* plays a big part in the Buddhist Tantra, the number seven, and the whole notion of a "book with seals" has its roots rather in the Judæo-Roman than in the Indian tradition. The second possibility is therefore the most improbable. The third seems to me the one most likely. The remark about the "seven seals" may then have been incorporated into the *Aṣṭa°* at any time up to about A.D. 250.

II

A set of four additions can be inferred from the fact that the name of *Akṣobhya* occurs in them. Originally the innovations of the *Prajñāpāramitā* literature were metaphysical. Its mythology remained that of the older Buddhism. In the bulk of the *Aṣṭa°* the names of persons and deities are common to both traditions, Hīnayāna and Mahāyāna. In the later part of the *Aṣṭa°*, however, names occur—sometimes in rather an abrupt manner—which belong to a different tradition, that of the Buddha Akṣobhya. I first set out a list of the proper names belonging to the cycle of Akṣobhya, as they are found in the *Aṣṭa°*:

xix,	365–9	Gaṅgādevi Bhāginī
	366–7	Akṣobhya
	366	Tārakopama kalpa
	366–9	Suvarṇapuṣpa (a Tathāgata)
xxvii,	450–2	Akṣobhya
	449, 452	Ratnaketu (a Bodhisattva)
	449	Śikhin (a Bodhisattva)
xxviii,	458	Avakīrṇakusuma (a Tathāgata)
		Tārakopama kalpa
	464*a*–5	Akṣobhya
	474	Akṣobhya
		Gandhahastin (a Bodhisattva)

An examination of these four passages will show that the text was worked over at a time when the cult of Akṣobhya came into vogue, and that a follower of Akṣobhya has inserted a number of references to him. Akṣobhya, as is well known, is a Buddha in the East, with *Abhirati* as his kingdom, or Buddha-field. He was very popular at the beginning of the Christian era, but only fragments of his legend have survived. In China he was known already in the *Han* period.[1] Even in the much later developments of the Tantra the *prajñāpāramitā* has always retained a special connection with Akṣobhya.

We must now consider these four passages one by one:

1. *The prediction of Bhāginī, A* xix 365, 7–369. The Ganges Goddess Bhāginī[2] is linked here with Akṣobhya, in whose Buddha-field she will be reborn. Her prediction to Buddahood, which is like the similar story about the daughter of Sāgara, the Nāga king, in the *Saddharmapuṇḍarīka*,[3] a concession of the Mahāyāna to women, interrupts the course of the argument. The sentence immediately preceding it runs: *tathā ca prajñāpāramitāyāṃ parijayaṃ kariṣyāmi sarva-sattvānāṃ kṛtaśo yathā prajñāpāramitāpi me tasmin samaye paripūriṃ gamiṣyatīti.* "Thus will I master the perfection of wisdom for the sake of all beings that also the perfection of wisdom shall be at that time fulfilled in me." The sentence which immediately follows on the story, i.e. xx, 370, runs: Subhūti: *prajñāpāramitāyāṃ Bhagavaṃś caratā bodhisattvena mahāsattvena kathaṃ śūnyatāyāṃ parijayaḥ kartavyaḥ kathaṃ śūnyatā-samādhiḥ samāpattavyaḥ?* "A Bodhisattva, a great being who moves in the perfection of wisdom, how should he master emptiness, how attain to the emptiness-concentration?" The joints are here still quite clearly visible. When the text was later on expanded into the *Śata°*, the pages immediately preceding the prediction of Bhāginī were completely rewritten,[4] so as to make the development of thought lead up to the story, which is absent in *Rgs.*

2. xxvii, 449, 12—453, 5, is a stereotyped passage which says that the Buddhas will praise the Bodhisattva who dwells in perfect wisdom. The references to Akṣobhya are inserted quite

[1] Cf. Hobogirin, s.v. Ashuku.

[2] Cf. A. K. Maitra, "The river goddess Gaṅgā," *Rūpam*, 6, 1921. Vogel, "Gaṅgā et Yamuna dans l'iconographie bouddhique," *Etudes Asiatiques*, 1925, ii, pp. 385–402. A. Coomaraswamy, *Yakshas*, i, 36.

[3] Ed. U. Wogihara and C. Tsuchida, 1933–5, chap. xi, pp. 226–8.

[4] Ś, MS. Cambr. Add. 1632, chap. 42, folios 97b–102a; *P*, MS. Cambr. Add. 1628, folios 400a 8–404b 4.

mechanically in three places, and they contribute nothing to the progress of the argument. The first part of the passage, 449, 12—452, 9, is not mentioned in *Rgs*. The last part of it is (452, 9–453, 5 = v, 4) but without the reference to Akṣobhya. Judging from the distorted and involved grammatical structure of the relevant sentence in *Aṣṭa*° the reference to Akṣobhya may well have been inserted later.

3. xxviii, 457–8, is a short narrative note about the prediction of *Avakīrṇakusuma* which has given the name to the chapter. That it is a later insertion is evident not only from its contents, and from its absence in *Rgs*, but also when we compare the last sentence of chap. 27 with the first sentence which follows the story. At *A*, xxvii, 456, 6–12, we read: *tasmāt tarhi Kauśika sarva-sattvānām agratām gantu-kāmena . . . kulaputreṇa vā kuladuhitrā vā anena vihāreṇa vihartavyaṃ yo'yaṃ bodhisattvānāṃ mahāsattvānāṃ prajñāpāramitāyāṃ caratāṃ viharatāṃ vihāra iti*. "Therefore, Kauśika, a son or daughter of good family who wishes to go to the highest state possible for any being . . . should live this life which is the life of Bodhisattvas, of great beings who move in the perfection of wisdom, who live in it." And then, at xxviii, 459, 1–2: *tasmāt tarhy Ānanda bodhisattvair mahāsattvair uttamena vihāreṇa vihartukāmaiḥ prajñāpāramitāvihāreṇa vihartavyaṃ*. "Therefore, Ānanda, the Bodhisattvas, the great beings who wish to live the best life, should live the life of perfect wisdom." The story breaks up the sequence of the two sentences[1].

4. xxviii, 464*a* to 474, the end of the chapter, is marked at beginning and end by a reference to Akṣobhya. The first reference occurs in the description of the magical apparition of Akṣobhya's Buddha-field (pp. 464*a*–6), which is clearly an insertion and absent from *Rgs*. The second is added quite mechanically at the end of an exposition of the advantages of perfect wisdom (pp. 471, 6–474), which is again lacking in *Rgs*.

[1] It is not easy to explain why the first sentence should be spoken to Śakra and the second to Ānanda. A solution is offered by *Rgs*, where the last verse of chap. 27 (v. 9) refers to *A* xxvii, 456, and the next verse (chap. 28, v. 1) to *A* xxviii 466, 2–9, which also follows smoothly on p. 456 and is also addressed to *Ānanda*. It may therefore be that the bulk of the whole passage from pp. 457 to 466 was added at a later time, with the exception of a reference to the *dharmakośa* (cf. *A*, p. 464, 12, and *Rgs*, chap. 28, v. 2), which would naturally be addressed to *Ānanda*.

The large *Prajñāpāramitā* has reproduced all the passages just mentioned relating to the cycle of Akṣobhya except xxviii, 474, 2–4. In addition, the same circle of devotees of Akṣobhya is responsible there for an insertion in the text which breaks the sequence of the argument at *S* 308 = *P* 91. The large *Prajñāpāramitā* does not begin immediately with the argument of the *Aṣṭa*°. It adds a long preliminary discourse on the aspects of the perfection of wisdom which are of special interest to the "Disciples". This preliminary discourse ends with the Venerable Śāriputra, and the other great disciples, exclaiming: *mahāpāramiteyaṃ Bhagavan bodhisattvānāṃ mahāsattvānāṃ yaduta prajñāpāramitā*, etc. "A great perfection of the Bodhisattvas, the great beings, O Lord, is this, i.e. the perfection of wisdom." The praise of the perfection of wisdom is then followed (at *S* 316 = *P* 95) by a short narrative, showing that the Buddhas in all directions endorse the sermon of the Buddha Śākyamuni. Now, at the beginning and end of this passage a follower of Akṣobhya has added, in the same mechanical fashion as in the *Aṣṭa*°, two propagandistic references to Akṣobhya. They are similar to the Akṣobhya passages in the *Aṣṭa*°. The same conception of *Abhirati* as the Buddha-field, and of the *Tārakopama kalpa*, the same idea that many Tathāgatas are reborn at the same time with the same name, and the same concern to find a place for women, by stating that "these 300 nuns, Ānanda, will be reborn in the 61st aeon as Tathāgatas, etc., Mahāketu by name."

III

We now come to the evidence of the *Ratnaguṇasaṃcayagāthā*. I have listed in Table 1 those arguments and passages of the *Aṣṭa*° which are absent in it. It is noteworthy that *Rgs* omits all those parts of the *Aṣṭa*° which have, on internal grounds, been suspected as later additions. In addition, a number of further passages are missing from *Rgs*. It would be rash to assume that none of them formed part of the *Aṣṭa*° at the time when the *Rgs* was composed. The omissions consist of episodes, separate arguments, and elaborations of arguments. Some of the episodes might have been considered as too insignificant,[1] and some of

[1] E.g. ii, 33–4, 41.

the elaborations as too tedious[1] for inclusion in the summary of the *Rgs*. Some of the arguments may be covered by the similes in which *Rgs* abounds. In the early chapters the verse summaries follow the text fairly closely. It is quite possible that, as the text of *Aṣṭa*° expanded, verse summaries to the new chapters were added by different authors, who were often content to pick out one sentence here and there. Moreover, the ordinary standards of literary criticism cannot be always applied, since in a *Prajñāpāramitā* text one must be prepared for a fair amount of inconsequential reasoning.

A comparison of *Aṣṭa*° and *Rgs* therefore can by itself not decide any particular issue. But in those cases where the text of the *Aṣṭa*° appears to have been recast at some time or other, the *Rgs* can often furnish important corroborative evidence. If we turn, for instance, to chaps. 8 and 9 we find large parts of them unrepresented in *Rgs*. Here the evidence of the large *Prajñāpāramitā* is curious in that the chaps. 26 to 28 of the *Śatasāhasrikā* omit most of the portions of *Aṣṭa*° which are absent in *Rgs*. Or, to take another point, chap. 13 of the *Aṣṭa*° has all the features of an independent treatise.[2] *Rgs* reproduces only one short simile,[3] which may easily have belonged to the end of chap. 12. It may be that at one time something was omitted from the *Aṣṭa*° to make room for chap. 13, as the chap. 12 of *Rgs* ends with four verses which have no counterpart in *Aṣṭa*°. These and other considerations must be left to others.

On the other hand, even the text envisaged by *Rgs* is not all of one piece. Some of it bears all the marks of later insertion. One unmistakable example is the end of *A* chap. 20, from p. 380, onwards, together with chap. 21, up to p. 395. The passage begins quite abruptly and breaks up the trend of the argument. The argumentation is laborious and fairly incoherent. The style is fumbling and clumsy and the thought mediocre. The rambling

[1] E.g. iii, 75–6, vi, 138–42.

[2] The chap. shows great similarities to chaps. 1–4 of the *Sandhinirmocana*, which also deal with the five marks of the Absolute. Cf. pp. 21 and 182 of E. Lamotte's translation, 1935.

[3] *A* 281, 8–14. *Rgs* xiii, 1:

yo eva paśyati sa paśyati sarva-dharmān
sarvān amātya kariyāti upekṣya rājā /
yāvanti Buddha-kriya dharmata srāvakānāṃ
prajñāya pāramita sarva karoti tāni / /

discourse is held together by concern with the subject of irreversibility and prediction to Buddhahood. It seems to constitute a kind of afterthought to chap. 17. The connection with chap. 17 is particularly evident in the passage xx, 383, 13–15, which sets the topic for the rest of xx and for xxi, and which repeats the formula characteristic of chap. 17, i.e. *punar aparaṃ Subhūte yair ākārair yair lingair yair nimittair avinivartanīyo bodhisattvo mahāsattvo dhārayitavyas tān ākārāṃs tāni liṅgāni tāni nimittāni deśayiṣyāmi* . . . "And again, Subhuti, the attributes, tokens and signs by which one should know the Bodhisattva, the great being, as irreversible, those attributes, tokens and signs I will demonstrate." That a complete break in the argument takes place at xx, 380, has been perceived by the *Abhisamayālaṅkāra*, which at this point starts the 5th *abhisamaya*, and by the larger recensions of the *Prajñāpāramitā*, which here begin a new chapter.[1]

IV

With the help of the foregoing analysis we can I think determine how the *Aṣṭa*° ended at a certain stage of its development. Chapters 25 to 28, incoherent as they seem at present, do,when freed of accretions, represent two different treatises, one (I) on the supreme excellence of the perfection of wisdom (marked SE in Table 2), and another (II) on the "Entrusting" of the *Sūtra* to Ānanda (marked P in Table 2).

I. A praising of the excellence of perfect wisdom would be a fitting conclusion to the work, just as in *Saddharmapuṇḍarīka* the exposition of the principal message in chap. 15 is followed, in chap. 16 to 20 by a praising of its advantages. In *Aṣṭa*°, likewise, this is the recurring theme from chap. 25 onwards. This is obvious in chap. 25, especially when we pay attention to such expressions as *sarva-sattva-sārā* on p. 426, 10, *sarva-sattvānām agratāyāṃ śikṣate* at p. 431, 15, and to the praise, in xxvi, 434–8, of the great merit of the *sattva-sārā*. At the end of chap.26 this trend of thought is interrupted by a short essay on the illusory nature of all things (pp. 438–443), which may be one of the *Sūtra's* inconsequential turns, or may have been inserted at

[1] I.e. Sanskrit *Śata*, chap. 45, Tibetan *P*, chap. 45, Tibetan *Ad*, chap. 55, *P* trsl. *Mokṣala*, chap. 62, *P*, trsl. *Kumārajīva*, chap. 61, *P*, trsl. *Hiuen tsiang*, chap. 60.

a later date.[1] Chapter 27 continues the argument when it acclaims the Bodhisattvas as "doers of what is hard" (*duṣkara-kārakā*), and expounds (pp. 444–456) the sublimity of their achievement, which it attributes to their capacity for winning complete detachment, and for practising "non-apprehension". In consequence the Bodhisattva is honoured and protected (pp. 446–9), and the Buddhas laud him because he "dwells" in perfect wisdom (pp. 449–452). Page 453 then resumes the topic of "doers of what is hard", returns to "detachment", "non-apprehension", and the "dwelling in the perfection of wisdom" and the chapter concludes with a tribute to the supreme excellence of the *prajñāpāramitā* (p. 456). After a short interruption (see above II, no. 3) the theme of supreme excellence is resumed in xxviii, 459, 1, and continued until p. 460, 14, where it gives way to the "transmission" of the perfection of wisdom to Ānanda.

II. The *Parīndanā* begins at xxviii, 460, 14, goes on to p. 464a, and is resumed again in Chapter xxxii, 527. Page 527, 15, follows logically immediately on p. 464a. In the printed editions of the *Aṣṭa°* the context of the argument has been here obscured by the omission of a palm leaf. I reproduce the missing portion of the text in an Appendix.

The authenticity of the *Sūtras* of the Great Vehicle was disputed by the followers of the old tradition, who maintained that they were "not the Buddha word but poetry made by poets".[2] Since, according to tradition, Ānanda was the repository of the Scriptures and of the *Sūtras* in particular,[3] this accusation was countered by the claim that the Buddha had entrusted the *Sūtra* in question to Ānanda. A *parīndanā* is also given in the *Saddharmapuṇḍarīka*,[4] and in *Daśabhūmika*,[5] though the

[1] The little treatise begins quite abruptly on p. 438, 16. After it, chap. 27 has first two sentences which refer back to xxvi, 434, 6, and the third, 444, 8–11, refers back and links up with xxvi, 438, 10–15, the sentence immediately preceding the suspected insertion. On the other hand, the *api* at 444, 11, refers to xxvi, 440, 17, right in the middle of the treatise. A definite decision seems at present not possible here.

[2] *naitad buddhavacanaṁ kavi-kṛtaṃ kāvyam etat. Aṣṭa°*, xvii, 328, an echo of *Saṁyutta Nikāya*, ii, 267. Cf. *A.N.*, iii, 107.

[3] E. Lamotte, *Le traité de la grande vertue de sagesse*, i, pp. 101–5, 223.

[4] Chapter 27, pp. 392–3, *anuparīndanā*.

[5] Chapter 9.

Saddharmapuṇḍarīka is entrusted not to Ānanda but to the Bodhisattvas. For the rest the situation in the *Saddharmapuṇḍarīka* is analogous to that of the *Aṣṭa*°. At the end of the prose version of chap. 20 we have a remark on the *parīndanā* of this *dharmaparyāya*,[1] and it is probable that originally chap. 27 followed immediately on chap. 20.[2]

The suggestions which I have put forward in the course of this article have dealt in the main with the latter part of the *Sūtra* as that most likely to have been remodelled in the course of time. The problems which touch on the remainder of the *Aṣṭa*° must be left to the efforts of others.

TABLE I

CORRESPONDENCE BETWEEN *Aṣṭa*° AND *Rgs*

Pages of Aṣṭa° *represented in* Rgs.	*Omissions.*[3]	*Verses of* Rgs *which do not correspond to* Aṣṭa°.
i, 1–32		
	ii, 33–4, Introduction	
ii, 34–41		
	ii, 41, Śakra's flowers	
ii, 41–9		
	iii, 50–7, 10, various guṇas, and prajñāpāramitā as a vidyā (cf. v. 5)	
iii, 57–75		
	iii, 75–80, various guṇas (75–6); episode of heretics and Māra's attack (76–80)	
iii, 80–2		
	iii, 82–92, various advantages from perfect wisdom (cf. v. 8)	
iv, 94–101		
	v, 102–112, Merit	v, vv. 2, 5–8
v, 112–13		
	v, 114–122, Merit	
v, 122–134		
vi, 135–8		
	vi, 138, 12–142, 12, Metaphysical questions on "turning over" (cf. v. 5)	
vi, 142–3		
	vi, 143, 3–150, 11, Further metaphysics (cf. v. 6)	

[1] Ed. Wogihara-Tsuchida, pp. 330–1.

[2] H. Kern, *The Saddharma puṇḍarīka*, 1909, Introduction, pp. xxxi, xi–xxii. W. E. Soothill, *The Lotus of the Wonderful Law*, 1930, p. 28.

[3] The omissions discussed in sections I and II are marked with an asterisk.

Pages of Aṣṭa° *represented in* Rgs.	*Omissions.*[1]	*Verses of* Rgs *which do not correspond to* Aṣṭa°.
vi, 150–161		
	vi, 161–9, Further elaboration of anumodanā, etc.	
	vii, 170–1, Litany	vii, v. 7
viii, 186–195		
	viii, 196–9, Like space and an echo. Conclusion	
	ix, 200, Episode of Maitreya	ix, v. 1
ix, 200–1		
	ix, 201–7, Great gain from perfect wisdom; second turning of the wheel of dharma; Litany	
	x, 208–211, 5, Past deeds account for present attitude to perfection of wisdom	
x, 211–220		
	x, 221–230, Bodhisattvas sustained by Buddhas; prediction about spread of the prajñāpāramitā; description of Bodhisattvas who in the future will study it	
xi, 232–5		
	xi, 235–8, Three similes	
xi, 239–240		
	xi, 240–2, Elaboration of Māra's deeds	
xi, 242–4		
	xi, 244–8, Elaboration of Māra's deeds	
xi, 248–252		
xii, 253–7		
	xii, 257–270, How the Tathāgata views the world	xii, vv. 6–9
	xiii, 277–281, 8, The perfection of wisdom is unthinkable, etc.; narrative	
xiii, 281, 9–14		
	xiii, 281–3, Nothing to take hold of; narrative	xiii, v. 2
xiv, 284–291		
xv, 292–305		
xvi, 306–311		
	xvi, 312–321, Perfect wisdom and skill in means; enlightenment and emptiness; the three vehicles; requisites of going forth to enlightenment	
xvi, 321, 13–322		
xvii, 323–340		
xviii, 341–351		
xix, 352–6		
	xix, 357–360, No objective support and no own-being	xix, vv. 3–5

[1] See footnote on previous page.

Pages of Aṣṭa represented in Rgs.	Omissions.[1]	Verses of Rg which do not correspond to Aṣṭa°.
xix, 361–5		
	xix, 365–9, *Prediction of Bhāginī	
xx, 370–384 xxi, 385–395 xxii, 396–405		xx, vv. 5–7, 11–16?, 17–20
	xxii, 405–9, Emptiness and growth in enlightenment	xxii, v. 6
	xxiii, 410–13, How the Bodhisattvas are superior to Śakra	xxiii, vv. 1, 3
xxiii, 413		
	xxiii, 414–15, Rewards of perfect wisdom	
xxiv, 416		xxiv, vv. 2, 6
	xxiv, 417–420, Conditions which lay a Bodhisattva open to the influence of Māra	
xxiv, 420		
	xxiv, 421–3, The Bodhisattva's right attitude to other Bodhisattvas	
xxv, 424–8		
	xxv, 428–430, Fewness of Bodhisattvas	
xxv, 430–3		
	xxvi, 434–5, 14, Śakra praises the Bodhisattvas	xxvi, vv. 2, 3
xxvi, 435–443		
	xxvii, 444–6, What is hard to do, and the Bodhisattva's courage in doing it	
xxvii, 446, 19–449, 19		
	xxvii, 449, 19–452, 9, *The Buddhas praise the Bodhisattva	xxvii, v. 8
xxvii, 452–6		
	xxviii, 457–8, *Prediction of Avakīrṇakusuma	
	xxviii, 459–464a, Praise of perfect wisdom; transmission of prajñāpāramitā to Ānanda (but cf. v. 2, which refers to both p. 464 and pp. 467–8)	
	xxviii, 464a–466, *Akṣobhya's Buddhafield	
xxviii, 466–471		
	xxviii, 471–4, *Advantages derived from perfect wisdom	
	xxix, 475–480, *Litany	vv. 1–14
	xxx, 481–511, *Sadāprarudita	vv. 1–14
	xxxi, 512–526, *Dharmodgata	vv. 1–18
	xxxii, 527–9, *End of story of Sadāprarudita; transmission to Ānanda	vv. 1–6

[1] See footnote on p. 179.

TABLE 2

THE COMPOSITION OF THE LATER PARTS OF THE *Aṣṭasāhasrikā*[1]

"Original" Sūtra	III	II	I
i–xii			
	xiii		
xiv–xviii			
xix, 352–6			
	xix, 357–360		
xix, 361–5			
		xix, 365–9	
xx, 370–380			
xx, 380–xxi, 395?			
xxii, 396–405			
	xxii, 405–9		
	xxiii, 410–413		
xxiii, 413?			
	xxiii, 414–15?		
xxiv, 416?			
	xxiv, 417–420		
xxiv, 420?			
	xxiv, 421–3		
xxv, 424–8 SE			
	xxv, 428–430 SE		
xxv, 430–3 SE			
	xxvi, 434–5 SE		
xxvi, 435–8 SE			
xxvi, 438–443?			
	xxvii, 444–6 SE		
xxvii, 446–8 SE			
		xxvii, 449–452	
xxvii, 452–6 SE			
		xxviii, 457–8	
	xxviii, 459–460 SE		
	xxviii, 460–4a P		
		xxviii, 464a–6	
xxviii, 466–471 SE			
		xxviii, 471–4	
			xxix
			xxx
			xxxi
			xxxii, 527
	xxxii, 527–9 P		

[1] Column I shows the items eliminated by section I of this article, and by *Rgs*; column II gives those which contain a reference to *Akṣobhya* and are absent in *Rgs* (see section II); column III gives those which are missing in *Rgs* from chapter 19 onwards in full. A question-mark indicates a doubt about the inclusion. For SE and P see p. 177.

Appendix

Here I reproduce the palm leaf which is missing in Mitra's edition of the *Aṣṭa*, after the Bodleian MS. Sansk. a. 7 (R), fol. 165v–166a. A large part of the passage is quoted by *Śāntideva* in *Śikṣāsamuccaya* 351, 9–352, 6. The missing passage comes between pp. 464 and 465 of Mitra's edition, and I have marked it as 464a.

sacet tvam Ānanda śrāvaka-yāni- (p. 464a) kānāṃ pudgalānāṃ śrāvaka-bhūmau dharmaṃ deśayes, tasyāṃ ca dharma-deśanāyāṃ ye tri-sāhasra-mahāsāhasre loka-dhātau sattvās te sarve arhattvaṃ sākṣātkuryus, teṣām api tvayā me śrāvakeṇa dharma-cakra-pravarttanānupravarttanato dharmaṃ deśayato śrāvaka-kṛtyaṃ na kṛtaṃ syāt. sacet punas tvam Ānanda bodhisattvasya mahāsasttvasyaikam api prajñāpāramitā-pratisaṃyuktaṃ dharma-padaṃ deśayeḥ saṃprakāśayer, evam ahaṃ tvayā śrāvakeṇa dharma-cakra-pravarttanānupravarttanato dharmaṃ deśayata ārādhitaḥ syān, na tu tayā paurvikayā dharma-deśanayā yayā te tri-sāhasra-mahāsāhasre loka-dhātau sarva-sattvā arhattvaṃ prāpitās, teṣāṃ cārhatāṃ yad dānamayaṃ puṇya-kriyā-vastu śilamayaṃ puṇyakriyāvastu bhāvanāmayaṃ puṇya-kriyā-vastu, tat kiṃ manyase Ānandāpi nu sa bahuḥ puṇya-skandhaḥ?

(Ānanda) āha: Bahu Bhagavan bahu Sugata.

Bhagavān āha: Tatas sa Ānanda śrāvaka-yānikaḥ pudgalo bahutaraṃ puṇyaṃ prasavati yo bodhisattvānāṃ mahāsattvānāṃ prajñāpāramitā-pratisaṃyuktaṃ dharmaṃ deśayati. ato' pi sa Ānanda bahutaraṃ puṇyaṃ prasavati yo bodhisattvo mahāsattvo 'parasya bodhisattvasya mahāsattvasya prajñāpāramitā-pratisaṃyuktaṃ dharmaṃ deśayati, antaśa eka-divasam api. tiṣṭhatv Ānandaika-divasam antaśaḥ purobhaktam api. tiṣṭhatv Ānanda purobhaktaṃ dharmo deśitaḥ, antaśa eka-nālikām apy eka-nālikāntaram api vā. tiṣṭhatv Ānanda eka-nālikāntaram antaśo muhūrttam api. tiṣṭhatv Ānanda muhūrttam antaśa eka-lavam api. tiṣṭhatv Ānanda ekalavam antaśa eka-kṣaṇam api. tiṣṭhatv Ānandaikakṣaṇam antaśa eka-kṣaṇa-sannipātam api. yo hy Ānanda bodhisattvo mahāsattvo 'parasya bodhisattvasya mahāsattvasyaika-kṣaṇa-lava-muhūrttam api prajñāpāramitā-pratisaṃyuktaṃ dharma-padaṃ deśayaty, ayan tato ba .aṃ puṇyaṃ prasavati. idaṃ by Ānanda tasya bodhisattvasya mahāsattvasya dharma-dānaṃ sarva-śrāvaka-pratyekabuddha-yānikānāṃ kuśala-mūlāny abhibhavati. evam Ānanda kuśala-mūla-samanvāgato bodhisattvo mahāsattvaḥ, evam etat kuśala-mūlaṃ samanvāharann, asthānam etad Ānandānavakāśo yat sa bodhisattvo mahāsattvo vivarttetānuttarāyāḥ samyaksambodheḥ, na caitat sthānaṃ vidyate.

Atha khalu Bhagavāṃs tasyāṃ velāyāṃ tathārūpaṃ ṛddhy-abhisaṃskāram abhisaṃskṛtānyathārūpeṇa sarddhy-abhisaṃskāreṇābhisaṃskṛtena tāś catasraḥ parṣado bhikṣu-bhikṣuṇy-upāsakopāsikā deva-nāga-yakṣa-gandharva-asura-garuḍa-kinnara-mahoraga-manuṣyāmanuṣyā vā, sarve te Buddhā-nubhāvenākṣobhyaṃ tathā-

(p. 465) gatam arhantaṃ samyaksambuddhaṃ paśyanti sma, etc.

A similar enumeration with *tiṭṭhatu* is found in *Dīgha Nikāya* ii, 314. For *purobhakta*, *Śikṣāsamuccaya* gives *prāgbhakta*, Tib. *sṅa-dro* "forenoon". The lists of short divisions of time in *Abhidharmakośa* iii, 179, *Divyāvadāna* 643–4, and *Mahāvyutpatti* 253 differ from the one given here. *Aṅguttara Nikāya* iv, 137, has *khaṇo*, *layo*, and *muhutto*.

Hate, Love and Perfect Wisdom

Though the teachings of the Prajñāpāramitā have on the whole been set out quite clearly, this has been done in a terminology which one has slowly to get used to. Psychological considerations may, however, give some assistance in leading on to a better understanding of these texts. This is no mere concession to the interests of the present day. Centuries ago already has the metaphysics of the *Prajñāpāramitā* been rounded off by a profound psychological system, known as the Tantra. In this article I offer two brief psychological observations.

I. The Tantric system of the Five Jinas associates the *Prajñāpāramitā* with the Buddha Akshobhya. She belongs to Akshobhya's "family", and in two Sadhanas of the *Sādhanamālā*[1] it is stated that Akshobhya should be represented on the head-dress or crown of the images representing her. The basic Prajñāpāramitā Sūtras themselves ante-date by four or six centuries the emergence of the Tantra into the light of history. In them also Akshobyha is the one figure of a Mahayana Buddha to play any substantial rôle. It is therefore permissible to ask why just this Buddha should be brought into such close contact with the Prajñāpāramitā.

Buddhist Scriptures do not aim at expounding the nature of the universe for the satisfaction of disinterested curiosity. They are medicines, antidotes to specific ills and ailments, meant to counteract faults to which we are prone, and which keep us away from true reality and from a fruitful and abundant life. Some faults are more marked in some people than in others. In the third chapter of his *Visuddhimagga*[2] Buddhaghosa describes six distinct personality types (*puggala*). They differ according to whether their conduct is dominated by greed, hate or delusion, or by the corresponding virtues of faith, intelligence or thoughtfulness (*vitakka*). Buddhaghosa gives many good observations which allow us to recognize the different

[1] No. 153. 151 cf. also No. 159.
[2] Pp. 101–110. E. Conze, *Buddhist Scriptures*, 1959, pp. 116–21.

types, and he adds some advice about the mode of life and the kind of meditation which would suit each one of them. Similarly, the Tantra has classified aspirants into five families (*kula*), of which the first three are identical with those of Buddhaghosa. In this essay I am concerned only with the first two of these, i.e. with those who "walk in greed", and those who "walk in hate"

A simple Abhidharma exercise can help to determine whether one belongs to the hate or the greed class. The mindful recollection of feelings (*vedanā*) is an elementary and valuable practice. Three kinds of feelings are distinguished—pleasant, unpleasant, and neutral. They are associated with greed, hatred, and delusion, respectively. A pleasant feeling will obviously strengthen our greed, our desire to make ourselves at home in this world, and to taste more and more of sensuous enjoyment. Just so an unpleasant feeling will strengthen our hatred, providing or registering the frustration which leads to future aggressiveness. If one now observes the feelings which occur at a given time, one can mindfully recall them by saying, "There is a pleasant feeling, beware of greed! There is an unpleasant feeling, beware of hate!", and so on, just as they come up. If this is done repeatedly, and over a number of years, some people (like the late Prof. Flugel) will find that pleasant feelings preponderate, others that unpleasant feelings greatly outnumber the pleasant ones.

The Vajrayana associates Akshobhya with the hate family, whereas Amitābha is said to "preside" over the greed family. The bhaktic trends within Buddhism centred largely on Amitābha. As friendliness, or "love", is said to have greed for its "near-enemy" (*āsanna-paccatthiko*),[1] so the faith of Bhakti is a sublimation of greed, as witness the description of the sensuous bliss and beauty of Amida's Paradise, etc. As distinct from Bhakti, the Gnosis of the Prajñāpāramitā is an antidote to hate. Buddhaghosa[2] says about the kinship between hate and wisdom (*paññā*):

"As on the unwholesome plane hatred does not cling, does not stick to its object, so wisdom on the wholesome plane. As hate

[1] *Visuddhimagga*, p. 318.
[2] *Visuddhimagga*, p. 102.

seeks for faults, even though they do not exist, so wisdom seeks for the faults that do exist. As hate leads to the rejection of beings, so wisdom to that of all conditioned things".

The Prajñāpāramitā to some extent destroys hate by refining it into universal compassion, which is the reverse of cruelty. Nietzsche stressed the essential unity of the two when he stated that "one must be both pitiful and cruel in order to be really either". The Gnosis of perfect wisdom further helps to sublimate hatred. It is the aim and purpose of hatred to smash that which offends. While "nihilism" is by no means the last word of the Prajñāpāramitā, the thorough annihilation of the world, emotional and intellectual, is an important step on the way towards winning her. In the ontology of the Prajñāpāramitā texts the entire world, all entities, whatever they are, are completely smashed and done away with, not only ground to powder, but reduced to nothingness. This is a great triumph of universal hate. If one's own self is included in the universal annihilation, it is at the same time also a triumph of the spirit.

Experience shows that the Sūtras on *Perfect Wisdom* mean very little to some people, while they strike others with the force of an overwhelming and self-evident revelation. It would be sheer vanity to invariably blame lack of response on low spiritual endowment. Even where the required degree of spiritual awareness has been reached, these Sūtras will be helpful chiefly to one type of person, i.e. to the "hate-type". Without some "discernment of spirits" one cannot determine in a given case which one of the many approaches to salvation is salutary, which one might be ineffective, or even pernicious. The above considerations may provide at least one rule which might help to guide our intuitions on the subject.

II. My second observation concerns the feminity of the Prajñāpāramitā. Feminine by the grammatical form of her name, she is explicitly called a "mother" in the Sutras themselves, and, on statues and images, the femininity of her form is rarely in doubt. To be psychologically sound, a religion should take heed of the feminine principle in our psyche, which has at least three functions to fulfil: First of all, as a representation of the mother, it helps to dissolve hindering residues of infantile conflict. J. Campbell in *The Hero with a Thousand Faces* (1949) has dealt superbly with this aspect of the problem, and I must refer my readers to his book. Secondly, incorporation of the feminine force deals with sexual incompleteness in that it completes the male by bringing his own femininity to the fore. Finally, this approach deals with sexual insufficiency in that, on a spiritual level, it satisfies the perpetual hankering after union with the sexual opposite.

Individuals, while generally male or female, are composed of a mixture of masculine and feminine elements, dispositions and attitudes. Both men and women can be more or less "masculine" or "feminine". Persons are incomplete if they try to exclude either. They must aim at a balance between the two. In the words of a psychologist[1]:

"Either principle pursued exclusively leads to death. Whoever unites them in himself has the best chance of life. This is the ultimate meaning of 'the spiritual marriage'. In this sense God is both Father and Mother, and is therefore androgynous. Love-without-Law and Law-without-Love are both false positions. The true position is Love-creating-Law and Law-revealing-Love. The monistic principle is primary, but insufficient to itself."

Where meditation is carried on by men, they must complete themselves by fostering the feminine element in their personality. They must practise passivity and a loose softness. They must learn to open freely the gates of nature, and to let the mysterious and hidden forces of this world penetrate into them, stream in and through them. When they identify themselves with the Perfection of Wisdom, they merge with the principle of Femininity (Jung's *anima*), without which they would be mutilated men. Like a woman the *Perfection of Wisdom* deserves to be courted and wooed. Meditation on her as a Goddess has the purpose of getting inside her, identifying oneself with her, becoming her, as a man wishes to merge his body with that of a woman.

Nor should the fact be overlooked that the union of the Disciple with the Perfection of Wisdom, as described in the Sūtras, bears a close resemblance to the sexual union between man and woman. This applies as well to the stages which precede enlightenment, as to the act of enlightenment itself. And this loving union in its turn, paradoxically, brings about an

[1] H. D. Jennings-White, *Guide to Mental Health*, 1939, p. 258

annihilation of the world, just as hate did. The *Brihad-aranyaka Upanishad*: expresses this idea by saying that:

"As one in the embrace of a beloved wife is unconscious of internal or external occurrences, so also the spirit who is in the embrace of the primal Self".

Buddhist tradition, of course, avoids the use of the word "Self" for the Perfection of Wisdom, or for the Absolute. In Buddhist terminology, Tillopāda says the same thing in his *Dohās*[1]: "Where the mind and emptiness enter into the bliss arising out of this communion, the objects of the senses are not perceived at all", and he adds that[2] "The mind is the Lord and emptiness is the Lady; they should always be kept united in the Innate (*Sahaja*)".

In the *Yab-yum* images of the later Tantra a sexual attitude to Prajñāpāramitā is quite explicit. Disguised by the use of ambiguous terms it was already present in the older Prajñā-pāramitā Sūtras themselves.

The physical signs of masculinity and femininity are, of course, much easier to define than the mental ones. Nevertheless, even here students of the subject have reached wide agreement. Among recent writers I must mention Robert Graves as showing great insight into these problems. It is interesting to notice that the writings on Prajñāpāramitā show many feminine features, features in which we learn to participate by their recitation, and by meditation on them: The Sūtras almost entirely rely on intuition, and attempts at reasoning are scanty, and far from conclusive. The reasoning is, indeed, apt to be decidedly inconsequential. They show some of the amoralism which later on developed into the antinomianism of the Tantra, and which did not fail to provoke protests from the more tight laced monks. The Sūtras win over by fascination, and not by compulsion. Timeless, they are not obsessed with time, but ignore it. They urge on to a contemplation of the world, and not its conquest by manipulation. They are indifferent to 'sense data' and in vain do we search through thousands of pages for one single "hard fact". And in her ultimate core the Prajñā-pāramitā is described as for ever elusive, not possessed by anyone, but absorbing all.

The dominant interests of our age are aptly summed up in

[1] No. 5. [2] No. 17.

the title of an American film which was once shown in London, i.e., they are *Flesh and Fury*. We may perhaps bring the holy doctrine nearer to the hearts of our contemporaries if we can show them that we want the same things which they want, but that we are perhaps slightly more successful in getting them.

THE PERFECTION OF WISDOM IN SEVEN HUNDRED LINES

Oṃ! Homage to the perfection of Wisdom, the Lovely, the Holy!

Thus have I heard at one time. The Lord dwelt at Śrāvastī, in the park of Anāthapiṇḍada in the Jetavana, together with a large community of monks, with a thousand monks who were Arhats and with a million Bodhisattvas, great beings who were armed with the great armour and who were all irreversible from the utmost, right and perfect enlightenment, headed by Mañjuśrī (192) the Crown Prince, Maitreya, Asangapratibhāna and Anikshiptadhura.

Thereupon Mañjuśrī, the Crown Prince, rose from his peaceful seclusion, left his own dwelling, approached the dwelling of the Tathagata, and stood outside the door, so as to behold the Tathagata, to revere and honour him. The Ven. Śāradvatīputra also left his own dwelling and approached the dwelling of the Tathagata, so as to behold the Lord, to revere and honour Him. And likewise the Ven. Pūrṇa, son of Maitrāyanī, and the Ven. Mahāmaudgalyāyana, the Ven. Mahākāsyapa, the Ven. Mahākātyāyana, the Ven. Makākausṭhila and the other great Disciples left each one their own dwelling, approached the dwelling of the Lord, and stood on one side. (193).

Thereupon *The Lord*, having noticed that the assembly of the great Disciples had approached, left his own dwelling, seated himself on one side on the seat spread outside his door, and (although he knew the answer) asked the Ven. Śāradvatīputra: Where did you come from before you came at daybreak to the door of the Tathagata's dwelling?

Śāradvatīputra: In fact, O Lord, Mañjuśrī the Crown Prince was the first to stand at the door of the Tathagata's dwelling. We came afterwards, because we loved to see you.

Thereupon *The Lord* (although he knew the answer) asked Mañjuśrī the Crown Prince: Were you, Mañjuśrī, in fact the first to stand at the door of the Tathagata's dwelling, so as to behold the Tathagata, to revere and honour him? (194)

Mañjuśrī: So it is, O Lord, so it is, O Well-Gone! I was the first to arrive here. I left my own dwelling, approached the dwelling of the Tathagata, and have stood on one side, so as to behold the Lord, to revere and honour Him. Because I will never get tired of seeing the Tathagata, revering and honouring Him. But when I approach the Tathagata so as to behold, revere and honour Him, then I do so for the sake of all beings. If, O Lord, the Tathagata should be seen, revered and honoured, he should be seen, revered and honoured just as I do see, revere and honour Him. Then the Tathagata does in fact become seen, revered and honoured. For the sake of all beings I have come to see the Tathagata. (195)

The Lord: How then, Manjusri, should the Tathagata be seen, revered and honoured?

Mañjuśrī: Through the mode of Suchness (*tathatā*) do I see the Tathagata, through the mode of non-discrimination, in the manner of non-observation. I see Him through the aspect of non-production, through the aspect of non-existence. But Suchness does not attain (enlightenment)—thus do I see the Tathagata. Suchness does not become or cease to become—thus do I see the Tathagata. Suchness does not stand at any point or spot—thus do I see the Tathagata. Suchness is not past, future or present—thus do I see the Tathagata. Suchness is not brought about by duality or non-duality—thus do I see the Tathagata. Suchness is neither defiled nor purified—thus do I see the Tathagata. Suchness is neither produced nor stopped—thus do I see the Tathagata. In this way the Tathagata is seen, revered and honoured. (196)

The Lord: When you see this, Mañjuśrī, what do you see?

Mañjuśrī: When I see this, O Lord, I do not see anything, neither the production of a dharma nor its stopping.

Śāradvatīputra: When, Mañjuśrī, you thus see the Tathagata and honour Him, you are a doer of what is hard to do. Although you have set up the great friendliness towards all beings, yet you apprehend no being and are inclined to no being. Although you have progressed with the final Nirvana of all beings as your aim, yet there proceeds in you no inclination towards any being whatever. And although (197) you have put on the armour for the sake of all beings, you have done so by way of non-observation, etc. to : by way of non-existence.

Mañjuśrī: So it is, Rev. Śāradvatīputra, as you say. This armour has been put on so that all beings may win final Nirvana, and yet I have no apprehension of a being, no inclination towards one. This armour, Rev. Śāradvatīputra, has not been put on with the intention to effect the depletion of the world of beings, or its repletion. If, Rev. Śāradvatīputra, to put an imaginary case, in each single Buddhafield there were Buddhas and Lords countless as the sands of the Ganges, and if each single Tathagata were to abide for aeons countless as the sands of the Ganges, demonstrating Dharma night and day, and if each single Tathagata by each single demonstration of Dharma were to discipline as many beings as have been disciplined by each single demonstration of Dharma on the part of the Buddhas and Lords countless as the sands of the Ganges (198)—even if that were done one could not conceive of a depletion of the world of beings or its repletion. And why? Because of the isolatedness of beings, because of their non-beingness.

Śāradvatīputra: If, Mañjuśrī, because of the isolatedness of beings and because of their non-beingness one cannot conceive of the depletion or repletion of the world of beings, why then do you just now, having fully known enlightenment, demonstrate Dharma?

Mañjuśrī: If, Ven. Sāradvatīputra, there is absolutely no apprehension of a being, who then (199) will fully know (anything)? Or to whom will he demonstrate Dharma? Because absolutely no dharma can be apprehended.

The Lord: If, Mañjuśrī there is absolutely no apprehension of any dharma, how then can you speak meaningfully of a being? If someone were to ask you how many beings there are, what would you tell him?

Mañjuśrī: If he were to ask me that, I would tell him, "just as many as there are Buddhadharmas". If, O Lord, he would then further ask me how great the extent of the world of beings might be, I would tell him that it is as great as the extent of the Buddha's domain.

The Lord: If further again, Mañjuśrī, someone (200) were to ask you wherein the world of beings is included, what would you tell him?

Mañjuśrī: I would tell him that it is included wherein non-production and unthinkability are included.

The Lord: If, further again, Mañjuśrī, someone were to ask you whereon the world of beings is supported, what would you tell him?

Mañjuśrī: I would tell him that that which supports the element (*dhātu*) of non-production, that also supports the world (*dhātu*) of beings.

The Lord: Supported whereon do you then, Mañjuśrī, develop the perfection of wisdom at the time when you do so?

Mañjuśrī: I have no support at all at the time when I develop the perfection of wisdom. (201)

The Lord: When you are unsupported, Mañjuśrī, is that then your development of perfect wisdom?

Mañjuśrī: When one is not supported anywhere, just that, O Lord, is the development of perfect wisdom.

The Lord: At the time when you, Mañjuśrī, develop the perfection of wisdom, which wholesome root of yours does at that time accumulate or decrease?

Mañjuśrī: None, O Lord. No one can develop perfect wisdom as long as the accumulation or decrease of any dharma whatsoever happens to them. That should not be known as a development of perfect wisdom where any accumulation or decrease of any dharma whatsoever is set up. That, O Lord, (202) is a development of perfect wisdom, where one neither forsakes the dharmas of an ordinary person, nor grasps at the dharmas of a Buddha. Because the development of perfect wisdom is not set up by taking as one's basis any dharma which one could forsake or grasp at. That, O Lord, is a development of perfect wisdom when one approaches neither the faults of birth-and-death nor the virtues of Nirvana. For one does not review birth-and-death, how much less its faults! And I do not apprehend Nirvana, how much less can I see its virtues! That, O Lord, is a development of perfect wisdom, where one appropriates no dharma whatsoever, seizes on none and escapes from none. That, O Lord, is a development of perfect wisdom where one apprehends the diminution of no dharma whatsoever, nor its growth. For non-production neither diminishes nor grows. Such a (203) development is a development of perfect wisdom. That, O Lord, is a development of perfect wisdom whereby no dharma is either produced or stopped, whereby no dharma is either depleted or repleted. Moreover, that is a development of perfect wisdom, when one strives after neither unthinkable nor definitely tangible dharmas. That which is striven after does not exist, he who strives does not exist, that wherewith he strives does not exist. Such a development is set up as a development of perfect wisdom. One does not think that these dharmas are superior and that those dharmas are inferior (204), and one also does not apprehend the dharmas which might be superior or inferior. Thus giving himself up to the practice (*yoga*) of the development of perfect wisdom, a son of good family does not apprehend any dharma at all. The development of perfect wisdom, O Lord, does not imagine any dharma as superior or inferior. There is nothing superior or inferior about non-production, or about Suchness, the Reality Limit, or all dharmas. Such a development, O Lord, is a development of perfect wisdom.

The Lord: Are then again, Mañjuśrī, the Buddhadharmas not supreme?

Mañjuśrī: They are supreme (*agrā*), but just because they cannot be seized upon (*a-grāhyatvād*). Has again, O Lord, the Tathagata fully known all dharmas to be empty? (205)

The Lord: So he has, Mañjuśrī.

Mañjuśrī: But one cannot, O Lord, conceive of superiority or inferiority in emptiness?

The Lord: Well said, Mañjuśrī, well said! So it is, Mañjuśrī, as you say! Are then the Buddhadharmas not unsurpassed?

Mañjuśrī: They are unsurpassed (*anuttara*), O Lord. Because in them not even the least (*aṇu*) dharma is found nor apprehended, the Buddhadharmas have not surpassed anything. Moreover, O Lord, the development of perfect wisdom does not lead to the winning of the dharmas of a Buddha, nor to the forsaking of the dharmas of an ordinary person. It neither trains in the dharmas of a Buddha (206) nor upholds them. Such a development, O Lord, is a development of perfect wisdom. And again, O Lord, if one reflects on no dharma, nor discerns one, then that should be seen as a development of perfect wisdom.

The Lord: Do you, Mañjuśrī, reflect on the dharmas of a Buddha?

Mañjuśrī: No indeed, O Lord. If I could see the specific accomplishment of the dharmas of a Buddha, then I would reflect on them. But the development of perfect wisdom is not set up through discriminating any dharma and saying that "these are the dharmas of ordinary people, these are the dharmas of Disciples, these the dharmas of Pratyekabuddhas, these the dharmas of fully enlightened Buddhas". The son of good family who has given himself up to the Yoga of the development of perfect wisdom does just not apprehend that dharma which would allow him to describe these dharmas as dharmas of ordinary people, (207) or as dharmas of those in training, or as dharmas of the adepts, or as dharmas of fully enlightened Buddhas. Because as absolutely non-existent I do not review those dharmas. Such a development, O Lord, is a development of perfect wisdom. It does not occur, O Lord, to a son of good family who has given himself up to the Yoga of the development of perfect wisdom that "this is the world of sense-desire, this is the world of pure form, this is the formless world, etc. to: this is the world of stopping". Because, O Lord, there is not any dharma which reviews the dharma of stopping. As such a development, O Lord, should the development of perfect wisdom be known. And again, O Lord, the development of perfect wisdom neither benefits nor injures any dharma. For perfect wisdom, when developed, is not a donor of the dharmas of a Buddha, nor an eliminator of the dharmas of an ordinary person. Just that, O Lord, is the development of perfect wisdom (208) where there is neither the stopping of the dharmas of an ordinary person nor the acquisition of the dharmas of a Buddha.

The Lord: Well said, well said, Mañjuśrī, you who demonstrate this dharma which is so deep. You have set up this Seal of the Bodhisattvas, the great beings, so that the greatly conceited Disciples should wake up to what is really true, and also those among the followers of the Bodhisattva-vehicle who lean on a basis. Those sons and daughters of good family (209) who, on hearing this deep exposition of perfect wisdom, will not tremble, be frightened or terrified, are not people who have honoured just one single Buddha or have planted wholesome roots under just one single Buddha. When, on hearing this deep exposition of perfect wisdom, they will believe, and will not tremble, be frightened or terrified, then they are sure to have planted wholesome roots under more than a thousand Buddhas.

Mañjuśrī: The exposition of the perfection of wisdom becomes clearer and clearer to me.

"May it become quite clear to you, Mañjuśrī!"—said *the Lord* to Mañjuśrī.

Mañjuśrī: This development of the perfection of wisdom, O Lord, apprehends neither the stability nor the unstability of any dharma whatever. Because the notion of stability does not apply to all dharmas. (210) Just that should be known as the development of perfect wisdom that it is not set up for the sake of acquiring the support of any dharma whatever. Because all dharmas lack in objective support. Such a development is a development of perfect wisdom. Moreover, O Lord, that should be seen as a development of perfect wisdom wherein one does not come face to face even with the dharmas of the Buddhas, how much less with those of the Pratyekabuddhas, and wherein one does not come face to face with the dharmas of the Disciples, how much less with those of the ordinary people. Moreover, O Lord, that is a development of perfect wisdom where, in the course of this meditational development, one does not even discriminate the unthinkable dharmas of a Buddha as "the unthinkable dharmas of a Buddha". One should see that this development of perfect wisdom serves the non-discrimination of all dharmas on the part of the Bodhisattvas, the great beings. (211) Moreover, O Lord, that is a development of perfect wisdom where, in the course of this meditational development, one sees all dharmas as Buddhadharmas, as unthinkable dharmas, but without doing any reviewing. Those sons and daughters of good family who on hearing this exposition of perfect wisdom will believe, will not tremble, be frightened or terrified, they will be such as have honoured many hundreds of thousands of Buddhas. Moreover, O Lord, such is the development of perfect wisdom that no dharmas can defile or purify it, nor can it review any dharma. Such is the development of the perfection of wisdom. And this also, O Lord, is the development of perfect wisdom that it does not differentiate between ordinary persons, Disciples, Pratyekabuddhas, (212) and fully enlightened Buddhas. Such is the development of perfect wisdom.

The Lord: How many Tathagatas have you honoured, Mañjuśrī?

Mañjuśrī: As many as there are the mental actions which have been stopped in an illusory man.

The Lord: You have, Mañjuśrī, not yet completed the dharmas of a Buddha?

Mañjuśrī: Can one then, O Lord, possibly apprehend a dharma which has not yet completed the dharmas of a Buddha?

The Lord: Who then has got these dharmas of a Buddha? (213)

Mañjuśrī: Even in you, O Lord, these dharmas of a Buddha do not exist and cannot be apprehended, how much less in other people!

The Lord: Have you, Mañjuśrī, attained non-attachment?

Mañjuśrī: Since I have never been attached to anything, why should I any further reach out for non-attachment?

The Lord: Are you than seated on the terrace of enlightenment?

Mañjuśrī: Even the Lord is not seated on the terrace of enlightenment, how again will I be seated on it—when the Reality-limit is taken as a standard?

The Lord: "Reality-limit", Mañjuśrī, of what is that a synonym?

Mañjuśrī: It is a synonym of individuality (*satkāya*). (214)

The Lord: In what hidden sense do you say that?

Mañjuśrī: Non-existent (*asat*), O Lord, is that body (*kāyo*), not a true individual body (*satkāyo*). It neither transmigrates nor does it fail to do so. That is why that body is not a true individual body (*asatkāya*).

Śāradvatīputra: Destined for enlightenment, O Lord, will be those Bodhisattvas (215) who, on hearing this exposition of perfect wisdom, will believe, will not tremble, be frightened or terrified.

Maitreya: Quite near to enlightenment, O Lord, will be those Bodhisattvas, who, on hearing this exposition of perfect wisdom, will believe, will not tremble, be frightened or terrified. And why? Because the supreme enlightenment is nothing but the full understanding of these dharmas.

Mañjuśrī: As veritable Buddhas should one regard those Bodhisattvas who, on hearing this exposition of perfect wisdom, will believe, will not tremble, be frightened or terrified. And why? Because, in the ultimate sense of the word, "Buddha" is synonymous with non-production.

Nirālambā Bhaginī: Those Bodhisattvas who, on hearing this exposition of perfect wisdom, (216) will believe, will not tremble, be frightened, or terrified, they will not look for support in the dharmas of ordinary people, of Disciples, of Pratyekabuddhas or of fully enlightened Buddhas. And why? Because all dharmas have no objective support, since they do not exist. That is why no objective support can exist for them.

The Lord: So it is, Śāradvatīputra, so it is. Destined for enlightenment will be those sons and daughters of good family who, on hearing this exposition of perfect wisdom, will believe will not tremble, be frightened or terrified. You should know that those sons and daughters of good family are established on the irreversible stage, if, on hearing this exposition of perfect wisdom, they believe, do not tremble, are not frightened or terrified, (217) and if they accept it, placing it on their heads as a mark of respect. They will be most generous givers, perfect in morality, and endowed with the most excellent patience, vigour and trances, with the most excellent and quite unequalled wisdom, and with everything up to that cognition of the all-knowing which is possessed of the best of all modes. (218)

And *the Lord* said again to Mañjuśrī, the Crown Prince: On what grounds do you wish to fully know the utmost, right and perfect enlightenment?

Mañjuśrī: If I had set out for enlightenment, then I would wish to fully know it. But I do not strive after enlightenment, because enlightenment is just the same thing as this Mañjuśrī, the Crown Prince.

The Lord: You expound well, Mañjuśrī, these very deep stations. That is because you have performed your duties under the Jinas of the past, and have coursed for a long time in the holy life which is devoid of a basis. (219)

Mañjuśrī: If I were one who courses in the baseless, that would be equivalent to my having taken hold of a dharma.

The Lord: Do you see this my assembled company of accomplished Disciples?

Mañjuśrī: I do, O Lord.

The Lord: How do you see it?

Mañjuśrī: In such a way that I see no ordinary people, no learners, and no adepts. I do not see, and I also do not see. But I see in such a way that I see neither many nor few, neither those who are disciplined nor those who are undisciplined. (220)

Śāradvatīputra: If, Mañjuśrī, you see in such a way those who use the vehicle of the Disciples, how then do you see those who use that of the fully enlightened Buddhas?

Mañjuśrī: I do not review a dharma call "Bodhisattva", nor a dharma "set out towards enlightenment", nor a dharma called "he fully knows". It is in this fashion that I see those who use the vehicle of the fully enlightened Buddhas.

Śāradvatīputra: How then, Mañjuśrī, do you see the Tathāgata?

Mañjuśrī: Leave the great Nāga out of it, Rev. Śāradvatīputra! Do not busy yourself about the great Nāga! (221)

Śāradvatīputra: "Buddha", Mañjuśrī, of what is that a synonym?

Mañjuśrī: Of what then is the term "self" a synonym?

Śāradvatīputra: It is a synonym of non-production.

Mañjuśrī: So it is, Rev. Śāradvatīputra. The word "self' denotes the same thing which the word "Buddha" denotes. What is here called "the Buddha" is synonymous with 'the trackless' (*apada*; also: wordless). Because it cannot easily be intimated by words (*vāk*). It is not easy tó define speech (*vāk*), how much more so the Buddha! You want to know, Rev. Śāradvatīputra, how one can describe the Buddha. (222) He is the one who is not in full possession of enlightenment, who has not been produced, who will not be stopped, who is not endowed with any dharma, of whom there is not track, who is undifferentiated, and just equivalent to the trackless. Those who seek for the Tathagata should seek for the self. For "self" and "Buddha" are synonymous. Just as the self does absolutely not exist, and cannot be apprehended, so also the Buddha. As the self cannot be expressed by any dharma, so also the Buddha. One speaks of a Buddha where definitions fail. As it is not easy to understand what the word "self" means, so it is (223) also not easy to understand what the word "Buddha" means.

Śāradvatīputra: Bodhisattvas who are beginners, O Lord,

cannot understand what Mañjuśrī, the Crown Prince, has demonstrated!

Mañjuśrī: I do not, Rev. Śāradvatīputra, demonstrate in such a way that even Arhats who have done what had to be done can understand it. In fact I demonstrate in such a way that no one can discern what I have said. Because enlightenment cannot be discerned by anyone; nor can it be fully known, seen, heard, or recalled; it has not been produced or stopped, and it cannot be pointed out or described. Insofar as there is any enlightenment, it is neither existence nor non-existence. For there is nothing that should be fully known by enlightenment, nor does enlightenment fully know enlightenment. (224)

Śāradvatīputra: Has the Lord, then, not fully known the realm of Dharma?

Mañjuśrī: No, He has not. For the realm of Dharma is just the Lord. If the realm of Dharma were something that the Lord had fully known, then the realm of Non-production would be something that ought to be stopped. In fact, however, the realm of Dharma as such is enlightenment. Because there are no beings in it. Enlightenment is synonymous with the non-existence of all dharmas. It is thus that this realm of Dharma comes to be called thus. Because as the Buddha's domain all dharmas are undifferentiated. (225) The word "non-differentiation" does not intimate anything, since one cannot instruct anyone about it, either through the conditioned or the unconditioned. It carries no intimation, and that is why it is something which intimates nothing at all. For all dharmas intimate nothing at all. Because they do not manifest themselves in such a way that they could be objects of instruction.

Even[1] those who have engaged in the deadly sins have engaged in the unthinkable, and those who have engaged in the unthinkable have engaged in what is real. Because "real" is a word which implies no distinctions. Those who are endowed with the unthinkable Dharma are not destined for heaven, the states of woe, or Parinirvana. And why? Because neither the

[1] The following contains some puns based on Vinaya terms which lose their point in English. Nor am I quite sure that I have always properly understood these monastic jokes. It would, however, be undesirable to abbreviate this holy scripture to suit one's own convenience.

unthinkable nor Parinirvana has been set up for coming or going. (226) Even among those who have committed the four root-offences, the offences are quite groundless (lit. rootless). Because in non-production one can look for neither a root or a top. "A monk who has no roots" means a monk who is not established anywhere. That a dispute (*adhikaraṇam*) has arisen means that a surpassing (*adhika*) superimposition has taken place; and coursing in that surpassing superimposition one becomes worthy of the offerings of the world. Because that surpassing superimposition is self-identical. A believing monk is not worthy to enjoy gifts given in faith, whereas a non-believing monk is worthy to do so. (227) A proper monk is not worthy to enjoy those gifts, but an improper monk is worthy to do so. A monk whose clinging to existence is quite unimpaired (*asamupahatanetrīko*) is called "an Arhat whose outflows have dried up".

Śāradvatīputra: In what hidden sense, Mañjuśrī, do you say that?

Mañjuśrī: The sameness (*samatā*) is quite unimpaired, and it is the sameness which is the guide (*netrī*). Another synonym for an Arhat whose outflows have dried up is "one who has not risen above fear".

Śāradvatīputra: In what hidden sense, Mañjuśrī, do you say that? (228)

Mañjuśrī: He fears not even the least thing; what then will he rise above?

Śāradvatīputar: What then is a synonym for "the one who patiently accepts what fails to be produced"?

Mañjuśrī: He is so called because through him not even the least dharma has been produced.

Śāradvatīputra: What is a synonym for an "undisciplined monk"?

Mañjuśrī: It is the synonym of an Arhat whose outflows have dried up. (229). For what has been disciplined is the non-discipline, and not the discipline. With this hidden meaning do I say that "the monk who needs no discipline" is a synonym of an Arhat whose outflows have dried up.

Śāradvatīputra: What is a synonym for "someone who courses in the higher thought (*adhicitta*)"?

Mañjuśrī: That term is synonymous with "the ordinary people".

Śāradvatīputra: In what hidden sense, Mañjuśrī, do you say that?

Mañjuśrī: Because he is superior to them (?*adhikaroti*). (230)

Śāradvatīputra: Well said, Mañujuśri, well said! You speak like an Arhat whose outflows have dried up.

Mañjuśrī: So it is, Rev. Śāradvatīputra, as you say! And yet although I am one whose outflows (*āsrava*) have dried up, I am not an Arhat. Because my longings (*āsā*) for the level of a Disciple or Pratyekabuddha have also dried up.

The Lord: Is it possible that a Bodhisattva, seated on the terrace of enlightenment, might be incapable of fully knowing the utmost, right and perfect enlightenment?

Mañjuśrī: Yes, it is. (231) Because in enlightenment even the least (*aṇu*) dharma does not exist and cannot be apprehended. That is why it is called the utmost (*anuttara*), right and perfect enlightenment. And that enlightenment is unproduced. In it no dharma exists or can be apprehended which could be seated on the terrace of enlightenment, or which could fully know enlightenment, or by which enlightenment could be fully known, or which could rise from the terrace of enlightenment. By this method, O Lord, one can see that the Bodhisattva, when seated on the terrace of enlightenment, is incapable of fully knowing the utmost, right and perfect enlightenment.

The Lord: "Enlightenment", of what is that a synonym?

Mañjuśrī: Of the five deadly sins. Because as non-existent those five deadly sins have just the essential original nature of enlightenment, (232) and therefore this enlightenment has the essential original nature of the deadly sins. It fully knows the deadly sins, but it is not a meditational development which provides a direct intuition of all dharmas. For all dharmas are absolutely beyond all direct intuition. No one can fully know them, see, recognize or ascertain them. Such is this enlightenment. The conceited, however, put out that these dharmas can be fully known, etc. to: can be made into an object of direct intuition.

The Lord: In My presence does it occur to you, Mañjuśrī, that the Tathagata is with you?

Mañjuśrī: It does not, O Lord. And why? Because thus is Suchness (*tathatā*) (233), and as the Suchness is so is the Tathagata. For, O Lord, Suchness does not intimate the Tathagata, nor does the Tathagata intimate Suchness. And why? Because in the ultimate sense both Suchness and the Tathagata are non-existent. It does therefore not occur to me that the Tathagata is with me. On the contrary," Tathagata" is a mere designation. Which is the duality in this Tathagata with reference to which it would occur to me that the Tathagata is with me?

The Lord: Have you any uncertainties about the Tathagata?

Mañjuśrī: None indeed, O Lord! Though I would have such uncertainties if there were any accomplishment, genesis or Parinirvana of a Tathagata. (234)

The Lord: Does it not occur to you that the Tathagata has been produced?

Mañjuśrī: That might occur to me if there were a genesis of the realm of Dharma.

The Lord: Do you not firmly believe that "Buddhas and Lords countless like the sand of the Ganges have gone to Parinirvana"?

Mañjuśrī: Is it not so, O Lord, that the Buddhas and Lords have one single domain, i.e. the unthinkable domain?

The Lord: So it is Mañjuśrī?

Mañjuśrī: Is it not so that the Lord stands there just now?

The Lord: So it is, Mañjuśrī. (235)

Mañjuśrī: These Buddhas and Lords, countless like the sands of the Ganges, have therefore never entered Parinirvana. Because they have one single domain, i.e. the unthinkable domain. Unthinkability, however, is not produced or stopped. When the Lord won full enlightenment, those who will in the future be Tathagatas, Arhats and fully enlightened Buddhas have therefore also known full enlightenment. Because unthinkability is not past, future or present. Therefore, O Lord, those who form the notion that the Tathagata has been produced, or that he will go to Parinirvana, will in consequence still further whirl around in the world and stay in it, and they will thereby prolong their sojourn in the world.

The Lord: You may therefore, Mañjuśrī, announce the fact that this unthinkability of a Tathagata (236) is unthinkable and inconceivable in front of a Tathagata, or of an irreversible Bodhisattva, or of an Arhat whose outflows have dried up. Because, having heard it, they will neither sanction nor reject it. For that which they think about is unthinkable and inconceivable.

Mañjuśrī: When, O Lord, all dharmas are unthinkable and inconceivable, who will be able to do any sanctioning or rejecting?

The Lord: Just as the Tathagata, so also the ordinary people are inconceivable.

Mañjuśrī: Are the ordinary people also in just that way inconceivable?

The Lord: They are. (237) Because all that can be thought is inconceivable.

Mañjuśrī: If, just as the Tathagata, so also the ordinary people are inconceivable, because also their state, like all dharmas, is inconceivable, then those who have set out for Parinirvana must already dwell in it. Because Parinirvana and inconceivability are one and the same thing. In consequence there can be no differentiation in inconceivability. Those, O Lord, who spoke of these dharmas as dharmas of the ordinary people, and of those as the dharmas of holy men, should in fact have said: "Let us, to begin with, honour the good spiritual friend, and thereafter let us cognize, 'these are the dharmas of ordinary people and those are the dharmas of holy men'." (238)

The Lord: Do you, Mañjuśrī, look for a Tathagata who is the foremost of all beings?

Mañjuśrī: I would do so if one being could be more perfect than another.

The Lord: Do you look for a Tathagata who is endowed with unthinkable dharmas?

Mañjuśrī: I would do so if anyone could be endowed with unthinkable dharmas.

The Lord: Do you again look for Disciples who have been disciplined by the Tathagata?

Mañjuśrī: I would do so if anyone could be subjected to the discipline of the unthinkable element. The production of a Buddha has not been set up (239) by the bestowal or by the removal of anything. Because this unthinkable element is established and uncontaminated, and in it one can apprehend no differentiation between Disciples, ordinary people, and so on.

The Lord: Do you then, Mañjuśrī, not look upon the Tathagata as an unsurpassed field of merit?

Mañjuśrī: Because of his non-existence is the Tathagata a field of merit, and for that reason he is also an unsurpassed field of merit. This field of merit is unsurpassed, because it is a field of merit, and not a field of demerit. It is a field of merit in the sense that therein no dharma can reach the fullness of its perfection or wane away. (240) A seed placed into it neither grows nor diminishes.

The Lord: In what hidden sense do you say that, Mañjuśrī?

Mañjuśrī: Because, O Lord, this field is a field of merit in the sense that it is unthinkable.

Thereupon on that occasion, through the Buddha's might, the earth shook in six ways. And the thoughts of 16,000 monks were freed from the outflows without any further clinging, and 700 nuns, 300 laymen, 40,000 laywomen and 6,000 niyutas of kotis of gods of the sphere of sense-desire produced the dispassionate, unstained eye of Dharma in dharmas.

The *Ven. Ānanda* thereupon rose from his seat, (241) put his robe over one shoulder, placed his right knee on the ground, bent forth his folded hands to the Lord, and said to the Lord: "What, O Lord, is the cause, what the reason, for the manifestation in the world of this great shaking of the earth"?

The Lord: This discourse on Dharma, Ānanda, called "The Exposition of the Field of Merit" has been taught in this very place by the Buddhas and Lords of the past. That is the cause, that is the reason for the manifestation in the world of this great shaking of the earth.

Prajñā and Sophia

WORD AND WISDOM. Studies in the hypostatization of divine qualities and functions in the Ancient Near East. By Helmer Ringgren. Haken Ohlssons Boktryckeri. Lund, 1947, 234 pages.

Although *H. Ringgren's* book was written chiefly for theologians, it is invaluable to all students of Asiatic culture. *Ringgren* assumes that "monotheism is the primitive religion", and polytheism a later stage of religious development. "How then", he asks himself, "has the puzzling multitude of gods and goddesses, that we meet with in most peoples, arisen?" In "Word and Wisdom" he considers "one of the factors that have been active in this process, viz. the hypostatization of divine qualities and functions" (p. 8). In the course of his book he surveys the hypostases in the religions of ancient Egypt and Mesopotamia, among the Western Semites and ancient Jews, and in Pre-Islamic Arabia.

Whatever may be the merits of *Ringgren's* theological thesis, his long chapter on "Wisdom in the Old Testament and in Later Judaism" brings out the extraordinary fact that during the same period of time,—i.e. from ca 200 B.C. onwards—two distinct civilizations, one in the Mediterranean, the other in India, constructed a closely analogous set of ideas concerning "wisdom", each one apparently independently, from its own cultural antecedents. Not that *Ringgren*, a specialist in Near Eastern literature, is aware of this connection. His account of Jewish wisdom literature is unbiassed by any opinion about its relation to Indian thought. It may not be without interest to set out some of the parallels or coincidences which I observed between *Ringgren's* account of *Chochma* and *Sophia* (abbreviated as S.) on the one hand, and the Buddhist texts dealing with perfect wisdom, or *Prajñāpāramitā* (abbreviated as PP), on the other.

Both S and PP are feminine. S is a mother (*Ringgren* pp. 111, 124, 125), and the PP is repeatedly called the "mother" of the Buddhas and Bodhisattvas. S is equated with the law (*tōrā*) (pp.

110, 114); PP is identified with Dharma. Both have existed from all times (p. 100), and are described as extremely elusive (pp. 96, 107). They are the equivalent of God (pp. 110, 115), and of the Buddha respectively. S is a gift of God (p. 127); the PP is taught through "the Buddha's might". They are both praised by litanies, which enumerate their attributes—21 for S (p. 116), 32 for PP. S is related to the sky (p. 137), just as PP is again and again related to ether (*ākāśa*). Both dispense the waters of knowledge (p. 111, cf. 141; and *Ashta*, xix, 363), and the "food of life" (p. 141), "the food of the ambrosial (deathless) *Dharma*", as the *Pañcaśatikā* (ii, 744d) calls it. Both are connected with a tree, S with the tree of life in Paradise (p. 140), and PP with the Bodhi-tree. Both are extremely pure (pp. 112, 116 and *viśuddhi*), are compared to light (p. 116), and are called "nurse and nourisher" (p. 125, and *āhārikā*). We are urged to "lean upon" Sophia (p. 111; cf. 122), and to rely, or lean on (*āśritya*) the PP. We must accept the chastisement of S (p. 120), while the *Diamond Sūtra* tells us to allow ourselves to be "humbled, well humbled". S disappears in the chaos of the last days (p. 120), and the sutras on PP show a marked preoccupation with what they call "the future period, the last time, the last epoch, the last five hundred years, the time of the collapse of the good *Dharma*". S is of vital importance for kings and rulers (pp. 97, 141, etc.); this aspect of PP has been worked out in a special Sūtra of great renown, the *Ninnō-kyō*.

The sexual aspects of wisdom are only alluded to in the texts dealing with the PP. They come to the fore in the later development of the Buddhist *Tantra*. Just as Sophia is the *paredros* of *Jahwe*, his companion, or consort, his "darling" (Prov. 8, 30), just so in the *Tantra* Perfect Wisdom becomes the consort of *Vajradhara*, the supreme Buddha. Cults of ritual sexuality were widely practised among the populations with which the ancient Jews were in contact. Some sections of Jewry did not remain uninfluenced by such cults. We know from the *Elephantine* papyri that in the fifth century B.C. a number of Jews in the Nile delta believed that Jahwe had a wife, *Anath-Jahu*. As *Ringgren* (p. 147) and also *Rankin* (*Israel's Wisdom Literature*, pp. 229–230) point out, the notion which made Wisdom the associate of *Jahwe* partly incorporated, and partly combated such ideas of the popular imagination. In this connection

Ringgren ignores *S. H. Hooke's* valuable studies about the erotic element in ancient Judaism. As a final parallel I may mention that *Sophia* is described as suitable for sexual intercourse (p. 119, cf. 106); in the left-handed *Tantra* the girls who are used for ritual intercourse are called *Prajñā*, wisdom. In a similar spirit the Gnostic *Simon* called his "wife" *Helene* "Sophia", or "Ennoia" (=*jñāna*).

The number of parallels could easily be multiplied if one were to take into account the kindred literature of Hellenism, of Gnosticism, of Neo-Platonism. We find everywhere in the Mediterranean world at that period a fusion between the idea of wisdom and the idea of the *magna mater*, resulting in a new deity who is modelled on *Ishthar*, *Isis* and *Athene*, and who is placed by the side of the supreme male being. A study of the more philosophical authors—like *Philon* or *Proclus*—reveals a profusion of verbal coincidences with the *Prajñāpāramitā* texts. Here Sophia as the *οἰκία* (house) of the wise, there the *Prajñāpāramitā* as their *vihāra* (dwelling). The epithet *ψωσψόρος* (light-bringer) corresponds to *āloka-karī*, *ἀχράντος* (immaculate) to *anupaliptā*; etc., etc.

It cannot be the purpose of a review to try and exhaust a problem of this magnitude. Ringgren himself gives a very thorough survey of "foreign influences "on the Jewish conception of Wisdom" (pp. 1238–149), without coming to any very definite conclusion. I regretted, incidentally, that he does not discuss *Troje's* suggestion, as far back as 1925, that Sophia is derived from *Buddhi*.

In all this we may have to deal with parallel developments, under the influence of local conditions, from a general widely diffused culture pattern. Or it may, of course, be that there is some hidden rhythm in history which activates certain archetypes—as Jung would call them—at certain periods in widely distant places. All that I set out to do in this review was to remind readers that there is a problem here, which historians cannot ignore, and for which they find first-hand material in *Ringgren's* careful and painstaking survey of the facts concerning the ancient Near East.

Buddhist Philosophy and its European Parallels

The search for philosophical parallels is fraught with many pitfalls. Some parallels are fruitful and significant, others incidental and fortuitous. I now propose to discuss the European parallels to Buddhist thought in two articles, of which the first is devoted to the true, and the second to the spurious, parallels.

As for my interpretation of the basic principles of Buddhism, I have recently given it in some detail in *Buddhist Thought in India*.[1] Since my views differ to some extent from those of my predecessors, I will briefly sum them up so that the reader can see what kind of "Buddhism" I compare with European philosophy.

The basic teaching of the Buddha can be expressed in one sentence: The conditioned world as it appears to us is fundamentally and irreparably undesirable, and salvation can be found only through escape to the Unconditioned, also called "*Nirvāna*". Everything else is elaboration.

All conditioned things are marred by having three "marks," i.e. by being impermanent, "ill", and "alien to our true self".[2] Much thought has gone into determining the full meaning of those marks. "Ill", for instance, comprises not only pain and suffering, but also the unease which is nowadays known as "existential anxiety",[3] and the mark of "not-self" has given rise to interminable discussions.[4] Human beings fret against a world which is impermanent, ill, and not-self and are not content to live in it, because they believe that in the core of their

[1] *Buddhist Thought in India* (London: George Allen & Unwin Ltd., 1962). Hereafter *BThI*.

[2] *BThI*, pp. 34–43.

[3] This will be discussed on pages 237–9.

[4] About its relation to Hume's denial of a "self", see pages 239–42.

own being they are eternal, at ease, and in full control of everything.[1] This alienation of our empirical personality from our true being (i.e., from the "Tathāgata" within us[2]) is brought about by "craving".[3] If we want to return to our original state of purity, we must first regenerate ourselves by developing five cardinal virtues,[4] of which wisdom is the last and most important. After these virtues have sufficiently matured, we can slowly attempt a break-through to the Unconditioned,[5] which, through the three doors of deliverance, i.e., Emptiness, the Signless, and the Wishless,[6] leads to *Nirvāna*,[7] which is a state in which the self has become extinct, in which none of this world is any longer extant, and which therefore transcends all words and concepts.[8]

This is all quite simple to understand, though at time hard to believe. It is very much complicated, however, by being combined with an ontological theory of "*Dharma*" which requires a tremendous intellectual effort.[9] This theory distinguishes three levels of reality: 1. The one and single *Dharma*, which is the ultimate and unconditioned reality of *Nirvāṇa*. 2. A multiplicity of *dharmas*, or momentary and impersonal events, which, though illusory compared with the one single *Dharma*,[10] are more real than the things around us. 3. The things of the common-sense world, which are mere verbal constructions, in that they are combinations of *dharmas* held together by words.[11] The Buddhist "*dharma*-theory" is unique, and has no exact equivalent anywhere else.[12]

So much for the tenets of what I call "archaic" Buddhism. They were probably formulated by the time of Aśoka.[13] Two centuries later the further elaboration of these ideas led to two distinct schools, i.e., the "scholastic Hīnayāna" and the

[1] *BThI*, pp. 43–6.

[2] It is "A central peace, subsisting at the heart/Of endless agitation" (W. Wordsworth). See below, p. 221.

[3] See below, p. 223.

[4] *BThI*, pp. 47–55.

[5] *Ibid.*, pp. 56–8.

[6] *Ibid.*, pp. 59–69.

[7] *Ibid.*, pp. 69–79.

[8] The teachings of European mystics correspond to this doctrine in its general tone (see below, pp. 220–2), but only Schopenhauer matches it in many particulars (see below, pp. 222–4).

[9] *BThI*, pp. 92–106.

[10] *Ibid.*, pp. 223–5 (see below, p. 227).

[11] *Ibid.*, p. 97n.

[12] See below p. 236.

[13] 274–236 B.C.

"Mahāyāna", which, contrary to what is often said, did not significantly conflict in their doctrines but merely diverged in their range of interest. The "scholastic Hīnayāna"[1] concentrated on the conditioned *dharmas*, systematized their classification, defined more precisely their particular attributes and general marks, and worked out the relations pertaining among them.[2] The creative contributions of the Mahāyāna, on the other hand, almost exlcusively concern the Unconditioned. In particular, the notion of "Emptiness", which in "archaic" Buddhism had been one of the avenues to *Nirvāna*, was now immensely enriched.[3] It was also buttressed by a searching analysis of the "own-being" of *dharmas*,[4] using a type of logic which in Europe we would call "dialectical."[5] Equally applied to conditioned and unconditioned *dharmas*, "emptiness" led to their identification. The result is a "monistic" ontology which shows many analogies to European metaphysical systems of the same type,[6] while the descriptions of the bafflement experienced by the intellect when confronted with this one and unique Absolute resemble the position of the Greek skeptics in many ways.[7]

Of special interest for the theme of these articles is the chapter on "Tacit Assumptions",[8] in which I compare Buddhist with contemporary mentality, and try to establish that

> Buddhist thinkers made a number of tacit assumptions which are explicitly rejected by modern European philosophers. The first, common to nearly all Indian, as distinct from European, "scientific", thought treats the experiences of Yoga as the chief raw material for philosophical reflection. Secondly, all "perennial"[9] (as against "modern") philosophers, agree on the hierarchical structure of the universe, as shown in *a*) the distinction of a "triple world" and *b*) of degrees of "reality", and *c*) in the establishment of a hierarchy of insights dependent on spiritual maturity. Thirdly, all religious (as against a-religious) philosophies *a*) use "numinous" as distinct from "profane" terms, and *b*) treat revelation as the ultimate source of all valid knowledge.[10]

[1] *BThI*, pp. 119–91. [2] *Ibid.*, pp. 148–58. [3] *Ibid.*, pp. 242–9.
[4] *Ibid.*, pp. 239–41 (see below pp. 223–4).
[5] *BThI*, pp. 261–4; also below, pp. 227–8.
[6] See below, pp. 224–7. [7] See below, pp. 217–20.
[8] *BThI*, pp. 17–30. [9] For a definition, see below, pp. 213–5.
[10] *BThI*, p. 17.

This is not how everyone sees it, and the doubting reader must be referred to the arguments of my book.

The cornerstone of my interpretation of Buddhism is the conviction, shared by nearly everyone, that it is essentially a doctrine of salvation, and that all its philosophical statements are subordinate to its soteriological purpose. This implies, not only that many philosophical problems are dismissed as idle speculations,[1] but that each and every proposition must be considered in reference to its spiritual[2] intention and as a formulation of meditational experiences acquired in the course of the process of winning salvation. While I cannot imagine any scholar wishing to challenge this methodological postulate, I am aware that, next to D. T. Suzuki, I am almost alone in having applied it consistently.

Finally, any interpretation of Buddhism which goes beyond the indiscriminate accumulation of quotations, and attempts actually to understand Buddhist thought involves an element of choice, in that one has to decide which one among the numerous presentations of the Buddha's doctrine should be regarded as the most authentic. Bu-ston favours the Buddhism of the Pāla period, Frauwallner the Yogācārins, Oldenberg the Pāli Canon (minus the Abhidhamma), Stcherbatsky the scholastic Hīnayāna and the later logicians, D. T. Suzuki the early Mahāyāna and Zen, some Chinese schools the *Saddharma-puṇḍarīka*, and so on. With Prof. Murti, I regard the Mādhyamikas as representing the central tradition of Buddhism, and believe that with them Buddhist theorizing reached its full maturity. This preference colours much of what I have to say.

What, then, is the relation of these Buddhist teachings to European philosophy? From the outset, I must admit that I do not believe in a clear-cut distinction between "Eastern" and "Western" mentality. Until about 1450, as branches of the same "perennial philosophy,"[3] Indian and European philosophers disagreed less among themselves than with many of

[1] See below pp. 234–5, 242.

[2] For a definition, see below, p. 216, note 1.

[3] This term was originally invented by Catholics to describe the philosophy of St. Thomas and Aristotle. In all probability it was first used by Augustinus Steuchus, Episcopus Kisami, Bibliothecarius to Pope Paul III, in his *De perenni philosophia*, libri x, 723 pp., Basel 1542.

the later developments of European philosophy. The "perennial philosophy" is in this context defined as a doctrine which holds. 1. That as far as worth-while knowledge is concerned not all men are equal, but that there is a hierarchy of persons, some of whom, through what they are, can know much more than others. 2. That there is a hierarchy also of the levels of reality, some of which are more "real", because more exalted than others. 3. That the wise men of old have found a "wisdom" which is true, although it has no "empirical" basis in observations which can be made by everyone and everybody; and that in fact there is a rare and unordinary faculty in some of us by which we can attain direct contact with actual reality—through the *prajñā* (*pāramitā*) of the Buddhists, the *logos* of Parmenides,[1] the *sophia* of Aristotle[2] and others, Spinoza's *amor dei intellectualis*, Hegel's *Vernunft*, and so on. 4. That true teaching is based on an authority which legitimizes itself by the exemplary life and charismatic quality of its exponents.

Within the perennial philosophy Indian thought is marked off by two special features: 1. The reliance on *yoga* as providing

He states quite clearly the main presuppositions involved. The very first sentence formulates his program, i.e. *ut unum est omnium rerum principium, sic unam atque eandem de eo scientiam semper apud omnes fuisse ratio multarumque gentium ac literarum monimenta testantur*. On p. 7 and later he explains that the *Sapientia* was strongest in the beginning, when first given by God, and that later on it becomes more and more dissipated and weakened. Wherever it appears, this *sapientia*, or *veritas veniens ad homines*, agrees so much in essentials, *ut apparet necessario unam totius humani generis esse religionem*. Later on the term was adopted by Leibniz to designate his own brand of eclecticism (Lettre à Rémond, 1714, Gerhardt III 624–5), and about 1908 by Willmann in his *History of Idealism*, 3 vols. More recently it was taken over by Aldous Huxley and others, and my definition is akin to that of Ananda Coomaraswamy. A. Huxley in his famous book of 1946 envisaged only the mystical school, whereas here I include the intellectual and speculative trends, i.e., Plato and Aristotle as well as the German idealists. The only people before 1450 who are excluded are those who, like the Lokāyatikas in India, were deliberately antispiritual, but not necessarily the Epicureans who were anticlerical but no foes of a tranquil and serene life.

[1] Being for him is "one" *kata ton logon* (when seen by reason), "many" *kata tēn aisthēsin* (when seen by perception). Aristotle, *Metaphysics*, I 986^{b}33–4.

[2] In his *Metaphysics*, Aristotle has taken great pains to describe the subjective counterpart of "being as being", e.g., in Book I, 981^{b}–983^{a}.

the basic raw material of worth-while experience.[1] 2. The implicit belief in *karma* and rebirth. *Yoga*, of course, has its counterpart in the West in the spiritual and ecstatic practices of contemplatives, and belief in reincarnation is nearly world-wide,[2] though rare among philosophers accorded academic recognition.

Then, as I see it, by 1450, the East, in decline since A.D. 1,000, had fallen asleep and from thereon lived on its inherited capital, until in the end innate lethargy and aggression from the outside brought it to its present impasse. In the West, a large number of philosophers discarded the basic presuppositions of the "perennial philosophy", and developed by contrast what for want of a better term we may call a "sciential"[3] philosophy. That has the following features: 1. Natural science, particularly that dealing with inorganic matter, has a cognitive value, tells us about the actual structure of the universe, and provides the other branches of knowledge with an ideal standard in that they are the more "scientific" the more they are capable of mathematical formulation and the more they rely on repeatable and publicly verified observations. 2. No being higher than man is known to science, and man's power and convenience should be promoted at all costs. 3. The influence of spiritual and

[1] "*Notre philosophie est née de la curiosité et du besoin de savoir, d'expliquer le monde d'une façon cohérente. En Inde la philosophie est l'interpretation rationelle de l'expérience mystique.*" So Constantin Regamey, on page 251 of what is one of the most notable contributions so far made to comparative philosophy, i.e., "Tendences et méthodes de la philosophie indienne comparées à celles de la philosophie occidentale," *Revue de Théologie et de Philosophie*, IV (1951), 245–62. Regamey also shows how this difference in the *point de départ* leads to a radical divergence in the criteria of absolute truth.

[2] Joseph Head and S. L. Cranson, eds., *Reincarnation: An East-West Anthology* (New York: The Julian Press, Inc., 1961).

[3] The opponents of the perennial philosophy prefer to describe themselves as "scientific." There can be nothing more unscientific, however, than the drawing of extravagant and presumptuous conclusions about the mind, soul, and spirit of man, and about his destiny and the purpose of his life, from a few observations about the expansion of gases, the distribution of moths, and the reflections of the celestial bodies in little pieces of glass. If I were reduced to that part of myself which can be seen in bits of glass, I would certainly feel that most of my being was omitted. Why should this not be true also of other things apart from my own dear self?

magical forces, as well as life after death may safely be disregarded, because unproven by scientific methods. 4. In consequence, "life" means "man's" life in this world, and the task is to ameliorate this life by a social "technique" in harmony with the "welfare" or "will" of "the people". Buddhists must view all these tenets with the utmost distaste.

"Sciential" philosophy is an ideology which corresponds to a technological civilization. It arises in its purity only to the extent that its social substratum has freed itself from all pre-industrial influences, and in the end it must lead to the elimination of even the last traces of what could properly be called "philosophy" in the original sense of "love of wisdom". For centuries it existed only blended with elements from the traditional "perennial" philosophy. As philosophies, both the "perennial" and the "sciential" systems possess some degree of intellectuality, and up to a point they both use reasoning. But, considered in their purity, as ideal types, they differ in that the first is motivated by mans' spiritual[1] needs, and aims at his salvation from the world and its ways, whereas the second is motivated by his utilitarian needs, aims at his conquest of the world, and is therefore greatly concerned with the natural and social sciences. Between the two extremes there are, of course, numerous intermediary stages. They depend to some extent on the quality of the spirituality behind them, which is very high, say, in Buddhism, slightly lower in Plato and Aristotle, and still quite marked in such men as Spinoza, Leibniz, Berkeley, Kant, Goethe, Hegel, and Bergson. The general trend, however, has been a continuous loss of spiritual substance between 1450 and 1960, based on an increasing forgetfulness of age-old traditions, an increasing unawareness of

[1] I have defined the word "spiritual" in my *Buddhism* (3rd ed., Oxford: Bruno Cassirer, 1957) on page 11 as involving 1. The devaluation of sensory experience, 2. The renunciation of belongings; and 3. Impartiality towards other persons. The quintessence of the spiritual life, shorn of its usual accretions, was admirably formulated by Petrus Damiani in the eleventh century in two exceedingly fine poems which have recently been reprinted in F. J. E. Raby, ed., *The Oxford Book of Medieval Latin Verse* (Oxford: Clarendon Press, 1959), pp. 185–9. The second has also been translated into English in Frederick Brittain, ed., *The Penguin Book of Latin Verse* (Harmondsworth, England: Penguin Books, Ltd., 1962), pp. 176–80.

spiritual practices, and an increasing indifference to the spiritual life by the classes which dominate society.

Leaving aside the relative merits of the "perennial" and the "sciential" approaches to philosophy, all I want to establish at present is their mutual incompatibility, which is borne out by their mutual hostility. Our "sciential" philosophers are well aware of this. We need only peruse the writings of empiricists, logical positivists, and linguistic analysts, and it will become obvious that the animosity displayed toward a philosopher is almost a measure of his concern for spirituality.[1] And, in a way, the moderns are quite right. For "perennial" and "sciential" philosophies represent two qualitatively different kinds of thinking which have almost nothing in common, except perhaps for a certain degree of respect for rationality. Our contemporaries continually assure us that the spiritual philosophers of the past are not "philosophers" at all, but dreamers, mystics, poets, and so on. All we can conclude from this is that the word "philosophy" is being used in two quite disparate senses: 1. As the pursuit of "wisdom". 2. As a "rigorous" academic exercise without much ostensible purpose. The "wisdom" meant here is compounded of knowledge and a "good life", and to it apply the words of *Proverbs*: "Blessed is the man who has found wisdom. Her ways are good ways, and all her paths are peaceful. She is a tree of life to all that lay hold upon her."[2] It is not easy to see how such words could be used of "philosophy" in the second sense.

Having stated the general principles on which, I believe, the comparison of Buddhist and European thought must be based, I now speak of the only three currents of European philosophy which can significantly be compared with Buddhism, i.e., 1. The Greek Skeptics. 2. The wisdom-seeking mystics. 3. The monists and dialecticians.

1. The European system nearest to the Mādhyamikas is that of the Greek Skeptics. In my *Buddhism*,[3] I have shown their

[1] To mention just two easily accessible sources: In Bertrand Russell's *A History of Western Philosophy* (New York: Simon and Schuster, 1945) this attitude is expressed with some urbanity, and in J. O. Urmson, ed., *The Concise Encyclopedia of Western Philosophy* (London: Hutchinson, 1960) with blunt rudeness (e.g., the article on Schopenhauer is sheer personal abuse).

[2] Cf. III: 13–8.

[3] *Op. cit.*, pp. 140–2.

close similarity, both in intention and structure. They also agree in that the history of skepticism exhibits the same tendency to deviate into a purely theoretical intellectualism which has continually threatened the integrity of Buddhist thought. Greek Skepticism went through four stages, which R. G. Bury[1] has called the practical, the critical, the dialectical, and the empirical. The parallel with Buddhism is closest in the first stage, i.e., with Pyrrho (360–275 B.C.). In the last, with Sextus Empiricus (A.D. 160–210), it is barely perceptible. Indeed, taking the later developments as his norm, Bury can affirm that Pyrrho "was probably not at all a full-blown Sceptic, but rather a moralist of an austere and ascetic type who cultivated insensibility to externals and superiority to environment."[2] It was only in the New Academy, with Arcesilas (315–241 B.C.), that Skepticism "ceased to be purely practical and became mainly theoretical."[3] "Thus, while Pyrrho had renounced and Timon flouted the Dogmatists, Arcesilas started the practice of refuting them scientifically and systematically, and earned thereby the abuse of Timon for his lapse from pure Pyrrhonism."[4] In fact, when we read Sextus Empiricus, we find that, although some of the original message has remained intact,[5] it has been overlaid by a vast technical apparatus accumulated over five centuries and by numerous concessions to common sense. The bulk of Sextus' work is parasitical on the dogmatic philosophers, and seems to be motivated more by disputatiousness and the desire to score debating points than by a positive interest in mental repose. In many ways his attitude resembles that of the later Buddhist logicians.

At the time of Cicero, halfway between Pyrrho and Sextus Empiricus, this loss of spiritual commitment had not gone quite so far. Some of the statements which Cicero makes in his

[1] R. G. Bury, trans., *Sextus Empiricus*, 4 vols. Vol. I, *Outlines of Pyrrhonism* (New York: G. P. Putnam's Sons, 1933), p. xxx.

[2] *Ibid.*, p. xxx; Cf. also p. xxxi.

[3] *Ibid.*, p. xxxii.

[4] *Ibid.*, p. xxxiii.

[5] E.g., in what the *skeptikē agōgē* ("sceptical procedure") (Book I. Chap. 4) has to say about *ataraxia* (=*śamatha*) as the end of life (I. 25–30), or about the *svabhāva* (*physis* or *peri tōn exōthen hypokeimenōn*) (I. 15, 22, 93, 163), the relativity of everything (I. 135), or on non-assertion (I. 192–193), non-determination (I. 197), and non-apprehension (I. 200).

Academica,[1] on behalf of or in response to the Skeptics, are indeed strikingly similar to the teachings of the Mādhyamikas and other later Buddhists.

The Skeptics were people who "sanctioned nothing as proved" (*qui nihil probarent*[2]). "All those things you talk about are hidden, closely concealed (*occultata*) and enfolded in thick clouds of darkness, so that no human intellect has sufficiently powerful sight to be able to penetrate to heaven and get inside the earth."[3] Though "it is possibly the case that when exposed and uncovered they change their character" (*quia possit fieri ut patefacta et detecta mutentur*).[4] The Skeptics "have a habit of concealing (*occultandi*) their opinion, and do not usually disclose it to any one except those that had lived with them right up to old age".[5] And the opponent says, "What pray are those holy secrets (*mysteria*) of yours, or why should your school conceal (*celatis*) its doctrine as something disgraceful?"[6]

"It is the wise man (*sapiens*) that we are investigating",[7] and it is on him that "all this enquiry turns".[8] He "avoids being taken in and sees to it that he is not deceived".[9] They hold that "nothing can be perceived",[10] or grasped (*comprehendi, anupalabdhi*),[11] and the "wise man will restrain all acts of assent" (*adsensus, abhiniveśa*).[12] There is also a reference to the "perversity" (*pravitas*) of seeing the non-real as real,[13] and to arguments against the senses, which are said to be "full of darkness",[14] and against "everything that is approved in

[1] Cicero, *De Natura Deorum; Academica*, H. Rackham, ed. and trans. (Cambridge: Harvard University Press, 1961).
[2] *Ibid.*, pp. 488–9, *Academica*, II (Lucullus), vi, 17.
[3] *Ibid.*, pp. 624–5, *Academica*, II (Lucullus), xxxix, 122.
[4] *Ibid.*
[5] *Ibid.*, pp. 462–3, *Academica*, fragment No. 21.
[6] *Ibid.*, pp. 542–3, *Academica*, II (Lucullus), xviii, 60.
[7] *Ibid.*, pp. 550–1, *Academica*, II (Lucullus), xx, 66.
[8] *Ibid.*, pp. 614–5, *Academica*, II (Lucullus), xxxvi, 115.
[9] *Ibid.*, pp. 550–1, *Academica*, II (Lucullus), xx, 66.
[10] *Ibid.*, pp. 550–1, 554–5, 608–9, 489–90, 542–3. They "do not deny that some truth exists, but deny that it can be perceived" (*qui veri esse aliquid non negamus, percipi posse negamus*), II, xxiii, 73.
[11] *Ibid.*, pp. 620–1, *Academica*, II (Lucullus), xxxviii, 119.
[12] *Ibid.*, pp. 554–5, *Academica*, II (Lucullus), xxi, 68.
[13] *Ibid.*, pp. 566–7, *Academica*, II (Lucullus), xxv, 80.
[14] *Ibid.*, p. 559, *Academica*, II (Lucullus), xxiii, 73.

common experience" (*consuetudo = saṁvṛti*).[1] And, as though he had read the *Prajñāpāramitā* herself, an opponent points out that "as for wisdom herself, if she does not know whether she is wisdom or not, how in the first place will she make good her claim to the name of wisdom? Next, how will she venture with confidence to plan or execute any undertaking when there will be nothing certain for her to act upon?"[2]

2. Secondly, there is a close similarity with those ascetic, other-worldly, and "mystical" thinkers who assigned a decisive importance to "spiritual experience". They are represented by four main trends:

a) First, there are the *Wisdom* speculations of the *Near East* between 200 B.C. and A.D. 300. Their conception of *chochma* and *sophia* is closely analogous to that of *prajñāpāramitā*, and some of the similarities are really quite startling.[3]

b) Next, we must mention the kindred *Gnostic* and *Neo-Platonic* modes of thought, especially the later Neo-Platonists, like Proclus and Damascius,[4] and also their Christian form in Origenes and in Dionysius Areopagita, who in some passages of his *Mystical Theology*[5] gives what may well be called a Christian version of the *Heart Sūtra*.

c) Thirdly, there are the great *mystics* of the thirteenth and fourteenth centuries, such as Meister Eckhart,[6] Ruysbroeck, and Suso. Their kinship with Buddhism has been noted so

[1] *Ibid.*, pp. 562–3, *Academica*, II (Lucullus), xxiv, 75.

[2] *Ibid.*, p. 499; *Academica*, II (Lucullus), viii, 24.

[3] For some details, see my review of H. Ringgren, *Word and Wisdom*, on pp. 207–9.

[4] Some useful material has been collected by R. Gnoli in *La Parola del passato*, I (1961), fasc. LXXVII, 153–159. See also J. Rahder's suggestions on *śūnyatā* in *Indogaku Bukkyōgaku Kenkyū* (*Journal of Indian and Buddhist Studies*). IX, No. 2 (1961), 754. On the other hand, I can see no merit in E. Benz's attempt to establish a direct link by claiming that Plotinus' teacher, Ammonios "Sakkas", was either a member of the Indian dynasty of the "Saki", or a "Sakya" (Sakiya, Sakka), i.e., a Buddhist monk. *Orientalia Romana*, I (1958), 18–20 (Instituto Italiano per il Medio ed Estremo Oriente. Serie Orientale Roma, XVII).

[5] I.e., I.2, II.1, III.1, chaps. 4 and 5. The translations are apt to obscure the parallel, which becomes strikingly obvious as soon as the Greek text is consulted.

[6] Cf. Daisetz T. Suzuki, "Meister Eckhart and Buddhism," in *Mysticism, Christian and Buddhist* (London: George Allen & Unwin Ltd., 1957), pp. 7–35.

often that I can be quite brief. Ruysbroeck says of the "God-seeing man" that "his spirit is undifferentiated and without distinction, and therefore feels nothing without the unity". Among Western contemplatives, *śūnyatā* corresponds to the "desert of the Godhead", to Ruysbroeck's "idle emptiness", to Eckhart's still wilderness where no one is at home, to the "naked orison", the "naked intent stretching unto God", which becomes possible with entire self-surrender, and also to the fathomless abyss of Ruysbroeck and Tauler.[1] This "abyss" is wholeheartedly welcomed by those steeped in self-negation and self-naughting, but, later on, less selfless people like B. Pascal[2] and Ch. Baudelaire[3] felt rather ambivalent when confronted with it, since they were clearly none too enchanted with the implications of being "separated from all created things". The *Theologia Germanica*[4] (*ca.* 1425), as is well known, contains many formulations with a distinctly Buddhist flavour. The most striking similarity lies, of course, in the constant emphasis on "I-hood and selfhood", and "I, me, and mine" as the source of all alienation from true reality, and on the need to undo that "blindness and folly".[5] But this is not all. On re-reading the book I have been astounded to find how close it is in so many ways to Buddhist mentality, in spite of its author's "cautious limitation of his speculations to what is compatible with the Church",[6] and some minor concessions to theism, especially in the later parts. Apart from the subject of *satkāyadṛṣṭi* this is true of what is said about the Godhead (= *Nirvāṇa*), the "deified

[1] For a good description, see Tauler, "Sermon on St. John the Baptist", in *The Inner Way: 36 Sermons for Festivals*. New translation, edited with Introduction by Arthur Wollaston Hutton (London: Methuen & Co., Ltd., 1901), pp. 97–9. Cf. St. John of the Cross, *Noche Oscura*, Vol. I, Book 2, chap. 17.

[2] E.g., L. Brunschvicg, ed. *Pensées* (14th ed., Paris: Hachette, 1927), p. 350.

[3] It is quite interesting to note, when reading *Les Fleurs du Mal*, the varying and conflicting connotations of such key terms as *gouffre*, *abîme*, and *vide*.

[4] New York: Pantheon Books, Inc., 1949. London: Gollancz, 1950. This is the translation of S. Winkworth, revised by W. Trask, on the basis of J. Bernhart's translation into modern German: *Theologia Germanica* (New York: Pantheon Books, 1949).

[5] Chaps. 1–5, 20, 22, 24, 32, 34, 40, 44, 49, 51.

[6] Bernhart, *op. cit.*, p. 101.

man" (=the *bodhisattva*), activated by both "cognition" and a "love" wherein "there neither is nor can remain any I, Me, Mine, Thou, Thine, and the like",[1] non-attainment,[2] the perverted views,[3] self-deception (=*avidyā*),[4] Suchness,[5] faith,[6] the One,[7] emptiness,[8] desire,[9] and so on—in fact, quite an impressive list.

d) Towards the end of the seventeenth century, shortly after Galileo, European mysticism of this type lost its intellectual distinction, and faded away into the "Quietism" of Molinos and Mme. Guyon. In the aftermath of the French revolution, many of the basic laws of the spiritual life were re-discovered by great poets who were also fine thinkers, such as Blake, Shelley, Wordsworth, and Coleridge in England. Though often vitiated by a fatal rift between theory and practice, their thought offers many parallels to Buddhist thinking. To this generation of rebels against the Goddess of Reason belonged *Arthur Schopenhauer*, whose thought, partly under Indian influence, exhibits numerous, and almost miraculous, coincidences with the basic tenets of Buddhist philosophy.[10] The term "parallel" implies that two lines run parallel at more than one point, and the degree of affinity existing between Schopenhauer and Buddhism will give us a standard by which to judge other alleged "parallels."

As he himself said, Schopenhauer continued the triple tradition of "quietism, i.e. the giving up of all willing, asceticism, i.e. intentional mortification of one's own will, and mysticism, i.e. consciousness of the identity of one's own inner being with that of all beings, or with the kernel of the world."[11] He shows that life in the world is meaningless, essentially suffering, and bound

[1] *Ibid.*, pp. 191–2, 197.
[2] *Ibid.*, pp. 167, 180, 183.
[3] *Ibid.*, pp. 119, 186.
[4] *Ibid.*, p. 200.
[5] *Ibid.*, pp. 206, 240.
[6] *Ibid.*, p. 207.
[7] *Ibid.*, pp. 197, 204–6, 218–9.
[8] *Ibid.*, pp. 144, 219–20.
[9] *Ibid.*, p. 115, *liebheyt*.

[10] Cf. R. Russell, *The Nature and Purpose of the Ascetic Ideal* (Kandy, Ceylon: Buddhist Publication Society, 1960). H. v. Glasenapp, *Die Philosophie der Inder* (Stuttgart: Alfred Kroener Verlag, 1958), pp. 428–9.

[11] E. F. J. Payne, trans., *The World as Will and Representation* (*WWR*), 2 vols. (Indian Hills, Colorado: The Falcon's Wing Press, 1958), p. 613, Vol. II.

to disappoint the hope that our desires might be fulfilled. He attributes this suffering to "the will to live," which is the equivalent of *tṛṣnā*, and which "involves us in a delusion." He looks for salvation from this world by way of a "denial of the will to live," which is a "consequence of the dawning of better knowledge,"[1] and by an asceticism and self-renunciation exemplified in "the lives of saints, penitents, *samaṇas*, *sannyāsins*, and so on."[2] We may add his atheism, his denial of an immaterial, substantially unchanging, soul, his belief in reincarnation, his stress on compassion as the basis of morality, his indifference to the "achievements" or "rhythm" of human history,[3] as well as his insight into impermanence[4] and into the reasons why *Nirvāṇa* can be described only negatively, and yet it is not nothing.[5]

It is only on two points that he differs from Buddhism.

A. He fails to appreciate the importance of disciplined *meditation*. Educated non-Catholic Germans of the nineteenth century were quite unfamiliar with the tradition of spiritual contemplation. On the other hand, for relaxation they habitually visited art galleries and went for walks in the countryside. It is no wonder, therefore, that Schopenhauer sees the foretaste of "the exalted peace" of *Nirvāṇa*, not in the trances (*dhyāna*), but in "pure esthetic contemplation." Although the contemplation of beauty has some analogy to the conditions prevailing in trance, it is on the whole an undisciplined faculty, and its results are rather fleeting and have little power to transmute the personality. In this respect, the German bourgeois town-dweller was a lesser man than the Indian man in the forest.

B. Secondly, Schopenhauer teaches that the Will is the Thing-in-itself, whereas in Buddhism "craving" operates within the conditioned and phenomenal world, and the unconditioned noumenon lies in *Nirvāṇa*, which is quite calm as the result of the abolition of craving. Unacquainted with the practice of *yoga*, Schopenhauer did not know that at the bottom

[1] *WWR*, Vol. II, p. 608.

[2] Quoted in Fussell, *op. cit.*, p. 1. *Samaṇas* = recluses; *sannyāsins* = ascetics.

[3] *WWR*, Vol. II, chap. 38.

[4] *WWR*, Bk. I, par. 3; Bk. III, par. 33.

[5] *WWR*, Vol. II, pp. 608, 612.

of every mind there is a calm quietude which is the prototype of *Nirvāṇa*. His central metaphysical thesis is, however, incompatible, not only with Buddhism, but also with his own soteriological aspirations. It is, indeed, not only hard to see how any cognitive act can ever reach the Thing-in-itself, but it also remains incomprehensible how thought can ever have the strength to stand up against the Will, and, what is more, how as a part of the purely illusory phenomenal world it can possibly overcome and effectively "deny" it.[1] This was early on recognized by F. Nietzsche[2] and J. Bahnsen[3] (1881), Schopenhauer's immediate successors, and led them, respectively, into nihilism and a pessimism unrelieved by the hope of escape.

C. Furthermore, Buddhism has a distinct affinity with the "monistic" traditions of European thought. The Eleatic emphasis on the One[4] implied devaluation, depreciation, and at times even rejection of the plural and multiple world. However they may phrase it, all monistic systems are in tune with the feeling which Shelley formulated in the famous verse:

> Life, like a dome of many-coloured glass
> Stains the white radiance of eternity
> Until death tramples it to fragments.[5]

Parmenides (*ca.* 480 B.C., nearly the Buddha's contemporary) and his successors assume a radical difference between appearance and reality, between surface and depth, between what we see (*phainomena*) and what we can only think (*noumena*), between opinion and truth. For Parmenides, opinion (*dṛṣṭi*) is derived from the senses, which are deceptive and the basis of false information. Truth is derived from the *logos*, which has for its object Being (that which is and has no other attributes

[1] For an exceedingly clear and lucid survey of the many inconsistencies in Schopenhauer's philosophy, I must refer to H. M. Wolf, *Arthur Schopenhauer. Hundert Jahre Später* (Bern and Muenchen: Francke Verlag, 1960).

[2] H. M. Wolf, *op. cit.*, pp. 36, 70, 106–7.

[3] About his "miserabilism," see E. Conze, "The Objective Validity of the Principle of Contradiction", *Philosophy*, X (1935), 216.

[4] But the *panta chōrei* of Herakleitos fits none too well, because not everything flows; *Nirvāṇa*, the most important thing of all, being excepted.

[5] Good parallels can be found in P. Damiani, "The Glories of Paradise", referred to above, page 216 note 1.

but to be). Being is, non-being is not; and that which Is can never not be, either now or later (as in change). Nothing that Is can either arise or perish.[1]

All monistic systems are remarkably uniform, and they are all equally beset by at least four unavoidable difficulties. They must, first of all, try to guard against the misunderstanding that the One might be a datum within the world, or a part of the conglomeration. Both East and West acutely felt the difficulties of finding an adequate verbal expression for the essentially *transcendent* and elusive reality of the One, and both made many attempts to circumvent them by the use of paradoxes, absurdities, contradictions, tautologies, riddles, negations, and other devices. Secondly, the monists must attempt to maintain the *simplicity* of the One by redefining the meaning of predication in regard to it. In this context, scholastic philosophers explained that God *is* each of his predicates, whereas creatures *have* them, and that the predicates of God are not different from one another, since otherwise he would not be simple. "The absolute essence is not in one respect different from what it is in another; what it is , it is in the totality of its being."[2] Everything plural is itself and in addition something else, and only the completely free can be itself pure and simple.

A third problem concerns the relation between the One and *Being*. The old Eleatic school, which flourished between 540 and 300 B.C.,[3] identifies the two. One must bear in mind, however, that in doing so it uses a special archaic, pre-Aristotelian type of logic[4] which, among other things, employs "the principle of unlimited predication". This means that a predicate is either predicated without limitation of the subject or it is not valid

[1] "It never was, and it never will be, since it is, all of it together, only present in the Now, one and indivisible." (Diels-Kranz, Fr. 8 [Simpl. *Phys.* 145.I.3–6].)

[2] Plotinus, *Enneads*, VI. vii. 10.

[3] Also the Megarics and Antisthenes belonged to it. Pyrrho appears to have started with the Megaric position.

[4] S. Ranulf, *Der eleatische Satz vom Widerspruch* (Kopenhagen: Gyldendal, 1924). The archaic character of Parmenides' thinking is also shown in his belief that Being is a mass which, as a well-rounded sphere, fills space. Also the well-known works of Prantl, Apelt, Maier, E. Hoffmann (*Die Sprache und die archaische Logik* [Tubingen: J. C. B. Mohr, 1925]), and Cornford are helpful in this connection.

at all. This logic only knows statements of the type "All A are all B", which predicate the entire P of the entire S, without any qualification as to time, part, or respect, without any distinction being made between total and partial identity of S and P, or between their partial and total difference. The Eleatics also "assumed that one speaks only in one sense (*monachōs*) of 'one' and 'being'."[1] The victory of Aristotelian logic changed all that. Plotinus describes the One expressly as "beyond being"; for Meister Eckhart, who said that "in the Kingdom of Heaven all is in all, all is one, and all is ours" Pure Being, as the most general, becomes the richest of all terms;[2] and Hegel, again, treats "being" as the initial and minimal definition of the Absolute, which is later enriched by many further "attributes." The *Theologia Germanica*[3] says that "he who finds satisfaction in God, his satisfaction is the One, and is all in the One. And he to whom the One is not all and all not the One, *and to whom something and nothing are not one and the same,* cannot find satisfaction in God." The Buddhist non-dual One was in the same way by many devices transferred beyond all logical categories.

And, fourthly, monists must come to some decision on the *status of appearance*. It may well be that not all of them have, like most Buddhists, regarded multiple and manifold appearance as a mere illusion, and it is probably true that "there is never any suggestion in Plotinus that all things except the One are illusions or fleeting appearances."[4] But this is a distinction without much of a difference, because also in the Plotinian system the sensory and material world has an extremely low degree of reality, and is afflicted by a great loss of the original reality, near its point of extinction. In the same way, in the Hegelian system the natural world is a state of estrangement from the Absolute Spirit. In M. Eckhart, "all creatures, insofar as they are creatures, as they are in themselves (*quod sunt in et*

[1] Aristotle, *Physics*, 185^b33. In many passages (*Metaphysics*, Gamma 2, 4, E 1, Z 1, K 3), Aristotle points out that Being is said *pollachōs* (in many senses).

[2] See R. Otto, *Mysticism East and West* (London: Macmillan and Company, 1932), pp. 21–6.

[3] Pp. 204–5. Italics mine.

[4] A. H. Armstrong, *Plotinus* (London: G. Allen & Unwin Ltd., 1953), p. 41. For the ambiguities in Plotinus' own thought, compare Armstrong, p. 21 with p. 29.

per se), are not even an illusion, but they are a pure nothing."[1] And, for Spinoza, "a temporal existence insofar as it is purely temporal is the same as non-existence, and is perishing in proportion to its fragmentariness and exclusiveness; existence in every range insofar as it gains content moves already towards an ideal of perfection which is one with eternity itself."[2]

The background of all "monistic" views[3] is a religious contempt for the world of ordinary experience, for that which is not One or not He who Is. That world is held to be unsatisfactory—partly emotionally as a source of suffering, and partly logically as self-contradictory, and as therefore either simply non-existing[4] or unable to abide in the state in which it is. In this way monism is apt to beget the *dialectics* out of itself, as in Zeno, Hegel, and Bradley, to name only a few. In the case of Zeno of Elea (*ca.* 460 B.C.) whom Aristotle called the founder of the dialectics, the "paradoxes" (*aporiai*) he devised aimed at defending by indirect proofs the view of Parmenides, which held local movement to be impossible in the ultimate reality of the true world of being. All Zeno did was to show that, on assuming movement, the consequences which follow are contradictory and untenable,[5] and that, therefore, the information derived from sense-data is patently false, since self-contradictions are the marks of false appearance.

[1] For useful quotations see R. Otto, *op. cit.*, pp. 91–6.

[2] According to Harold F. Hallett, *Aeternitas* (Oxford: Clarendon Press, 1930), p. 45.

[3] It may be objected that the comparison of all this with Buddhism applies more to the "monistic" Mahayana than to the "pluralistic" Hinayana theories. But the difference should not be overstressed. As the Theravada had a latent idealism and an implicit bias toward a mentalistic interpretation of physical reality (Étienne Lamotte, *L'enseignement de Vimalakīrti*. Bibliothèque du Muséon, Vol. 51 [Louvain: Institut Orientaliste, Université Catholique de Louvain, 1962], pp. 52–60), so it teaches also the one *Dhamma* side by side with the multiple *dhammas* (see Buddhaghosa on *ekam hi saccam, na dutīyam atthi*, in *Visuddhimagga of Buddhaghosācariya*, H. C. Warren, ec.; rev. by Dh. Kosambi. Harvard Oriental Series, Vol. 41 (Cambridge: Harvard University Press, 1950), pp. 422, 421.

[4] A purely intellectual contradiction reduces thought to nothing. It results in nonsense. He who thinks a contradiction thinks nothing at all.

[5] Or, in other words, that his Pythagorean opponents cannot assert the reality of movement without coming into conflict with their own premises. These opponents assumed that a line consists of indivisible points in

Zeno's dialectics has had many successors. Among them, Bradley seems nearer to the Mādhyamikas than either Hegel or Marx. Both Hegel and Marx make two assumptions which must irritate Buddhists. The first is the insistence on human history,[1] which Buddhists hold to be utterly pointless. The second is the constant introduction of the tripartite scheme of thesis, antithesis, and synthesis, which postulates a relentless "progress" from one state to the other, culminating in the tyranny of the Prussian state or of the U.S.S.R. On the other hand, Bradley is, I believe, next to Schopenhauer, the nearest representative in modern Europe of at least one side of Buddhist thought. Even the procedure of *Appearance and Reality* is the same as that of the *Mādhyamikakārikā*, in that one currently accepted category after the other is taken up and shown to be self-contradictory and untenable. Nor can I agree with Professor Murti's[2] claim that they differ greatly "in their notion of the Real and its relation to appearance". In fact, they both treat the Real as ineffable, and "at once transcendent and immanent".[3] If Bradley takes care not to exclude entirely the appearance from the Real, and seeks somehow to identify the two,[4] then this is not a "rather inconsistent contention",[5] but the exact equivalent of the Mādhyamika position ("Form is emptiness", etc.). Both these books are essentially polemical treatises and their message seems to be identical.

juxtaposition, and the counter-arguments of Hobbes (*Works*, I. 110), Bergson, and Aristotle take no notice of the historical situation. The contradictions involved can be seen succinctly in Hegel, *History of Philosophy*, Haldane, trans., 1892, I. 273–4; cf. *Logic*, I. 191–3, II. 143, sq.; F. Engels, *Herrn Eugen Dührings Umwälzung der Wissenschaft*, 3rd ed. (Stuttgart: J. H. W. Dietz, 1894), 120; E. Conze, *Philosophy* (see page 224 note 3), p. 215.

[1] Hegel said that "comprehended history forms both the memorial and the calvary of the absolute Spirit—that without which it would be Lifeless (!) Solitude." He seems to have a strange view of "life", as composed of a long series of senseless oppressions and massacres perpetrated in the name of some fatuous "ideal" or other.

[2] *The Central Philosophy of Buddhism* (London: George Allen & Unwin Ltd., 1955), p. 308.

[3] Murti, *ibid.*, p. 310.

[4] *Appearance and Reality: A Metaphysical Study* (9th impression, corrected, Oxford: Oxford University Press, 1930), p. 404.

[5] Murti, *op. cit.*, p. 309.

Spurious Parallels to Buddhist Philosophy

After an examination of the genuine parallels between European and Buddhist philosophy, we shall now consider a few of the more widely advocated spurious parallels. They often originate from a wish to find affinities with philosophers recognized and admired by the exponents of current academic philosophy, and intend to make Buddhist thinkers interesting and respectable by current Western standards. Since this approach is not only objectively unsound, but has also failed in its purpose to interest Western philosophers in the philosophies of the East, the time has now come to abandon it. Modern academic philosophers normally have no interest in what Buddhists care for, and vice versa.

A philosophical doctrine can be viewed from at least four points of view: 1. As the *formulation* of certain propositions. 2. In terms of the *motivation* which induced their author to believe them to be true, his motives being connected with the *purpose* he had in mind. 3. In terms of the *argumentation* through which he tries to establish their truth—the reasons which he adduces being rarely those which actually impelled him. 4. In terms of the *context* in which the statements are made, a context which is determined by the philosopher's predecessors and contemporaries, and by his social, cultural, and religious background. When we compare Buddhist and European thought, it happens quite often that the formulations agree, whereas considerations of their context, of the motives behind them, and of the conclusions drawn from them suggest wide discrepancies. Verbal coincidences frequently mask fundamental divergences in the concepts underlying them. For pages upon pages Shinran Shōnin and Martin Luther in almost the same words expound the primacy of "faith," and yet in fact their two systems disagree in almost every other respect.[1] Berkeley's denial of matter

[1] See H. Butschkus, *Luther's Religion und ihre Entsprechung im japanischen Amida-Buddhismus* (Elmsdetten: Verlags-Anstalt Heinr. & L. Lechte, n.d., probably 1950).

seems to re-state literally the absolute idealism of the Yogācārins,[1] but, nevertheless, *a*) his immaterialism sets out to deny a conception of matter derived from Locke, etc., and unknown in India; *b*) his idea of Mind agrees none too well with that of the Vijñānavādins; *c*) his uncritical acceptance of sense-data conflicts with the *dharma*-theory; and *d*) his idea of "God" would not commend itself to Buddhists.

Far too often "soteriological". are confused with "philosophical" concepts, and the Buddhist "Void"[2] is thus regarded as being on the same level with the Aristotelian or Plotinian idea of "matter," or with the "pure potentiality" of the *Timaeus*, which is empty of all distinctions and full of infinite possibilities. Nor must it be forgotten that spiritual sickness is apt to ape or counterfeit (*prativarṇika, pratirūpaka*) the language of spiritual health. If the words alone are considered, the emptiness doctrine may be mistaken for one of the forms of European post-Nietzschean nihilism,[3] and the self-naughting of saints is to some extent mimicked by the self-destructive tendencies of German Romantics, like Schlegel, Tieck, Novalis, and so on,[4] who, as a result of vanity, self-reflection and self-centredness, *ressentiment*, *Widerstreit* and self-disgust could say that "I feel myself annihilated right in my inmost essence, and destroyed right up to the last depth of my thoughts"[5]. They, however, also maintained that "the reality behind things

[1] See the quotation in my *Buddhism* (New York: Harper & Brothers, 1959), p. 168.

[2] E. Conze, *Buddhist Thought in India* (London: George Allen & Unwin Ltd., 1962), pp. 242ff.

[3] In my *Der Satz vom Widerspruch* (Hamburg: Selbstverlag, 1932), I have, at no. 300, collected a few characteristic statements of Nietzsche, for example, "The only reason why we imagine a world other than this one is that we are motivated by an instinct which makes us calumniate life, belittle and suspect it". "It is not life which has created the other world, but the having become weary of life". "It is of the utmost importance that one should abolish the true world. It is that which has made us doubt the world which we are, and has made us diminish its value; it has so far been the most dangerous assault on life". Whatever this "life" may be, it is surely not the spiritual life.

[4] See Fritz Brüggemann, *Die Ironie als entwicklungsgeschichtliches Moment* (Jena: E. Diederichs, 1909). Eckart von Sydow, *Die Kultur der Dekadenz* (Dresden: Sibyllen Verlag, 1921).

[5] L. Tieck, *William Lovell*, III, 379.

destroys us spiritually when we look upon it"[1]—and that had not been the experience of the sages who had found themselves actually perfected by the contemplation of reality. Likewise, we could in recent years observe in the Anglo-Saxon countries certain of D. T. Suzuki's followers using the Master's sayings to justify a way of life diametrically opposed to the one envisaged by him.[2]

These examples might be multiplied almost indefinitely. In this article I will confine myself to three kinds of false parallels. 1. Some, like Kant, are not "parallel" at all, but *tangential*. 2. Others, such a Bergson and the existentialists, are *preliminary*. 3. Others, again, like David Hume, are merely *deceptive*.

1. Professor T. R. V. Murti[3] has found between *Kant* and the Mādhyamikas close similarities, which Jacques May[4] has rejected as "*perfides*," or "treacherous." In judging this issue, we must first of all bear in mind that it is the whole *purpose* of Kant's philosophy to show that morality and religion, as understood by the German Protestantism of East Prussia, can survive, even though Newtonian physics be true and Hume's skepticism significant. So great had the pressure of natural science become by his time that he is a man divided against himself. On the one hand, he longs to preserve the decencies of the perennial philosophy. It seemed vital to him to confine the intellect, conceived as the progenitor of natural science and therefore the foe of all human values, to the phenomenal

[1] L. Tieck, *Kritische Schriften*, VII, 278. He also said: "All objects around me appeared to me as mere empty forms or insubstantial things", *Ibid.*, III, 36.

[2] N. M. Jacobs, in *The Times Literary Supplement*, May 3, 1963, p. 325, speaks appositely of "Miller and those Beat writers who abandon practical affairs for the inner life and self-realization—or destruction—by means of Zen, Sex or Drugs."

[3] *The Central Philosophy of Buddhism* (Hereafter, *CPB*) (London: George Allen & Unwin Ltd., 1955), pp. 294–301, though with serious reservations. Stcherbatsky, on the other hand, had seen Kant as closely similar to the later Buddhist logicians, and had likened the Mādhyamikas to Hegel and Bradley. See Conze, *Buddhist Thought in India*, pp. 264–9.

[4] 1. "Kant et les Mādhyamika", *Indo-Iranian Journal*, III (1959), 102–11. 2. "La philosophie bouddhique de la vacuité", *Studia Philosophica*, XVIII (1958), 131–4. Some valuable comments by J. W. de Jong are in *Indo-Iranian Journal*, V (1961), 161–3.

world. In consequence, he resembles the perennial philosophers insofar as he maintains that true reality cannot be known through sense-data or concepts, but must be contacted by a pure spiritual intent—in his case, a completely disinterested act of the will. On the other hand, he takes the assertions of natural science very seriously, and is concerned as much to find reasons for their universal validity as to define their limits.[1]

Kant's great specific contribution to philosophy stems from his insight into the problems posed by the tension between traditional values and the implications of natural science, and in his having found a solution acceptable to many for a long time. This tension was quite unknown in India. Since he answers a question no pre-Macaulayan Indian could ever ask, his answer can have no real correspondences in Indian thought, which never underwent the onslaught of the "mechanical" method. Therefore, all those modern thinkers who either accept the ideal of "mechanical" knowledge or give it great weight cannot have much affinity with Buddhist thought. Kant's position in regard to Buddhist philosophy is the exact reverse of Schopenhauer's. There the analogies were essential, and the discrepancies fortuitous, whereas here the similarities are incidental and the differences vital.

To begin with, it seems to me wrong to describe Nāgārjuna's position as *epistemological*, when it is clearly ontological.[2] For

[1] This is one reason why the Kantian "phenomena" cannot be simply equated with the Buddhist "*saṃsāra*". From the point of view of the Absolute, both Kantian empirical and Buddhist conventional knowledge are non-valid. But Kant never questioned the value of empirical knowledge. In Buddhism, however, the *saṁvṛtisatya* (conventional truth) is a mere error due to nescience (*a-vidyā, a-jñāna*), and conventional knowledge represents no more than a deplorable estrangement from our true destiny. In its uncompromising monastic form, Buddhism maintains that the empirical world is not worth exploring, that all one has to know about it is its worthlessness and inanity; its scientific exploration, as irrelevant to the escape from the terrors of *saṁsāra*, is deemed unworthy of attention. A second reason why the Kantian phenomena/noumena cannot be equated with the Mādhyamika *saṁsāra/Nirvāṇa* is that the latter are identical, whereas the first clearly are not. The one dichotomy, in any case, is defined by its relation to science, the other by its relation to salvation.

[2] On this subject, see also the excellent remarks of Jacques May 1. 104–8, 2. 135–8.

perennial philosophers everywhere, philosophy is a way of life based on an understanding of reality as reality, of being as being. They all agree with Aristotle's famous remark according to which "The question which was raised long ago, is still and always will be, and which always baffles us—'What is Being?' —is in other words 'What is substance?'"[1] The whole theme of Nāgārjuna's work is the search for the own-being (*svabhāva*) of *dharmas*.[2] Epistemology, by contrast, is a branch of "sciential" philosophy, and became an object of inquiry only in modern times. Following the hints of the nominalists, Descartes tore apart thought and being, and then decided that we are more immediately aware of our thoughts about things than of the things themselves, that the data of inner experience are more immediate and clear to us than the experience of outward things.[3] Kant succinctly expressed the shift from the ontological to the epistemological approach in his famous remark about the "Copernican Revolution", which Murti has surely misunderstood.[4] Kant there says[5] that "hitherto it has been assumed that all our knowledge must conform to objects", whereas he himself prefers "to suppose that objects must conform to our knowledge". This assertion of the primacy of the subjective over the objective assumes a separation between subject and object which is alien to Indian thinking. In the Mādhyamika system, on the highest level, i.e., on that of the fully realized perfect wisdom, they are one and identical. On the lower levels, they are occasionally distinguished, but never with the rigidity of post-Cartesian philosophy. The division between subjective and objective facts is always incidental and never fundamental.

[1] *Metaphysics*, Z 1, 1028b. H. Tredennick, trans. (New York: G. P. Putnam's Sons, 1933), p. 312. Kai dē kai to palai te kai nȳn kai aei dzētoumenon kai aei aporoumenon, ti to on, touto esti, tis hē ousia.

[2] Conze, *Buddhist Thought in India*, pp. 239–41.

[3] This is not a psychological but a philosophical statement, because psychologically it is manifestly untrue. The normal and untutored mind is usually quite at ease among external objects, and, unable to even understand this doctrine of the "primacy of internal experience", is much more immediately aware of a chair than of its awareness of a chair.

[4] *CPB*, pp. 123–4, 274.

[5] *Critique of Pure Reason*, N. K. Smith, trans. (London: Macmillan & Co., Ltd., 1961), p. 22.

Their basic unity lies in their all being *dharmic* facts. Just as truth (*sat-ya*) does not describe a particular kind of knowledge, but a state of being, so all cognitive acts are viewed as factors in the interplay of objective facts (*dharma*) which bring about, not just a false view of the world, but the origination (*samudaya*) of a false world alienated from true reality. There is no room here for me to show the existential character of *avidyā* (ignorance), *dṛṣṭi* (false views), *prapañca* (idle speculations), etc., but the reader should always bear in mind that false views are not merely wrong knowledge, but wrong knowledge on the part of a viewer who is in a false position and surrounded by distorted objects.

All Mādhyamika reasoning has the one single *purpose* of enabling *transcendental wisdom to* function freely. In his remarks about "intellectual intuition", Kant questions the possibility of such a faculty, and, in addition, he could not possibly formulate a spiritual discipline which could lead to it,[1] because no man can be much wiser than his age. The essence of Buddhism concerns the one true reality (*Dharma*), which can be realized only in the discipline of a traditional system of meditation, of which the Christian counterparts vanished from sight in Northern Europe soon after the Reformation.

There remains the apparent analogy between Kant's *antinomies* and the Buddhist treatment of speculative questions (*avyākṛtavastūni*). They agree in a few details, i.e., in that they are both concerned with whether the world is finite or infinite etc., and in that they are both left undecided. The difference, however, is the following: The antinomies are insoluble because one can argue convincingly on both sides, and so no decision is possible. The deadlock of reason indicates that it has overstepped its boundaries. The argument concerning the "indeterminate topics" is totally different. They "are not explained, but set aside and ignored", because they are not conducive to salvation. There are answers to them, and the Tathāgata knows them, but he does not reveal them because they are of

[1] *Ibid.*, pp. 268, 270–1. Murti, *CPB*, p. 300. May (1) 108: "*La dialectique kantienne est le jeu de l'impuissance de la raison. . . . Au contraire, la dialectique mādhyamika es véritablement constitutive de la réalité, elle accomplit en abolissant*".

no use to us.[1] In the one case, these questions fall outside the scope of scientific, in the other of salutary, experience. The similarity is purely formal, and quite trivial when the formulations are viewed in their respective contexts.

2. We now come to those who go but part of the way. Bergson and the existentialists, among others, agree with the Buddhists in their revulsion from the nightmare of a sinister and useless world, but cannot follow them into the transcendental world, just for lack of *expertise* and because of their unfamiliarity with any definite spiritual tradition—whereas Kant had still stood squarely in the Protestant tradition, however impoverished that may have been by his time.

2a. Bergson, like Kant, strives hard to show that spiritual values can co-exist with the findings of science. He does this by contrasting the largely false world of common sense and science (in which he, nevertheless, takes a keen interest) with the true world of intuition. He is perfectly lucid and even superb so long as he demonstrates that both the intellect and our practical preoccupations manifestly distort the world-view both of everyday experience and of mechanical science. But, when he comes to the way out, to his *durée réelle* and his "intuition", vagueness envelops all and everything. His positive views have therefore been rightly described as "tantalising", for "as soon as one reaches out to grasp his body of thought it seems to disappear within a teasing ambiguity".[2] Mature and accomplished spritual knowledge can be had only within a living tradition. But how could a Polish Jew, transplanted to Paris, find such a tradition in the corridors of the Collège de France or in the *salons* of the sixteenth *arrondissement*? It is the tragedy of our time that so many of those who thirst for spiritual wisdom are forced to think it out for themselves—always in vain. There is no such thing as a pure spirituality in the abstract. There are only separate lineages handed down traditionally from the past. If any proof were needed, Bergson, a first-class intellect,

[1] This is perfectly clear from *Majjhima Nikāya*, no. 63, and the fuller account of Nāgārjuna, Étienne Lamotte, trans., *Le traité le grande vertu de sagesse* (Louvain: Bureau du Muséon, 1944), Vol. I, pp. 154–8.

[2] Th. Hanna, ed., *The Bergsonian Heritage* (Hereafter, *BH*) (New York and London: Columbia University Press, 1962), p. 1; also pp. 27, 53.

would provide it. His views on religion are a mixture of vague adumbrations and jumbled reminiscences which catch some of the general principles of spirituality but miss its concrete manifestations. Tradition furnished at least two worlds composed of objects of pure disinterested contemplation—the Buddhist world of *dharmas* and the Platonic ideas in their pagan, Christian, or Jewish form. Here Bergson would have had an opportunity to "go beyond intellectual analysis and to recapture by an act of intuitive sympathy the being and the existence in their original quality."[1] But for various reasons he could not accept either of these traditions. Like Schopenhauer, he regarded art as one of the avenues to the truth,[2] but, otherwise, his "intuition," this "ecstatic identification with the object,"[3] this "spiritual sympathy by which one places oneself within an object in order to coincide with what is unique in it, and consequently inexpressible,"[4] is never explained as a disciplined faculty.

Because of this disseverance from a concrete spiritual practice, Bergson has now no disciples, and his work belongs to the past. As Raïssa Maritain put it so well, "Bergson travelled *uncertainly* towards God, *still far off*, but the light of whom has already reached him".[5] Unable, like Moses, to reach the promised land, he, nevertheless, cleared the way for the Catholic revival of the twentieth century, which enabled many French intellectuals to regain contact with at least one living spiritual tradition. At the same time, he realized that the inanition of the spiritual impulse slowly deprives life of its savor among the more finely organized minds of Europe, and he wrote in 1932, "Mankind lies groaning, half-crushed beneath the weight of its own progress. Men do not sufficiently realize that their future is in their own hands. Theirs is the task of determining first whether they want to go on living or not (!) . . ."[6]

[1] *BH*, p. 40.

[2] "So art . . . has no other object than to brush aside the utilitarian symbols, the conventional and socially accepted generalities, in short, everything that veils reality from us, in order to bring us face to face with reality itself". *Le Rire*, quoted in *BH*, p. 88.

[3] *Ibid.*, p. 158.

[4] *Ibid.*, p. 87.

[5] *Ibid.*, p. 92 (my italics, but not my translation from the French.)

[6] *Ibid.*, p. 99. If this statement, which goes on to speak of the "universe" as "a machine for the making of gods", is collated with that which

2b. It is at this point of despondency that the *existentialists* had, after the first World War, arrived on the scene. By that time the speculative vigour of European philosophers had declined so much that they got the worst of both worlds. As for the world of science, they rejected its pretensions with a lordly disdain. As for the world of the spirit, they did not know where to find it.[1] Their beliefs reflect to perfection the social position of the post-1918 intelligentsia on the European Continent. In the provincial perspective of England both logical positivism and existentialism are often explained as reactions against German idealism. This is not the case. Logical positivism is descended from the philistinism of the English commercial middle classes,[2] and long before the days of Messrs Ayer, Wittgenstein, and Wollheim, the "British school of philosophy" had found its classical and superbly brilliant expression in Macaulay's essay on Lord Bacon.[3] As for existentialism, it is derived from the hopeless anxieties of the more intelligent European intellectuals. Their *Sorge* and *existentielle Angst* spring, not from their reading of Pascal and Kierkegaard, but from their own objective social situation. Bertrand Russell was certainly not under the influence of either Pascal or Kierkegaard when he wrote in 1903 that "only on the firm foundation of unyielding despair, can the soul's habitation

Italo Svevo (Ettore Schmitz) made in 1924 in his *Confessions of Zeno* (New York: G. P. Putnam's Sons), pp. 411–2, it must become clear that we do not owe our present plight merely to the brilliant achievements of our able technicians. The progressive decline of spiritual wisdom may well have weakened the will to live and correspondingly strengthened the death wish. On this subject I must refer to Erich Heller, *The Disinherited Mind* (London: Penguin Books, 1961), whose conclusions I take for granted throughout.

[1] I speak here only of the "secular" existentialists. The "religious" existentialists would require separate treatment.

[2] Matthew Arnold, after dividing the English population of his time into "barbarians, philistines, and populace", well defined the philistine as "a strong, dogged unenlightened opponent of the chosen people, of the children of light", in A. C. Ward, *Illustrated History of English Literature* (London: Longmans, Green & Co., 1955), Vol. III, p. 227.

[3] July, 1837, Th. B. Macaulay, *Literary Essays* (Oxford: Oxford University Press), pp. 364–410.

henceforth (!) be safely built".[1] We naturally ask ourselves what might have happened to "henceforth" necessitate so much despair. By way of reply we are told that "the world which Science presents for our belief" is "purposeless" and "void of meaning."[2] If Lord Russell had realized that the methods of Science, with a capital S, preclude it from ever recognizing any objective purpose or meaning even if there is one, he might have saved himself much unnecessary worry. Millions of people like him take the conventions and hypotheses of mechanical "Science" for "truths",[3] and are plunged into deep gloom for ever after. Existentialism, like logical positivism, arose primarily from social conditions. Secondarily, of course, when these two movements reached the universities, their followers naturally rubbed themselves against the professors who were entrenched there and who were then in the habit of expounding the tenets of German idealism, and they also added a few frills of their own, such as Moore's characteristically Cambridge "preciousness" and so on.

The existentialist diagnosis of the plight of human existence agrees with that of the Buddhists. "So human life is nothing but a perpetual illusion. Man is nothing but disguise, lie and hypocrisy, with respect to himself and with respect to others",[4] and so on and so on. In terms of the Four Truths, the existentialists have only got the first, which teaches that everything is

[1] *Mysticism and Logic* (London: Penguin Books, 1951), p. 51. The whole essay (pp. 50–9) is worth re-reading because now, sixty years later, it shows clearly the grotesque irrationalities of a "sciential" philosophy, which in nearly every sentence blandly went beyond all scientific observations made even up to the present day.—May I explain that my attitude cannot be called "anti-scientific", because nowhere have I said anything about "science" as such, either for or against. My strictures concern only extravagant philosophical conclusions drawn from a few inconclusive scientific data. Sir Isaac Newton, as is well known, said at the close of his life, when all his work was done, that he had only played with pebbles on the sea shore, and that "the great ocean of truth lay all undiscovered before me". This is all I try to say, neither less nor more.

[2] *Ibid.*, p. 51.

[3] *Ibid.*, p. 51.

[4] Blaise Pascal, *Pensées*, no. 100. For a good comparison in some detail see Constantin Regamey, "Tendances et méthodes de la philosophie indienne comparées à celles de la philosophie occidentale", *Revue de théologie et de philosophie*, IV (1950), 258–9.

ill. Of the second, which assigns the origin of ill to craving, they have only a very imperfect grasp. As for the third and fourth, they are quite unheard of. They just do not believe that "there is, O monks, an Unborn, an Unbecome, an Unmade, an Unconditioned; for if there were not this Unborn, Unbecome, Unmade, Unconditioned, no escape from this born, become, made and conditioned would be apparent".[1] Knowing no way out, they are manufacturers of their own woes. As distinct from their world weariness, that of the Buddhists is cheered by the hope of ultimate release and lightened by multifarious meditational experiences which ease the burden of life. Denied inspiration from the spiritual world existentialists are apt to seek it from authoritarian social groups (Nazis, Communists, the Roman Catholic hierarchy). They are prone to ascribe their disbelief in a spiritual world to their own "unblinking love of truth". I myself was brought up among them, and they were clearly the bedraggled victims of a society which had become oppressive to them through the triple effect of Science, technology, and social decomposition, and in which no authoritative spiritual teaching could any longer be encountered, except in some obscure nooks and corners inaccessible to the metropolitan intelligentsia.

3. By "*deceptive*" comparisons I mean those which concern statements that are negative in either form or content. A negative proposition derives its true meaning from what it is directed against, and its message thus entirely depends on its context. In different contexts two identical negative statements may, therefore, have nothing in common. One single example must suffice.

David Hume's denial of a "self" seems literally to agree with the *anattā* doctrine. Buddhists are certainly at one with him when he rejects the notion of a permanent self-identical substance in favour of a succession of impermanent states and events.[2] Furthermore, his assertion that our mind is "nothing but a bundle or collection of different perceptions,[3] united

[1] *Udāna*, viii, 3: *no . . . nissaraṇaṃ paññāyetha.*

[2] So, Murti, *CPB*, p. 130.

[3] "For my part, when I enter most intimately into what I call *myself*, I always stumble on some particular perception or other, of heat or cold,

together by certain relations" would win at least their qualified approval. The unity of the personality is a fairly loose one for Hume, just as for Democritus and the Epicureans it was a mere assemblage (*concilium*) of subtle moving atoms, and all that Hume did was to substitute "perceptions" for the "atoms" of the ancient materialists. He understood our personality after the image of inanimate objects,[1] which also have no "self," or true inwardness, of any kind. In addition, those inanimate objects, as well as the human personality, were subjected to the mechanical method, which discarded Aristotle's "substantial forms" and "intelligible substances", and which, in accordance with the "law of inertia", allows for no centre of inward initiative. For Hume, only a stream of successive ideas exists, and there is no permanent self within, nor is any subject of experience needed to hold the ideas together, or to guide them. The mind, a mere stage for its contents and for their relations and interactions, is reduced to the drifting passage of an aimless temporality,

All this corresponds well to the picture of Pali Buddhism which British civil servants gave us about eighty years ago. It takes no account, however, of the *context* of Hume's statements. When applied to the human personality, the Aristotelian synthesis used the term "substance" to indicate that some features of man are more essential to him than others, closer to his true being.[2] For Hume, on the other hand, all mental contents are of equal value, and for him it makes no sense to speak of "surface" or "depth", of "inwardness" or "alienation". In consequence, from his point of view, there can be no

light or shade, love or hatred, pain or pleasure. I never can catch *myself* at any time without a perception, and never can observe any thing but the perceptions". David Hume, *A Treatise on Human Nature*, T. H. Green, ed. (London: Longmans, Green & Co., 1874), Vol. I, p. 534. When I first saw this sentence forty years ago, I thought it unanswerable. What now strikes me is the immense vagueness of the word "perception".

[1] *Ibid.*, pp. 537–40.

[2] For Aristotle, intelligence (*dianoētikon*) was a man's true self (*E.N.*, 1166a8), and, for Porphyry (*de abst.*, I, 29), the *Nous* is his *ontōs auton*. The *Nous* is man's sovereign (*kyriotaton*) and his better part (*ameinon*) (*E.N.*, 1178a2). The connection between man's *ousia* (essence) and his proper objective purpose is made particularly clear in Aristotle's *Protreptikos*. For the quotations, see E. Conze, *Der Satz vom Widerspruch* (Hamburg: Selbstverlag, 1932), no. 141.

sense in the spiritual approach of which S. Augustine has so well said, *In te ipsum redi, in interiore homine habitat veritas.*[1] Although Aristotle's theory of substance may have been a rather clumsy way of providing an ontological basis for the spiritual life, its rejection by Hume meant that he dropped all quest for the transcendental, and, appalled by his own nihilism, turned away from philosophy and occupied himself with re-writing the history of England in the interest of the Tory Party.

Whereas Hume reduced selfhood to the level of the sub-personal, the Buddhist doctrine of *anattā* invites us to search for the super-personal. Its whole point lies in that, since everything in this empirical self is impermanent, unsatisfactory, etc., therefore it constitutes a false self, and none of it can be mine, me, or myself. In consequence, I must look beyond the *skandhas* (heaps) to find my true and abiding transcendental self (which is the Tathāgata).[2] The *Dhammapada* says that, if the egolessness of all dharmas is seen with the eye of wisdom, it will then lead to a turning away from all ill.[3] Suzuki, commenting on this verse, defines the *prajñā*-eye as "a special kind of intuition enabling us to penetrate right into the bedrock of Reality itself."[4] To D. Hume, such a penetration would not have been a particularly meaningful undertaking, and he would have been still more displeased by Suzuki's sequel, when he says: "The

[1] Approximately: "Enter into yourself, for the truth dwells in the inmost heart of man." Seneca: *prope est a te deus, tecum est, intus est.* More about this in Proclus, *The Elements of Theology*, ed. E. R. Dodds, Oxford, 1933, p. 203. Likewise, in the Far East, Ch'an taught that "a man could be a Buddha by immediately taking hold of his inmost nature". D. T. Suzuki, *The Essentials of Zen Buddhism*, Bernard Phillips, ed., (London: Rider & Co., 1963), p. 175. Also George Grimm, *The Doctrine of the Buddha* (Berlin: Akademic-Verlag, 1958), p. 175. "We must retire from the world back into ourselves, to the 'centre of our vital birth', and by persistent introspection seek to find out how we have come into all this Becoming in which we find ourselves enmeshed".

[2] This side of the *anattā* doctrine has been explained with great subtlety and acumen by Grimm, *op. cit.*, pp. 115–6, 140, 147, 149, 175, 369–72. For my own views, see *Buddhist Thought in India*, pp. 36–9, 42, 122–34, 208–9.

[3] *Dhammapada*, v. 279: *yadā paññāya passati, atha nibbindati dukkhe.*

[4] *Mysticism, Christian and Buddhist* (London: George Allen & Unwin Ltd., 1957), p. 39.

problem of the ego must be carried on to the field of metaphysics. To really understand what Buddha meant by saying that there is no *ātman*, we must leave psychology behind." Those who equate Hume and Buddhism on the subject of the "self" overlook the fact that no passage in the Buddhist scriptures teaches that there is no self, (although the self is often called "inconceivable" and inaccessible to verbalized knowledge), that the whole subject of the existence and non-existence of a self is relegated to the class of the fruitless "indeterminate topics",[1] and that the fixed conviction that "there is not for me a self" is expressly condemned as a false view.[2]

These comparisons with European philosophers could be continued for many more pages, but enough has been said to clarify the general principles which in my view a comparative study of Buddhist and European philosophy must observe.

[1] Grimm, *op. cit.*, p. 140n.

[2] The *Majjhima Nikāya*, I, p. 8. Edited by V. Trenckner. (London: Pali Text Society, 1888).

The Iconography of the Prajñāpāramitā

Although European scholars have now for about half a century studied the Buddhist iconography of the later period, a great deal remains to be done. In the vast area of Buddhist influence we are confronted with a profusion of images and mythological systems, about which much is still unknown or in doubt. Innumerable works of art have been described. The descriptions are, however, widely scattered in all kinds of publications, often difficult of access, and not always correct. When we wish to gain certainty on some particular point, we all too frequently find ourselves enveloped in a dense fog of bewildered conjecture. At the present stage of our knowledge, a comprehensive survey of the knowledge accumulated about particular deities would be a distinct step forward. In due course we may then be able to build up an accurate survey of the whole pantheon.

In this article I propose to give an account of what is known at present about the images of the *Prajñāpāramitā*. Although the somewhat unspiritual West has so far failed to even translate the work, the *Prajñāpāramitā-sūtra* is the most important text of the Mahayana form of Buddhism, and it has remained its abiding inspiration. The mythological consciousness has personified as a deity the book, its doctrine, and the virtues it represents. In the pantheon of Tantric Buddhism this deity occupies a distinguished, though somewhat subordinate place. It would not be easy to give a comprehensive survey of the images of, say *Avalokiteśvara* or *Mañjuśrī*, which must be counted in thousands. The images of *Prajñāpāramitā*, which have come down to us, can be counted in dozens. The subject is therefore manageable, it is of interest as showing in a definite example the relation between the literary and the iconographic documents, and the often intricate problems involved in the identification of images, while finally its discussion affords a contribution to the long and varied history of the Mother-goddess who, from the Palaeolithic onwards, has occupied so great a place in human affection.

Statues of the *Prajñāpāramitā* are attested in India as early as A.D. 400 by *Fa-hsien's* account. All the early representations of the Prajñāpāramitā are now lost. No surviving example seems to be older than ca A.D.800. All the documents of the historical development which must have taken place in those four centuries between A.D. 400 and 800 are no longer available to us. We are therefore unable to say anything very definite about the historical sequence of the various types.

Before we turn to a description of those types, a few words must be said about the symbols by which the artist tries to give some visible form to the spiritual qualities of perfect wisdom.

The Symbolism Employed

The *ritual gestures* employed are three: The gesture of teaching (*dharma-cakra-mudrā*, or *vyākhyāna-mudrā*) is obviously fitting for a deity whose central function is the exposition of doctrine. Akin to it is the gesture of argument (*vitarka*)—the hand is raised and the ring finger touches the tip of the thumb. Finally there is the gesture which re-assures (*abhaya*)—the arm is raised, and the palm turned outward. This gesture symbolizes two aspects of Prajñāpāramitā. She is the supreme source of protection.[1] At the same time, the absence of all fear is very often stated to be the sign that perfect wisdom has been understood. I quote just one typical sentence. "If, when this doctrine is being taught, demonstrated and expounded, the thought of a Bodhisattva does not become cowed, nor stolid, does not despair nor despond, and if his mind is not dejected, or has its back broken, if he does not tremble, is not frightened nor terrified, then he is to be known as a Bodhisattva, a great Being, who is not lacking in the perfection of wisdom."[2]

Six kinds of *attributes* occur in the images of Prajñāpāramitā. There is, first of all, the *lotus*, which chiefly signifies purity, but also stands for many other ideas, which have been lucidly

[1] In the words of the *Sādhanamālā*, p. 226, 4: saiva Bhagavatī prajñāpāramitā saiva paramā raskhā.

[2] *Ashta* I 10.

explained by *Coomeraswamy*[1] and *H. Zimmer*.[2] The *book* is, of course, the Prajñāpāramitā-sūtra. The *Sādhanamālā* prescribes the Prajñāpāramitā-book also for *Mañjuśrī*[3] and *Sarasvatī*.[4] It also occurs in images of *Avalokiteśvara*, *Vasudhārā* and *Cundā*. B. Bhattacharya[5] assumes that in the case of *Cundā* it is the *Cundā-dhāraṇī*. But this *dhāraṇī*, preserved in Chinese and Tibetan, covers only one or two leaves, whereas the statues show a full-sized manuscript. The *rosary* has a threefold use in connection with the Prajñāpāramitā-sūtra. 1. A great deal of the text consists in applying certain formulas to a great number of items. For instance, a formula like "x is empty of x", is applied to long lists of categories, i.e. "form is empty of form", "feeling is empty of feeling", etc., etc. In meditation on such a formula a rosary would ensure that none of the repetitions is omitted. 2. The sūtra contains a chapter on "dharani-doors"[6] in which, on the principle of "A for apple, C for cat" etc., forty-two letters of a mystical alphabet—the *Arapacana*—sum up the doctrine in all its aspects; e.g., the letter *B* is the door to the insight that the *b*onds have departed from all dharmas. 3. Later on, from ca A.D. 400 onwards, the teaching was summed up in a number of short mantras, which had to be repeated as often as possible. A rosary was used to count the number of repetitions.

The *sword*, more usual with *Mañjuśrī*, is said to cut through the darkness of ignorance. The sword is a symbol of wisdom already in Pali Buddhism. The *thunderbolt* (*vajra*) is a well-known symbol of the emptiness which constitutes the core of the doctrine of perfect wisdom. The *begging bowl*, finally, reminds us that renunciation of all possessions is held to be a necessary prerequisite to full understanding.

The Types

The artistic representations of Prajñāpāramitā can be roughly classified according to the number of arms which the deity

[1] *Elements of Buddhist iconography*, 1935, p. 17 sq.

[2] *Myths and symbols in Indian art and civilization*, 1946, p. 98 sq.

[3] Vādirād Mañjughosha, pp. 107, 111. Dharmadhātuvāgiśvara, pp. 127, 128. Mañjunātha, p. 148. Mañjuśrī, p. 151.

[4] Pp. 332, 340; 339.

[5] India Antiqua, 1947, p. 28.

[6] Dhāraṇī-mukhāni. Śata-s, ix, 1450–3. Pañcaviṃś, 148–52.

possesses. It is of course, not always easy to know whether we have to deal with an image of Prajñāpāramitā, or of another deity. For the purposes of identification we have at our disposal only three sources of information: 1. Inscriptions on the images themselves. 2. The literary descriptions of the deities in the sādhanas. 3. The context in which the images are found. In quite a number of cases, these sources, as we shall see, fail us, and we cannot then easily arrive at complete certainty. Inscribed images are comparatively rare. Many of the works of art which can be studied in museums, etc., have been removed from their original context. And the sādhanas which have come down to us are not by any means complete, nor do we know really very much about their affiliation to the various schools of Tantric initiates.

1. We begin our survey with the *two-armed* form, with *book* and *lotus* as the decisive attributes. The details of the arrangement of book and lotus vary greatly. The figure is either sitting or standing.

The *Sādhanamālā* (before A.D. 1100) has preserved for us eight sādhanas (151–155, 157–159) of the two-armed Prajñāpāramitā. They are distributed as follows:

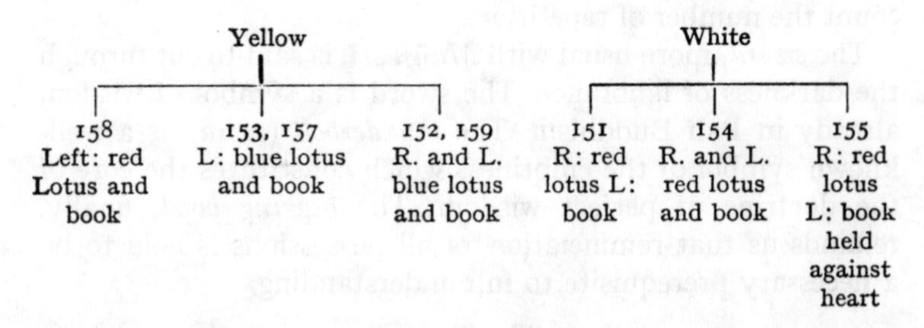

I. A. All the yellow forms have the hands in the gesture of teaching. Sometimes there is one lotus, with a book on top of it, on the left side of the seated figure. In the famous statue from *Singhasāri* in East Java (1 A a)[1] this is a red lotus, as required by sādhana 158. Several bronzes from Java (1 A b–d) conform, on the contrary, to sādhanas 153 and 157, giving a blue lotus.

In other cases two lotuses rise on both right and left, the stalks twisted round the arms, with a book on top of each lotus.

[1] The numbers refer to the Inventory at the end.

This type is the Prajñāpāramitā of the Vulture Peak (*Gṛdhra-kūṭa*) in *Magadha*. The Vulture Peak is a mountain near *Rājagṛha*[1] on which the Prajñāpāramitā-sūtra was traditionally preached. It was, as *Nāgārjuna* informs us,[2] the seat of a Vihāra, which was remote and undisturbed, and on which the Saints (*āryā*) like to dwell, as all the Buddhas of the past have done.[3] In former times, a well-known statue of the Prajñāpāramitā seems, on the evidence of two illuminated manuscripts of the *Pāla* period (1 A i, k) to have stood there. The lotuses are not always blue ones, as the sādhanas (152, 159) demand, and in some cases two red lotuses are shown (e.g., 1. Ai). A drawing of the white Prajñāpāramitā (A 1. Ar) corresponds to sādhana 154.

(1 B). In *Cambodia* we often find a *standing* Prajñāpāramitā, who holds a book in the right, and a lotus bud in the left hand. The deity is bare to the waist. The sarong is held by an ornate belt, and falls to the ankles. A crown is worn on the head. In some cases (e.g., 1 Bd, and also 1. Bc?) a Buddha in meditation is found in the crown. Two sādhanas (151 and 153) place the Buddha *Akshobhya* in the crown of Prajñāpāramitā. Sometimes (1. B l–o)[4] the figure holds a lotus in each hand.

1. C. There are, in addition, a few other forms. A graceful bronze from Sumatra (1 Ca) shows the two-armed form in the gesture of teaching, but without either lotus or book. A *Chu Fo P'usa* in the series of wood cuts which Clark[5] has reproduced, has lotuses to the right and left, outside the halo. The two arms hold lotus and book in front of the body (1. C b).

One of the earliest literary descriptions of a Prajñāpāramitā image is found in a commentary to the *Prajñāpāramitā-sūtra of a benevolent king*,[6] which was translated into Chinese about A.D. 750. She is said to sit cross-legged on a white lotus. The body is golden yellow, grave and majestic, with a precious necklace and a crown from which silken bands hang down on both sides. Her left hand, near her heart, carries the book.

[1] Visited by Fa hsien (Legge 82–3), and Hiuen-tsiang (Watters, ii, 151).
[2] Le traité de la grande vertu de sagesse, trad. Lamotte, I, 190.
[3] Ibid., p. 196.
[4] Acc. to Finot, Etudes Asiatiques, I, 1925, p. 254.
[5] Two Lamaistic Pantheons, 1937, Two vols.
[6] T 994.

Her right hand, near her breasts, makes the gesture of argumentation.[1] A statue (1. C c) in the Lama Temple in Peking is the one surviving work of art which corresponds to this description.

In addition, in the *garbha-dhātu-mandala* of the *Shingon* sect, a Prajñāpāramitā (1. C d) with a sword as its only symbol appears in the assembly of *Ākāśagarbha*.[2] Finally there is statue from Java (1. C e), of which I have seen no reproduction, with a Buddha image in the crown, where the right hand holds the rosary (?), and the left a book without a lotus.

2. A *four-armed* form is mentioned in the *Sādhanamālā* (no. 158, *kanakavarṇā*). She is there described as follows: "She bears a head-dress of twisted hair; she has four arms and one face. With two of her hands she makes the gesture of expounding the dharma and she is adorned with various jewelled ornaments. She blazes like the colour of gold and in her (second) left hand she holds a blue lotus with the Prajñāpāramitā-book upon it. She wears various garments both below and above and with her (second) right hand she makes the gesture of fearlessness."[3]

This form is apparently not found amongst the images which have survived.

2. A. Usually, in the four-armed images, two hands are in the gesture of teaching, while the second right hand holds a *rosary*, and the second left hand a *book*. We know this form either from manuscripts (2.Aa-g, q-r), or from paintings and statues from Nepal and Tibet (2. A l–p). Where the colour is shown, it is a golden yellow or a reddish brown.

2. B. A few four-armed forms in Nepal and the Lamaist world, all of them very late, show a different pattern. An illumination in a fairly modern Nepalese collection of dhāraṇīs (2. B a) shows a four-armed figure which has the right hand in *abhaya*; the left rests on the lap and holds a bowl; the second

[1] Seppō-in cf. de Visser, p. 173. The term *seppō-in* is not as unambiguous as we would wish it to be. This can be seen when we consider the very unsatisfactory explanations which E. Dale Saunders (*Mudrā*, 1960) gives on the basis of his Japanese material.

[2] Kokūzō-in.

[3] Trsl. D. L. Snellgrove, in *Buddhist Texts Through the Ages*, ed. E. Conze, 1954, p. 253. The entire *sādhana* 156 is there translated as no. 191, "An Evocation of Prajñāpāramitā".

right hand is just raised, and seems to bear no attribute; the second left hand holds the book. It is probable that this figure represents Prajñāpāramitā, because on this page the *Prajñā-pāramitā-hridaya* commences. It is also fairly similar to 2. C a, a statue in the Lamaist temple in Peking. The right hand holds a *vajra*, the left rests in the lap, holding a bowl. The second right hand holds the rosary, the second left the book. *R. Linossier*[1] mentions a quite similar yellow figure on a Tibetan banner. She tentatively identifies it as a *Cundā*. 2. D a, a Lamaist wood cut could possibly be the image described in the *Sādhanamālā*. The second right hand is in *abhaya*, the second left holds lotus and book, but the two central hands are just held up side by side against the chest. If this is not a new, otherwise unknown, ritual gesture, but a way of representing the gesture of teaching, we would have here the one four-armed image to carry out the instructions of the *Sādhanamālā*. Finally, *Tsuibikow* gives a reproduction of a Tibetan woodcut, 2. D c, where two hands are in the gesture of teaching, while the second right holds a thunderbolt, and the second left the book.

3. A *six-armed* form is preserved only in the *Shingon* sect in Japan. It came to Japan, of course, from China, and to China from India through *Śubhākarasiṃha*, a monk from *Nālandā*, who arrived in 716 at *Ch'ang-an*, and translated the *Mahāvairocana-sūtra* in 724. A magical circle of outstanding importance, the *garbha-dhātu-mandala*, derives from that text. The Prajñāpāramitā sits there in the centre of the "Light-bearing assembly".[2] Her six hands are said to represent the six perfections (*pāramitā*). The *Hizōki* describes her: "The Bodhisattva is of heavenly female form, of white flesh colour with six hands. One hand on the left holds a Sanskrit manuscript, the other five hands form mūdrās. She wears a kind of armour on her shoulder. She destroys the karma seed of ignorance".[3]

4. A *ten-armed* form is found in *Cambodia*, with four or five heads. The figure is standing, but the attributes cannot be distinctly made out.

5. A *twelve-armed* form is preserved in a statue from

[1] *Etudes d'orientalisme*, 1932, Les peintures tibetaines de la Collection Loo, I, 25.
[2] Tejo-dhara-parshad; ji-myō-in. Also Vidyādhara-vriti.
[3] B. L. Suzuki, Eastern Buddhist, vii, 1936, pp. 32–3.

Nālandā. Two of the hands are in the gesture of teaching, the others hold various attributes. I do not know on what grounds types 4 and 5 are regarded as Prajñāpāramitās.

6. Finally, in Cambodia, we have a form of *Prajñāpāramitā* with eleven heads, and *twenty-two* arms. She is either standing (6 a–c) or seated (6 d). The identification seems assured by the inscription on the pedestal of one of the statues, which reads: *Vrah rūpa vrah prajñāpāramitā*, "holy image of the holy perfection of wisdom" (6 b). Two of the images have a figure of a meditating Buddha in the crown (6 b, d).

We can sum up the *geographical distribution* of the images as follows: Under the *Pāla* dynasty a number of types was evolved in *Bengal*, which from there spread South East to *Java* and *Sumatra*, and North to *Nepal* and *Tibet*. *Khmer Cambodia* stands outside this main stream. The standing Prajñāpāramitā, and the ten-armed and twenty-two-armed forms are peculiar to it. No images seem to have been preserved in *Central Asia*. In *China* and *Japan* images of the Prajñāpāramitā are virtually unknown outside the sphere of influence of *Lamaism* and of the *Shingon* sect.[1]

Kindred Images

Representations of Prajñāpāramitā may be confused with images of Mañjuśrī, Sarasvatī, Avalokiteśvara, Tārā and Cundā. This results from an analysis of her qualities. Prajñāpāramitā[2] means first of all "perfect wisdom", and that asso-

[1] In addition that sect, according to de Visser, 491, traditionally identifies Prajñāpāramitā with Kongō-go Bodhisattva (Vajraraksha) of the four "near ones" (Shishingon) of Buddha Amoghasiddhi in the North side of the vajra-dhātumandala. Vajraraksha is illustrated in Clark, 4B, 52 and B 180.

[2] Professor Demiéville, of Paris, has very kindly sent me a number of observations on the "iconographie sino-japonaise" of the Prajñāpāramitā. His notes will, we hope, in due course appear in the *Hobogirin*. The Letter (D.) marks the material which I owe to him. For those who come after me I must mention some sources which I could not explore. They are in Chinese the "Dharaṇīsamuccaya" trsl. 625, T. 901, iii, 804c sq., and T 259 and T 1152, a Sutra and a ritual, both translated about A.D. 1000 and dealing with a six-armed form (D.). In Tibetan a number of Sādhanas are preserved in the Tanjur. They are, in Ui's Catalogue, no. 2326, 2640–1, 3219–22, 3352–5, 3542–8, 3550. Some further information in E. Conze, *The Prajñāpāramitā Literature*, 1960. pp. 22–4, 87 sq.

ciates her with Mañjuśrī, while the element of intellectual power and erudition involved in "wisdom" makes her resemble Sarasvatī. It is, however, of the essence of Prajñāpāramitā that wisdom is fused with an all-comprehensive compassion—and that naturally leads to similarities with Avalokiteśvara. It is the function of Prajñāpāramitā to save people, and that makes her close to Tārā, the popular saviouress. Finally, Prajñāpāramitā is the "mother of all the Buddhas", and that has led to a fusion, and even confusion, with Cundā, "the mother of seven koṭis of Buddhas", as her *dhāraṇī*[1] calls her.

DIAGRAM

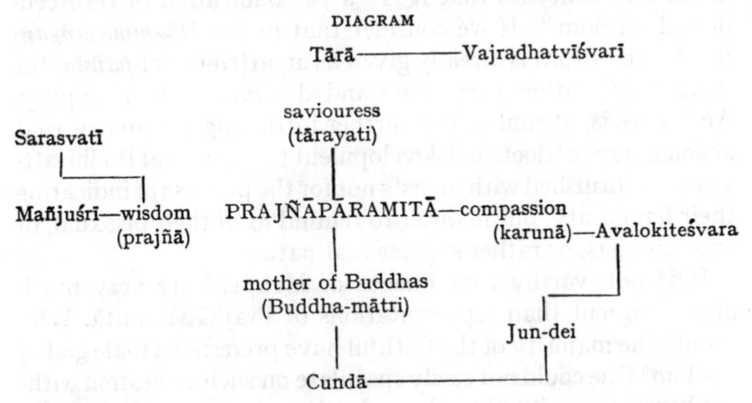

Mañjuśrī is the male personification of wisdom. His images frequently carry a lotus and book, and sometimes closely resemble those of Prajñāpāramitā. There is, however, always some distinguishing feature. Either a sword is added to the other symbols, or the posture differs,[2] or the figure is masculine.[3] The femininity of Prajñāpāramitā is usually fairly obvious. She is normally bare to the waist. As she is essentially a mother-goddess, her full breasts are conspicuous. Nevertheless there are a few borderline cases where a decision is not easy. In spite

[1] S. Beal, *Catena*, 1871, p. 413.

[2] E.g. some images of Mañjuvara are differentiated by the *lalita* or *ardhaparyanka* posture; or the image in Tsuibikow, p. 20 is standing and masculine.

[3] The statue from Tibet which Visser, Asiatic Art, 1948, no. 263, tentatively regards as a Prajñāpāramitā, is more likely to be a Mañjuśrī. It carries a book and a pearl (bindu?), but is not feminine. In addition, according to Getty, p. 111, the pearl is frequently associated with the book which Mañjuśrī carries.

of the existence of I. C d it is generally assumed that a Mongol or Tibetan figure with a sword must be a Mañjuśrī. But can we be really quite certain? For instance, the frontispiece of G. Schulemann, *Geschichte der Dalai-Lamas*, 1958, shows a very interesting modern temple flag, probably Mongol. Schulemann himself (p. 485) identifies it as the Bodhisattva Mañjuśrī, reddish-yellow in colour, with the sword of knowledge in his right hand, and the P.P. book on a lotus-flower in his left. But the figure is clearly and unmistakably *feminine*, and Schulemann also concedes that it is "a personification of transcendental wisdom". If we consider that in the *Dhammasaṅgani* (no 16) the sword is already given as an attribute of *paññā*, the situation is rather perplexing and deserves further enquiry. And there is, of course, the further intriguing possibility that at some stage of doctrinal development the images of Bodhisattvas were furnished with breasts not for the purpose of indicating their femininity, but in order to remind us of their bisexual, or androgynous, or rather supersexual nature.

It is noteworthy that images of Mañjuśrī are very much more frequent than representations of Prajñāpāramitā. Why should the majority of the faithful have preferred a male god of wisdom? One could not easily speculate on such a question without being drawn into lengthy reflections on comparative mythology, which abounds in both gods and goddesses of wisdom.

Sarasvatī is the Hindu goddess of learning, eloquence and intelligence. She goes back to Vedic times, and was taken over by the Buddhists, often under the name of *Vajra-Sarasvatī*. She is usually easily recognized by the lute which is her distinctive symbol. In one of her forms, described in *Sādhanamālā* no. 168 she is, however, practically identical with the somewhat elusive *white* form of the two-armed Prajñāpāramitā. Not only is her outward visible form indistinguishable from that of the white Prajñāpāramitā, but, what is more, even the mantras of the two deities are exactly the same.[1] An illustration is found among *Clark's* wood cuts,[2] and in Cambodia Sarasvatī is often shown with lotus and book.

[1] *Sādhanamālā*, p. 340, compared with sādhanas 151 and 153, cf. also pp. 331 and 335.

[2] B 254. Lotus in right hand, book in left in front of body, just as in *sādhana* 155 of *prajñāpāramitā*.

The iconography of *Avalokiteśvara* comes at several points into close contact with that of Prajñāpāramitā. Most Mahayana countries know of a four-armed form of Avalokiteśvara which is very similar to the normal four-armed Prajñāpāramitā. The four-armed Avalokiteśvara is subject to great variations, but usually some detail permits us to know that we have to deal with an Avalokiteśvara—e.g. the white colour of the body, or the flask in one hand, or the posture of the body. In Nepal and Tibet the hands are sometimes clasped in front of the chest in such a way that they resemble the gesture of teaching.[1] The similarity with Prajñāpāramitā is sometimes so close that even scholars have been deceived.[2] Ārya-Avalokiteśvara with eleven heads and twenty-two arms[3] is very similar to form (6) of Prajñāpāramitā, and a statue with eighteen arms, very much like a Prajñāpāramitā, has, as we shall see (p. 255), arisen as a result of a fusion between Cundā and Avalokiteśvara.

The notion of *Tārā* is, as I showed before,[4] very similar to that of Prajñāpāramitā. In most cases a Tārā can, however, with some care be identified by the gesture of the hands as the important criterion. A two-armed feminine deity in padmāsana with

[1] Getty plate, xxi c. Foucher, Mém. Acad. Inscr. Belles Lettres, i, xi, 1902, p. 23 mentions a Tibetan painting of a figure in dharmacakra, with rosary and lotus, which is inscribed as Lokeśvara. A Dhāraṇīsamgraha of 1719, i.e. Cambr. Add. 1326, seems, on the other hand, to show the golden four-armed Prajñāpāramitā on fol. 1 with hands in namaskāra. It seems, to me, in fact, that from the eighteenth century onwards some of the Buddhist craftsmen of Nepal, China and Mongolia had no longer the competence to draw the *dharmacakramudrā* properly, as is shown, for instance, by the figure of Vairocana in *A New Tibeto-Mongol Pantheon*, 1961, ed. R. Vira and L. Chandra (plate 61; cf. H. V. Guenther's comment on p. 15).

[2] E.g. Tucci, Indo-Tibetica, iii, i, p. 120, believes that a statue in the Shalun Temple, at Spyi-ti, Western Tibet, represents the four-armed kanakavarṇā prajñāpāramitā of sādhana 158. Local tradition, as reported by H. Lee Shuttleworth, Mem. Arch. Survey India, no. 39, 1929, regards the statue as one of Avalokiteśvara, and this identification seems confirmed by the presence of Amitabha above the image. Fig. e in Shuttleworth gives a better view than Tucci's photo (tav. lxviii), on which the body is partly hidden by a cloak. The symbols of the two extra hands are lost.

[3] Getty, 1st ed., p. 65, and pl. xxiii a. A. K. Gordon. The Iconography of Tibetan Lamaism, 1939, p. 67.

[4] Oriental Art, i, 1948, p. 12.

a lotus on her left, even though the lotus may carry a book, is not a Prajñāpāramitā, but a Tārā, or a Māmakī,[1] if and when the right hand is in the gesture of giving (varada mudrā). If the left hand in addition holds a lotus *without* a book no confusion should really take place.[2] Things are more difficult with the Tārā *Vajradhātvīśvarī*, who is white, and the consort of *Vairocana*. Her hands are in *dhvaja-mudrā*, which is very similar to the gesture of teaching. Where such a statue is found together with Vairocana, the identification is, of course, easy.[3] Little is known about the many-armed forms of Tārā, and there remains the possibility that they have had some influence on the many-armed forms of Prajñāpāramitā.

Prajñaparamita is closely related to *Cundā*, who shares her gesture, the book and the rosary. Cundā has up to now remained a rather mysterious deity. Literary documents concerning her are scarce, and we know next to nothing about either her origin or her later functions. Even the name of this deity shows a considerable range of variation. Sanskrit manuscripts give it as Cuṇḍā, Cundrā, Candra, Cuṇḍrā and Cundā. The Chinese[4] and Tibetan equivalents Tchouen-t'i (T'siuen-d'ie) or Tchouen-tche, and Tsundahi or Tsundehi—may go back to a sanskrit Cundī, Caṇḍī (=Durgā!), Cunda, Chundi, or Cuṇṭi. The Japanese Shingon sect is in doubt as to whether the name of *Jundei Butsumo*, or *Jundei* Kwannon, is derived from the

[1] A plate to Raffle's History of Java, 1817, shows a statue from Singasāri, very similar to 1Aa, but with the right hand in varada, while the left holds a lotus. It is inscribed Śrī-Māmakī.

[2] This is the case of a statue from East Java in the Musée Guimet, of ca. 800, which the Histoire générale des religions, iv, 1947, p. 420, wrongly describes as a Prajñāpāramitā. P. C. Bagchi, in *J.I.S.O.A.I.*, 1933, 1–5 describes a Nepalese painted banner of 1570 A.D., and believes that the two chief figures represent Mañjuśrī and the white Prajñāpāramitā. The male figure, white, has the book and rosary, but the two central arms are not, as Bagchi asserts, in dharmacakra, but are just lifted up together in front of the chest. The figure is a four-armed Avalokiteśvara. The female figure has one hand in varada, and the other in vitarka, and obviously shows the white Tārā (Getty, p. 122), the usual consort of Avalokiteśvara. This is also the opinion of S. Kramrisch, *The art of Nepal*, 1964, p. 148, who reproduces the painting on p. 108.

[3] An example is Leyden 2862, illustrated in Oudheidkundig Verslag 1930, plaat 50. Another example is Leyden 1703.

[4] Pelliot, T'oung Pao, 1931, 435–6.

sanskrit *śundhi* (purity), *sunda* (bright and beautiful), *cuṇṭi* (a well), or *cuṇḍī*(to become smaller).[1]

Images of Cundā exist probably with two arms,[2] and certainly with four, six, sixteen and eighteen arms. With some care the four-armed Cundā is easily distinguished from the four-armed Prajñāpāramitā by the gesture of the original hands, which are either in *dhyānamudrā*, or hold the begging bowl. Difficulties arise, however, about the many-armed forms. From the sixteen-armed images of Cundā we know that what the *Sādhanamālā* calls the *mūla-mudrā* of the many-armed Cundā is similar to the gesture of teaching. This similarity causes difficulties when we come to an eighteen-armed feminine deity from Nālandā and Java, who has two hands in what closely resembles the gesture of teaching, and who has sometimes been identified as a Prajñāpāramitā.[3]

It is difficult to be quite certain in this matter, but I believe that we have here to deal with a fusion between *Cundā* and *Avalokiteśvara*. The statue in Java is reddish.[4] It appears that Prajñāpāramitā is usually either yellow or white, whereas we have red images of Cundā.[5] The Indian and Javanese statues in question represent, I think, the same deity as the *Jundei Kwannon*, with eighteen arms, who holds the original arms against the breast, in the gesture *renge-no-in*,[6] and who is well-known from Japan.[7]

[1] Eastern Buddhist, vii, 1936, p. 30.

[2] The sādhanas do not mention such a form. A two-armed statue in the Batavia Museum, no. 639a (Rapporten 1912, plaat 18b) is very like a *prajñāpāramitā*, but the hands are in *dyhāna-mudrā*. A Java bronze, no. 3614 of the Rotterdam Museum, holds a bowl and is not a Prajñāpāramitā, as usually assumed.

[3] 1. Nālandā, ill. Annual A.S.I. 1927–28, pl. xlivb. Shastri, pl. xiii, h.-2. Java ill in Heine-Geldern, *Altjavanische Bronzen* (Vienna), 1925, pl. 12. 3. Hist. Bengal xxvi, ill. 64. 4. Bodh Gaya, ill. Foucher, *Iconographie*, p. 145.

[4] Dunkelroetlich getoent, acc. to Heine-Geldern, p. 21.

[5] E.g. Cambridge Add. 1643, no. 58.

[6] Getty, 1st ed., p. 82, and plate xii c.

[7] In the *sarvajña-vritta* of the *garbha-dhātu-mandala*. Ill. in Taishō Issaikyō, Illustrations, vol. 1, no. 14. Other images in *Shoshū Butsuzō-zu-ye* I, 37f, and 378 (Daigoji Temple).

The Context

The context often helps in the identification of images and throws light on the ideas associated with the various deities. Prajñāpāramitā forms either a part of 1). *a trinity*, or other numerical series,[1] or 2) of *mandalas*.

1. In *Nepal* we frequently[2] find the trinity Dharma, Buddha and Sangha[3]. The Dharma is there represented by the normal four-armed Prajñāpāramitā (2A), the Sangha by a four-armed male Bodhisattva, Avalokiteśvara, with two arms held in front of the chest, while the other two hold, like the Prajñāpāramitā, a rosary, and lotus or book, respectively. In the earlier periods the "three jewels" were represented by aniconic symbols, such as wheels, tridents, etc.[4] In the later Mahayana, the Prajñāpāramitā came to be considered as the quintessence of the doctrine (*dharma*), and the compassionate activity of Avalokiteśvara as the model for the duties of the monastic community (*saṃgha*). The trinity Avalokita, Buddha, Prajñāpāramitā occurs frequently in *Khmer* sculptures and inscriptions of the tenth and eleventh centuries, on many votive tablets (Brah Bimb) of the same period in *Siam*,[5] and sometimes in *Tibet*. The votive tablets show the Buddha in meditation on a Nāga; on his right a four-armed Avalokiteśvara, and on his left a two-armed Prajñāpāramitā. In Cambodia, between 950 and 1,000, several inscriptions link the Prajñāpāramitā, called Prajñādevī, or Divya-devī, with Lokeśvara[6] and also, in some cases, with Vajrapāṇi and the Buddha.[7] The four-faced monolithic *caityas* of Cambodia often show Prajñāpāramitā together with Lokeśvara.[8] In Cambodia, in any case, Buddhist theology was strongly influenced by Shivaism, and Lokeśvara corresponded

[1] Such as the 10 *pāramitās* with 1cd.
[2] E.g. Temple of Sambhunath, and 2 Am (?).
[3] H. A. Oldfield, *Sketches from Nepal*, ii, 1880, pp. 158–9.
[4] Foucher, Vol. 1, pp. 428–9.
[5] G. Coedès, *Tablettes votives bouddhiques du Siam*, Études Asiatiques, I, 1925, pp. 158–9, pls. 10 and 1 (= 1 Bf.g).
[6] E.g. Bantay Nang 975; Pràsàt Cikren 972; Battambang 982. Stele of Srei Santhor 975–80.
[7] So in the inscriptions of Bàt Čum (near Angkor Thom). J. As. 1908, ii, 247–8, 223–4.
[8] L. Finot, in *Études Asiatiques*, i, 1925, pp. 251–5.

to Maheśvara, just as the Prajñā-devī to the Shivaite Devī. Sometimes the Buddha on a Nāga is added as a third, and Vajrapāṇi,[1] and Hayagrīva[2] as a fourth.

The covers of Prajñāpāramitā manuscripts usually show a Prajñāpāramitā in the centre, accompanied by various attendants. The cover of the manuscript in the Bodleian (2. A a), which was described in *Oriental Art*, I, 1948–9, pp. 5–12 depicts ten attendants, whom Mlle de Mallmann has lately identified as the nine *pāramitās* plus the green Vārendra Tārā[3]. In other cases, the attendants are not easily identified. On 2 A l, for instance, we have, on each side, first six deities worshipping, then an eight armed figure, and then again four standing figures. Other elaborate *parivāras* can be seen on 1. A m, 2. A b and 2. A q. On the illuminations in the body of the manuscripts the attendants appear to be mostly Tārās, for instance a white and a green one on I. A i, 4 and a green and a yellow female Bodhisattva on each side in 1. Ak. In Cambr. Add. 1643, fol. 40v, the four-armed Prajñāpāramitā may be, according to Foucher, one of the attendants of Avalokiteśvara.

2. In a few mandalas (magical circles) the Prajñāpāramitā is the central figure. Three texts describing such a mandala are preserved, one in Chinese,[4] and two in Tibetan.[5] In a ritual text, translated by Amoghavajra (T 1151), the Prajñāpāramitā is represented as a Bodhisattva, encircled by the ten Pāramitās, and surrounded by sixteen deities. I do not know of any pictorial representation of a Prajñāpāramitā Mandala which has come down to us. In a few cases Prajñāpāramitā occurs as a subordinate figure. The *Mañjusrī-mūla-kalpa* describes two such mandalas,[6] one of them being a very elaborate one of Śākyamuni in which the Prajñāpāramitā figures twice. A detailed discussion of the subject would lead us here too far.

[1] E.g. 4a.

[2] Or Heruka, or Hevajra?—e.g. no 7, 9.

[3] A propos d'un MS. Illustré du xi^es. Oriental Art. N.S. xi, 4, 1965, pp. 2–12.

[4] T 1151. The persons of the Mandala are indicated in Mikkyōdaijiten, p. 1840a (D).

[5] *Prajñāpāramitā-mandala-vidhi*, Ui's Catalogue no. 2644 (13 pp.) and 2645 (10 pp.; by Ratnakīrti).

[6] Chap. 2, p. 40, Trsl. BEFEO, xxiii, 313–4, chap. 28, p. 318, trsl. in Lalou, Étoffes peintes, pp. 64–5.

The arrangement of deities in the *garbha-dhātu-mandala*, on the other hand, gives such a clear indication of the ideas associated with the conception of Prajñāpāramitā in the eighth century, that I give a diagram of the central portion of his mandala, and add a few remarks on those deities who are immediately related to the Prajñāpāramitā.

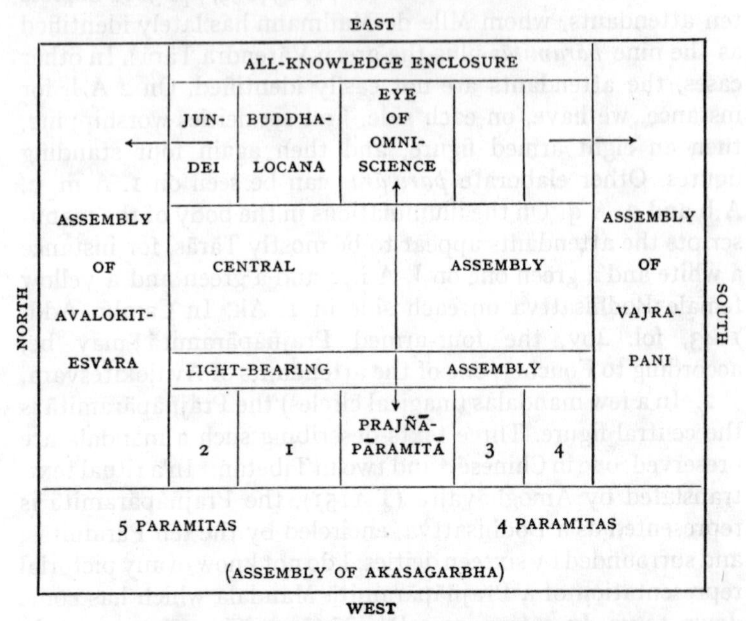

It should be remembered that this diagram refers to the current *genzu-mandara*—the mandala as depicted graphically—which comprises 414 deities. The *genzumandara* is attested in Japan from the days of Kōbō Daishi onwards (ca. A.D. 830), and it is therefore likely to be still older in China where the *Mahāvairocana-sūtra*, on which this mandala is based, was translated in 724 by Śubhākarasiṃha.[1] The Sūtra itself, however, in chap. 2, envisages only 110 deities in the garbha-dhātu-mandala. The contemporary oral commentary of Śubhākarasiṃha[2] provides for 164 figures. The remaining 240 deities must be derived from oral traditions which have not always been preserved in writing.

[1] Taisho Issaikyō, no. 848.

[2] Written down by Yi-ching in 725–727. *Taishō*, no. 1797.

The *Mahāvairocana-sūtra*, as well as the nearly contemporary *Manjuśrī-mūla-kalpa*, divides the spiritually significant forces in the universe—personified as deities—into three main families, or clans (*kula*). The principle behind this threefold division is fairly intelligible. The first family, that of the Buddhas, corresponds to those aspects of the Tantric rites which attempt to appease and to remove suffering (*śāntika*). The Lotus family (*padma*, *abja*), again, corresponds to the *paushthika* rites, which attempt to increase happiness, and to make it grow. It is represented by the assembly of Avalokiteśvara. The Thunderbolt family (*vajra-kula*), finally, is related to the *ābhicāruka* rites, which exorcise and annihilate evil, and it is represented by the assembly of Vajrapāṇi.

The six-armed Prajñāpāramitā in the Light-bearing assembly corresponds to the Eye of Omniscience in the All-knowledge Enclosure. The Prajñāpāramitā is the mother of all the Buddhas, just as the Eye of Omniscience is their father. The Eye of Omniscience is, in the All-knowledge-enclosure, associated with two other mothers of the Buddha—*Buddha-locanā*, and the *Jundei* whose affinity with the Prajñāpāramitā we have noted previously (p. 254). Buddha-locanā is called a "mother" of the Buddha, not in the sense that she creates or engenders the Buddha—for the Buddha is uncreated—but in the sense that "this Eye allows the Buddhas to discern the differences in the condition of the various beings whom they wish to save, and, as a consequence, to engender from it, as from a mother, different manifestations which are adapted to the needs of the different categories of beings."[1] From Jundei, again, spring the twenty-one forms of Avalokiteśvara to the left, or North side, of the Central Assembly.

The six-armed Prajñāpāramitā is flanked by four *vidyārājās* (kings of knowledge), two on each side. This gives five figures for the Light-bearing assembly, as against two in the text of the Mahāvairocana-sūtra itself. Only Acala-nātha-vidyārāja and Trailokya-vijaya-vidyārāja (also Vajra-huṃ-kara-vidyārāja) are mentioned in the Sūtra and in Śubhākarasiṃha's commentary. All the five persons of this enclosure are, however, mentioned already in a ritual which is as old as the Sūtra itself, and

[1] *Hobogirin*, p. 205.

which is attributed to Śubhākarasiṃha.[1] According to B. L. Suzuki,[2] the four vidyārājās represent the power of subduing, while the Prajñāpāramitā herself represents the power of accepting. Yamāntaka's (=1) virtue consists in removing all hindrances; Trailokavidyārāja (=2) represents the virtue attained by destroying evil passions; *Vajrahuṃkara Trailokavijaya* (=3) stands for the conquest of the triple world, i.e. over greed, hate and delusion; *Acalavidyārāja* (=4) likewise aims at removing hindrances and obstacles from all sentient beings. According to Tajima[3] Acalavidyārāja personifies the firmness of the heart of enlightenment. He should be invoked whenever either the unwholesome after-effects of our past, or the impurities of our hearts, place obstacles in the path of our spiritual progress.

It is difficult at present to say much more than this about the position of the Prajñāpāramitā in the garbha-dhātu-mandala. Much preliminary work has still to be done with regard to the detailed interpretation of the magical circles which play such a large part in the Buddhism of Japan and Tibet. What we need first of all is a careful and amply annotated translation of the second chapter of the *Mahāvairocana-sūtra*, which should be compared with the pictorial representations of the mandala.[4] The idea of representing spiritual forces by diagrams of deities has become rather unfamiliar to our contemporary habits of thought. The work of Ananda K. Coomaraswamy has recently again provided us with a key to this varied and beautiful world of the past, which, if we can believe some modern psychologists, still slumbers in the depths of our collective, or racial, sub-conscious mind.

[1] T 851, pp. 100 b–c, 106b (D).

[2] The Eastern Buddhist, vii, 1936, p. 32.

[3] *Étude sur le Mahavairocana-sutra*, 1936, p. 116.

[4] Quite a number of pictorial representations of the mandala exist in Japan, some of them in colour. They differ from each other in many details. The picture of 3a which I reproduced from Taishō Issaikyō, Zuzō 1 in my first article, derives from the painting of the mandala which Kūkai made between 824 and 833 in the Takaosan Temple near Kyōto, in gold and silver on purple silk (D).

INVENTORY OF THE IMAGES

The Types

1. *Two-armed*

1.1. Seated, padmāsana, dharmacakra, lotus with book on left
1.1a. Red lotus (sādhana 158)
1 Aa. Statue, stone, East Java, Singhasāri, ca 1300.
1.1b. Blue lotus (sādhanas 153, 157)
1 Ab. Bronze, Java.—1 Ac, Bronze, Java, Kedoe.—1 Ad, Bronze, Java.
1.1c. Two lotuses (with book) on right and left. (sādh. 152, 159, 154)
Statues: 1 Ae, Nālandā, 1200.—1 Af, India, 1200.—1 Ag, India, 1200.—Illuminations, *Aṣṭas.*: 1 Ah, Vikramaśīla.—1 Ai, Nepal, 1015.—1 Ak, Nepal, ca 1070.—1 Al (back cover), Nepal?, ca 1100.—1 Am (back cover), Nepal, 1136.—1 An, East India, ca 1200.—1 Ao, Wood cut, Tibet, ca 1750.—1 Ap, Illumination, ca 1000.—1 Aq, Illumination, Kashmir.—1 Ar, wood cut, Tibet (white form).—1 As, Ill. Ms. *Aṣṭas.*—1 At, cover to Ms. *Aṣṭas*, (white form).
1.2 Standing, lotus and book
1.2a. One lotus
Bronzes, Cambodia, 1300: 1 Ba, 1 Bb, 1 Bc, 1 Bd, 1 Be.—Votive tablets: 1 Bf, Siam, 900–1100.—1 Bg, Siam, Vat Dao Gotr, 900–1100.—1 Bh, Siam, Subarnapurī.—Stele: 1 Bk, Cambodia, 1300.
1,2b. Two lotuses
Stele, Cambodia: 1 Bl, 1300.—1 Bm, 1300.—1 Bn, Prah Khan, 1300.—Sculpture, 1 Bo. Angkor Wat, 1300.
1.3 Others, all seated
1.3a. Dharmacakra, neither lotus nor book
1 Ca. Bronze, Sumatra, Padang Sawas, ca 1200?
1.3b. Cintāmaṇi (lotus?) and book in front of body
1 Cb. Wood cut, China, ca 1750.
1.3c. Vitarka and book
1 Cc. Statue, Peking, 1653.
1.3d. Sword
1 Cd. Wood cut, Japan (China), 725+.
1.3e. Rosary(?) and book
1 Ce. Statue, Java.
1.3f. Lotus and book (=sādhana 151?)
1 Cf. Wood cut, Tibet.

1.3g. Sūtrabox in LH; RH in abhayadada
1 Cg. Described in *Dhāraṇīsamuccaya*, A.D. 653–4.

2. *Four-armed*

2 A. Seated, dharmacakra, rosary and book
Illuminations, Ms. *Aṣṭas.*: 2 Aa, back cover to Ms. Nālandā, A.D. 1092.—2 Ab, Nepal, 1015.—2 Ac, Nepal, 1247.—2 Ad, Vikramaśīla, 1100.—2 Ae. Ms. *Pañcarakṣā*, Bengal?, 1104.—2Af, Ms. *Pañcaviṃśatis.*, Nepal, ca 1800.—2 Ag, Ill., *Aṣṭas.*, Bengal, A.D. 1020.—2 Ah, back cover, Ms. *Aṣṭas.*, 1028.—2 Ai, Ms. *Pañcaviṃśatis.*, Nepal, 1750.—2 Ak, Ms. *Aṣṭas.*, Nepal? ca 1100.—2 Al; Bronze, Nepal, ca 1350.—2 Am, Statue, Nepal, Kirtipur.—2 An, Temple banner, Tibet.—2 Ao, Stucco statue, W. Tibet.—2 Ap, Bronze, Nepal.— 2 Aq, Front cover to Ms. *Aṣṭas.*, Bengal, 1020.—2 Ar, ill., Ms. *Pañcaviṃśatis.*, Nepal, ca 1750.
2 B–H. Other forms, all seated
2 B. Rosary, book; vitarka, bowl
2 Ba. Ill. *Dhāraṇīsaṃgraha*, Nepal, ca 1750 (UR: no rosary in raised arm?).—2 Bb, Ill., *Śatas.*, Nepal.
2 C. Rosary, book; vajra, vase
2 Ca. Statue, Peking, 1653.
2 D. Dharmacakra, and various arrangements of other two hands
2 Da, Wood cut, China, ca 1750. UR, *varada;* UL holds book lying on lotus.—2 Db, Stone statue, Orissa, ca 1050. LR: *varada*, LL: broken. 2 lotuses (?), or lotus and book(?).—2 Dc, Wood cut, Tibet. Other two hands: *vajra* and book.
2 E. Book, vase; double vajra, lotus
2 Ea. Painting, Tibet, Mahākālamaṇḍala?
2 F. Vajra, book; LL in lap; LR, vitarka
2 Fa. Book cover of Ms of *Śatasāhasrikā*, Tibet, 17th c.
2 G. Two hands in lap; UR book, UL, vajra (?)
2 Ga. Tibetan thangka of five *ḍākiṇīs.*—2 Gb. Lhasa print of *Aṣṭasāhasrikā.*
2 H. Rosary, book; LR, vitarka, LL in lap
2 Ha. Fresco, White Temple of Toling.—2 Hb. Drawing, Tibet ca 1750.

3. *Six-armed*

3a. Wood cut, China, Japan, 725+.—3b. First RH: rosary, LH: Sūtra; 2nd RH: arrow, LH: bow; 3rd RH: *varada*, LH: *cintāmaṇi.*—3c. *Dharmacakramudrā.* 4 others hold: book, *utpala*, small lance, etc.

4. *Ten-armed*

4a. Statue, Cambodia, Phnom Srok. 1300.

5. *Twelve-armed*

5a. Statue, Nālandā, 1200.

6. *Twenty-two-armed*

6.1. Standing

Bronzes: 6a, Cambodia, Pnom Penh, 1300.—6b, Cambodia, Korat, 1300.—6c, Cambodia, Surindr, prov. Ubon, 1300.

6.2. Seated

6d. Bronze, Cambodia, 1300.

Sources and Reproductions

1 *Aa*. Leiden Mus. 1587. 1.26 m. high. Found in the Shivaite temple. Illustrations are very numerous, e.g. B. Bhattacharya, pl. xxviii C.—Havell, *Indian Sculpture and Painting*, pl. xiv.—N. J. Krom, *L'Art Javanais*, 1926, pl. 28.—V. A. Smith, *A History of Fine Art in India and Ceylon*, 1930, pl. 112 (from side).—A. K. Coomaraswamy, *Viśvakarma*, 1914, pl. 4 (side view); pl. 5 (front view).—N. J. Krom, *Inleiding*, 1923, pl. 54.—Or. Art II, 1949, p. 46.—Colour photograph in D. Seckel, *The Art of Buddhism*, 1964, p. 237 (which, however, fails to bring out the warm golden glow of the original andesite stone); side, *ibid*. p. 239 (very striking and good).

1 Ab. Leiden Mus. 1697. 16.6 cm. high.—H. H. Juynboll, *Katalog des Ethnograph. Reichsmus.*, 5, Javanische Altertümer, 1909, p. 105 (drawing).—Photo: T. B. Boorda, *Kleur v. Indische Beeldhouwkunst*, I, 1923, xvii.—Cf. Tobi, Oudheidkundig Verslag, 1930, p. 196 (*dhvajamudrā*), 198.

1 Ac. Batavia Mus. no. 639.—13 cm. high. Described in *Rapporten v. d. Commissie in Nederl.-Indie v. Oudheidkundig onderzoek*, 1912, p. 71.—Ill. pl. 18a. cf. *Verhand*. 21 p. 35 no. 49.

1 Ad. Batavia Mus. no. 602a.—*Rapporten*, 1912, pl. 13a.—Trinity: Buddha and Prajñāpāramitā, right and left(?). Described *Rapporten* pp. 20–1. Ill.—also Foto Oudheidkundig Comm. 872, 873.

1 Ae. Ill.: Kempers, fig. 17.

1 Af. Calcutta, Indian Mus. no. 3817.—Ill. Bhattacharya pl. xxxvi C.—R. D. Banerjee, ASI XLVII, 1933, pl. XLI C.—The arms are broken off.

1 Ag. Maldah Mus.—Ill. *Dacca Hist. Bengal*, I, ill. 62. Descr. *ibid*. I p. 472.—The arms are broken off.

1 Ah. B. M. Or. 6902, fol. 2.—The body is yellow, the lotuses white. —A blue halo behind the body.

1 Ai. Cambridge Add. 1643, fol. 13v. Inscription: Gṛdhakūṭa-parvate prajñāpāramitā.—Descr. by Foucher, *Etude sur l'Iconographie Bouddhique de l'Inde*, 1900, p. 190.—Ill. in Oriental Art III, 1951, p. 106.—Yellow body, red lotuses. L: white, R: green figure (Tārā).

1 Ak. Calcutta, RASB A 15, fol. 12r. Gṛdhrakūṭe prajñāpāramitā. —Foucher p. 207, ill. pl. IX, 3.—*Dacca History of Bengal*, I, ill. 188, reddish yellow; four assistants.

1 Al. Japan, S. Sawamura.—Ill. Ostas. Zeitschr., N. F., 3, 1926, pl. 9, 10 (details); cf. 119–123.
1 Am. Boston Mus. no. 20.589.—Ostas. Zeitschr., N. F. 3, 1926, Tafel 11.
1 An. Detroit Inst. of Arts no. 27.586.—*Bulletin* XXI, 1942, p. 66.—S. Kramrisch, *The Art of Nepal*, 1964, p. 144.
1 Ao. Śer-phyin-ma. From the Pantheon of the Changtsha Hutuktu Lalitavajra (1736–96?). In: S. F. Oldenburg, *Sbornik izobrazenii 300 burkhanov*, Bibl. Buddh. V, 1903, no. 158.—Also: Or. Art, III, 1951, p. 105.
1 Ap. RASB Ms. 4713.—Photo: M. Mookerjee's London Thesis, pl. V, 12 (blurred).
1 *Aq.* G. Tucci, *Tibetan Painted Scrolls.* Two green attendants.
1 Ar. "Five hundred Gods of Narthang", Rin-'byuṅ 67a śer-phyin-ma dkar-mo.-Lokesh Chandra, *Tibetan-Sanskrit Dictionary*, p. 2361. Also: *A New Tibeto-Mongol Pantheon*, vol. 8, 1963, p. 64.
1 As. Boston Mus. of Fine Arts. (Check whether = 1 Am???).
1 At. Boston Mus. of Fine Arts.
1 Ba. 6 inches high.—A. Getty, *The Gods of Northern Buddhism*, 1928, pl. xxv d.
1 Bb. Bangkok, 46 cm.—G. Coedès, *Bronzes Khmers*, Ars Asiatica., V, 1923, pl. xxxiv, 1.
1 Bc. Bangkok?, 29 cm.—Coedès, pl. xxxiv, 2.
1 Bd. Coedès, pl. xxxiv, 3.
1 Be. L. Fournerau, *Le Siam Ancien*, I, 1895, pl. xxviii, 1, who describes it as a Lakṣmī.
1 Bf. Coedès, *Etudes Asiatiques*, I, 1925, pl. 1.
1 Bg. *Ibid.* pl. 10b.
1 Bh. *Ibid.* pl. 10c.
1 Bi. Fournerau, *Le Siam*, pl. xxiii.
1 Bk. Musée du Trocadero (now: Guimet?)
1 Bl. Musée Guimet, B.C.A.I., 1910, p. 55, no. 54.
1Bm. *Ibid.* no. 55.
1 Bn. Musée Guimet 18 118. Dupont (X) 3.36 (Photo in M. G. Not good.)—This is a stele, with four sides, showing the Buddha, a four-armed Lokeśvara (lotus, book, rosary, flask), the Buddha, the Prajñāpāramitā, *à chaque main longue tige terminée par un bouton de lotus.*—The illustration in Fournerau, *Les Ruines Khmères*, 1890, pl. 78, does not show the Prajñāpāramitā. cf. Coedès no. T 20, 10 pl. viii m. de Crozier, *L'Art Khmer*, 1875, no. xxxvi, 115.
1 Bo. Fournerau, *Les Ruines Khmères*, 1890, pl. 77.
1 Ca. A.B.I.A., 1939, pl. III, a, b.—The halo, and perhaps a parasol, is lost.
1 Cb. Clark, *Two Lamaistic Pantheons*, 1937, 2 vols, no. 251.—Inscript.: Śer-phyin phyag gñis-ma. Ch 23: Erh-pei pan-jo fo-mu.
1 Cc. Lama Temple.—Clark 4 A 17.—This statue is part of a set of ten *pāramitās* (A, 4 A 1–4, 14–17, 4 B 33–36), and there is some

difficulty about identifying the *prajñāpāramitā* among them. Clark gives 4 B 34, which is inscribed (Ch 446): *chih po-lo-mi-mu*, which I take to be *jñānapāramitā*, the last one in the list of ten pāramitās. 4 A 17 is inscribed (Ch 443): *Chih-hui po-lo-mi-mu*, which seems to come nearer to *prajñāpāramitā*.—Cf. Soothill-Hodous p. 375a on *chih-hui*, and p. 193b and 228a on *mātṛ*.—On the other hand, in the *garbhadhātumaṇḍala* it is the *jñānapāramitā* which is represented with a book. The reference to T 994 seems, however, to decide the identification.

1 Cd. Outline drawing in Taishō Issaikyō, Illustrations, vol. I, no. 129.—Eastern Buddhist, vii, 1937, p. 186.—*Bukkyō Daijiten*, 4269.—This figure illustrates the extraordinary fluidity of the Shingon images. While Shunnyū's (890–927) *Taizōkai-shichishū* prescribes that this Prajñāpāramitā should hold a sword in her right hand, T 853 (a ritual on T 848, by a Chinese of the 9th c) tells us that the left hand holds a book and that the right hand is in *abhayandada* (so *Mikkyō Daijiten* p. 1839), and other sources (quot, *ibid.*) again give the *dharmacakramudrā* for the right hand. (D).

1 Ce. Ned. Indie Oud en Nieuw, I, 1916–17, fig. 18 (cf. p. 394).

1 Cf. *Śer-phyin-ma.* "Five Hundred Gods of Narthang", section sNarthaṅ, 11b (fo-mu). Ill. in Lokesh Chandra, *Tibetan-Sanskrit Dict.* p. 2361.

1 Cg. T 901. See E. Conze, *The Prajñāpāramitā Literature*, 1960, pp. 87–8.

2 Aa. Oxford, Bodleian, Ms. a 7(R).—Ill. Or. Art I, 1948, p. 8.—Seated on a throne with geese and lions.

2 Ab. Cambridge Add. 1643 (cover 1 and 2).—Foucher pl. IX 4 (cover 2).—cf. Foucher, *Iconographie*, 1900, pp. 152–3.

2 Ac. British Mus. Or. 2203, fol. 2.—The colours are somewhat faded.

2 Ad. Cleveland.—Illustration, enlarged twofold, in: Bull. Cleveland Mus. of Art. Cleveland, Ohio, 26th year, no. 3, March 1939.

2 Ae. Asutosh Mus. of Indian Art. T 1055. fol. 60. Reddish.—Photo: M. Mookerjee, *Mediaeval Illustr. Manuscr. of Eastern India and Bengal*, Thesis for D.phil., London, 1951, (LSOAS). Plate xiv. Ill. 46.

2 Af. Paris, Bibl. Nat.—Ill. in N. Dutt, edition of *Pañcaviṃśatisāhasrikā*, 1934.—The figure is shown within a *stūpa*.

2 Ag. Ms. Cambridge Add. 1474. Front cover. Red brown.

2 Ah. Saraswati Coll., Calcutta.—Ill. M. Mookerjee's Thesis, plate xx, B 2. The P.P. has four attendants, and is accompanied, on the left, by a Tārā with two attendants and on the right by a Vasudhārā with two attendants.

2 Ai. Tokyo University Library, S. Maṭsunami's Catalogue (1965) no. 234. With two worshipping monks.

2 Ak. Cambridge Ms. Add 1163.—Cover, Body brown like clay.

2 *Al*. London, Christmas Humphreys.—The Middle Way xxix 2, 1954.—Frontispiece of E. Conze, *Selected Sayings from the Perfection of Wisdom*, 1955. Descr. *Ibid.* pp. 7–8.—Also in: Chintamoni Kar, *Indian Metal Sculpture*, 1952, no. 8 (wrongly ascribed to 9th–10th c.).

2 *Am*. Chillandeo Temple.—H. A. Oldfield, *Sketches from Nipal*, II, 1880, p. 156.—Line drawing in J. Burgess, *Notes on the Bauddha Rock Temples*, etc., 1879, pl. xxviii fig. 26. (=Bhagavan Lal, *Bauddha Mythology*, no. 9 of Misc. Series of Arch. Survey W. India, p. 99 and pl. xxii, fig. 2).

2 *An*. Boston no. 24.—On a Tibetan banner depicting Uṣṇīṣa-Sitātapatrā there is on top a trinity: A yellow four-armed Prajñāpāramitā, a Buddha in *bhūmisparśa* and with bowl, and a four-armed white Avalokiteśvara, with rosary, lotus flower and jewel. Illustr. in colour in G. Roerich, *Tibetan Paintings*, 1925, who wrongly identifies the Prajñāpāramitā as an Avalokiteśvara.

2 *Ao*. Temple of Nako.—Tucci-Ghersi, *Secrets of Tibet*, 1935, p. 71.—Francke had wrongly identified the statue as Padmasambhava.

2 *Ap*. From trinity in Nepalese shrine.—Ill.: Or. Art, III 3, 1951, p. 107.

2 *Aq*. Cambridge Ms. Add. 1464. Reddish brown. Book on white flower, Beautiful colours.

2 *Ar*. Cambridge Ms. Add. 1629. Front page.

2 *Ba*. Cambridge Add. 1553, fol. 18b. Ill.: Or. Art, II, 1949, p. 49

2 *Bb*. Cambridge Add. 1633, p. 1.

2 *Ca*. Lama Temple.—Clark 6 A 61. (Ch. 663): pan-jo fo-mu.

2 *Da*. Clark B 252.—Śer-phyin phyag bshi-ma. (Ch 154): Ssū-pei pan-jo fo-mu.

2 *Db*. 23½″ high.—Alice Boney, Or. Art, New York.—Ill. in advertisement in Oriental Art, N.S.I2. =sādhana 156?

2 *Dc*. Tsuibikow, *Buddist Palomnik u soyatnin' Tibeta*, 1919, p. 15.—Now confirmed as a P. P. by: *A new Tibeto-Mongol Pantheon*, 1962, ed. Raghu Vira, no. 162; before A.D. 1717.

2 *Ea*. *yum chen*. Ill. (and partly described) in: Or. Art, N. S. II 2, 1956, p. 69.

2 *Fa*. Exhibitions in the Yale University Library on the occasion of the 170th meeting of the American Oriental Society, 1960. p. 4, no. 18. Tibetan Ms of *Śatasāhasrikā* vol. 10, 17th c. in old orthography (Brda-sñiṅ). Top cover 11 1/4 by 28 5/8, with intricately carved panel. Numerous miniature figures, dominated by three larger figures. Centre: the crowned, four-armed Prajñāpāramitā. Left: crowned Bodhisattva, right: the Buddha.

2 *Ga*. J. Driver, Oxford.

2 *Gb*. J. Driver, Oxford.

2 *Ha*. Temple of Ye-śes 'od, Toling.—Ill. Tucci-Ghersi, p. 168.

2 *Hb*. *Śer-phyin-ma ser-mo*. "Five Hundred Gods of Narthang", Rin-'byuṅ 67b. Ill.: Lokesh Chandra, *Tibetan-Sanskrit Dict.*, p. 2362. Also: *A New Tibeto-Mongol Pantheon*, vol. 8, p. 64.

3a. Outline drawings in *Taishō Issaikyō*, Ill., vol. 1, no. 86. Eastern Buddhist, vii 1936, p. 13. *Bukkyō Daijiten*, 1931 sq., 4268. Or. Art II, 1949, p. 49. Painting in Getty, plate xvi.—A lid of a box of 1175 which contained the *Mahā-prajñāpāramitā-sūtra* is now in the Nanatsudera monastery in Nagoya. It is illustrated in *Japanese Temples and their Treasures*, pl. 380, in *Bukkyō Daijiten*, pl. 145(2414), and Or. Art II, 1949, p. 50. The lid shows the Prajñāpāramitā with two disciples, two Bodhisattvas and the sixteen guardians of the *Hannya* (=Prajñāpāramitā) Sūtra. According to M. W. de Visser, *Ancient Buddhism in Japan*, II, 1935, p. 493, sixteen good spirits guard the Sūtra, in accordance with the number of sermons (p. 492; also: E. Conze, *The Prajñāpāramitā Literature*, 1960, p. 28) it is held to contain. *Bukkyō Daijiten* 2412–2415 gives outline drawings of the sixteen good spirits.

3b. Descr. in T 259, trsl. ca A.D. 1000.

3c. Descr. in T 1152, trsl. ca A.D. 1000.

4a. Musée Guimet H.G. 17 487. Dupont 3.35.—A stele with Buddha, Vajrapāṇi, Prajñāpāramitā and Lokeśvara. cf. BEFEO xxii, 1922, 329. Coedès, *Indochine*, 1931, I 258. Ill. in Hackin-Grousset, *Le Musée Guimet*, 1928, p. xiv shows the side with the Buddha only. I have had no access to Grousset, Beaux Arts, no. 16, fig. 29–30.—Ill.: Or. Art II, 1949, p. 51.

5a. Ill. A.J.B. Kempers *The Bronzes of Nālandā*, 1933, fig. 18.

6a. Coedès, xxxv 1. O m. 125.

6b. *Ibid.* xxxv 2. O m. 255.

6c. *Ibid.* xxxv, 4.

6d. *Ibid.* xxxv, 3.

Unidentified Images

7.1. Illum., Ms *Aṣṭas.*, Vikramaśīla, 1100. Cleveland. Not seen.

7.2. dto. Not seen.

7.3. Statue, India. Dacca Mus.—Bhattasali p. 42.—Too decayed to be clearly recognizable.

7.4. Statue, Angkor.—cf. BEFEO xxxvi, 618.—Descr. as a small *statue addossée provenant d'une trinité bouddhique.*

7.5. Statue, Cambodia, 1300.—Musée Guimet 14908. Dupont 3.18.—This had twelve heads and six arms, but the identification as prajñāpāramitā is doubtful. Two hands are in *añjalimudrā*. Photo in Coedès no. G 52, 58 pl. xi, dr.

7.6. Stele, Cambodia, 1300.—M. G. 18117. Dupont 3.38. Two arms with lotus. (Uncertain identification).

7.7. Statue, Cambodia, Prah Khan (Bayon), 1200+. Dupont 4.37 (as 7.6.).

7.8. Head, Cambodia, Thma Pnok, 1200=. Dupont 4.40. (as 7.6).

7.9. Head, dto. 1200+. Dupont 4.41. (As 7.6.).

7.10. Relief, stele. Cambodia, 1200+. Dupont 4.56.9921. (As 7.6.).

7.11. Relief, silver. Angkor, 1200+. Dupont 5.1. Detail indistinct.

7.12. K. Khandalavala, Some Nepalese and Tibetan Bronzes in the Collection of Mr. R. S. Sethna of Bombay. Mārg iv no. 1, p. 27, fig. Prajñāpāramitā; with halo; on very high lotus in lalitāsana; + two extra arms! Sukhavatī Lokeśvara. 17th c.

7.13. Baroda Mus. and Pict. Gall, Baroda 1952, pl xxxi. Wooden book cover. Carved with figures of Buddha, Prajñāpāramitā and Vajradhara.

7.14. British Mus., Drawer G(1). 1906.12.27.12. Trinity: Buddha with bowl; Prajñāpāramitā; Vajrasattva.

7.15. F.D. Lessing, *Yung-ho-kung*, I, 1942, p. 75 mentions that the goddess Mahāprajñāpāramitā is found in Hall X of the Lamaist Cathedral in Peking.

7.16. F. D. K. Bosch, *Een Oorkonde van het groote Klooster te Nālandā*. T. B. G. 65, 1925, pp. 509–88.—Bosch, O. V., 1926, p. 31: 7 different Prajñāpāramitās; but six are Cundās, A. J. B. Kempers, *The Bronzes of Nālandā and Hindu-Javanese Art*, Leiden, 1933, p. 43.

7.17. Victoria and Albert Mus., Ind. Sect., IM 106=1929. Ādi-Buddha and Prajñāpāramitā. Vajrasattva and Prajñāpāramitā. Ill. H. Zimmer, *The Art of Indian Asia*, II, 510–11. Close-up.—Tibet. Late 18th c. From Chamdo, Khams province, East Tibet.—Ms inside hollow image. (I see no reason why this image should be regarded as a P.P.).

7.18. Ms. of *Aṣṭas.* in Freer Gallery of Art.

INDEX

nihilism 28, 137, 139, 140, 187, 224, 230, 241